A HISTORICAL AND ETYMOLOGICAL DICTIONARY OF AMERICAN SIGN LANGUAGE

✳

A HISTORICAL AND ETYMOLOGICAL DICTIONARY OF AMERICAN SIGN LANGUAGE

✷

The Origin and Evolution of
More Than 500 Signs

✷

Emily Shaw and Yves Delaporte

Gallaudet University Press
WASHINGTON, DC

Gallaudet University Press
Washington, DC 20002
http://gupress.gallaudet.edu

© 2015 by Gallaudet University
All rights reserved. Published 2015
Printed in the United States of America

Library of Congress Cataloging-in-Publication Data

Shaw, Emily.
　A historical and etymological dictionary of American Sign Language : the origin and evolution of more than 500 signs / Emily Shaw and Yves Delaporte ; illustrations by Carole Marion.
　　pages cm
　ISBN 978-1-56368-621-4 (hardback)—ISBN 978-1-56368-622-1 (ebook)
　1. American Sign Language—Dictionaries. 2. American Sign Language—History. 3. French Sign Language—History. I. Delaporte, Yves. II. Title.
　HV2475.S522 2014
　419′.703—dc23

　　　　　　　　　　　　　　　　　　　　　　　　　　　　　　2014031564

∞ This paper meets the requirements of ANSI/NISO Z39.48-1992 (Permanence of Paper).

CONTENTS

Preface	vii
Introduction	ix
Handshape Typology	xxv
American Manual Alphabet	xxvi
Symbols and Conventions	xxvii
Historical and Etymological Dictionary of ASL	3

   On Common Ground   28

   Meaning of the Thumb   63

   Handshape Change   148

   The Veiled Devil   176

   The Bundled Handshape   217

   UN *(One): The Hidden Number*   239

   Axis of Time   286

Illustration Credits	323
References	325

PREFACE

This work was precipitated by a profound curiosity about the historical relationship between American Sign Language (ASL) and French Sign Language (LSF). Deaf people from regions throughout France, too numerous to be cited here, provided Yves with information about their dialects that ultimately enabled him to publish his *Dictionnaire étymologique et historique de la langue des signes française* (*Etymological and Historical Dictionary of French Sign Language*) in 2007. After meeting Emily, some of this information proved relevant to reconstructing the history of ASL. It is thus a pleasure to thank again those who showed Yves these undocumented forms, especially the old signs from Chambéry and Clermont-Ferrand.

In Paris and surrounding suburbs, special mention is accorded Chantal Callen and Jean Spitéri for the richness and diversity of their personal knowledge of LSF. In addition, thanks go to Armand and Yvette Pelletier in Bourgogne, whose collaboration with Yves resulted in the publication of two books and the establishment of a museum on the History and Culture of the Deaf. Yves also thanks Annie Ravent, Marie-Jo Page, Michel Poensin, and Évelyne Dubourdeau, who were responsible for collecting photographs of signs in the regions of Le Puy, Chambéry, and Saint-Laurent-en-Royans, allowing us to redraw them in this publication. Finally, Yves wishes to thank Françoise Bonnal-Vergès, director of the magnificent collection "Archives de la langue des signes française" published by Lambert-Lucas, for her unwavering intellectual support.

Emily wishes to thank her Deaf neighbors and friends from her childhood home in Ohio, her ASL teachers in Columbus and Chicago who first exposed her to the language in a classroom, and her instructors in Paris at l'Académie de la Langue des Signes Française. She thanks her family, particularly Aimee Potter, for hosting her for extended periods of time during her research in France. Special thanks are due to Chantal Callen and Jean Spitéri, dear friends who generously embraced her and patiently introduced her to LSF. She also wishes to thank Edna Johnston whose initial interest in and passion about LSF's historical connection to ASL prompted her to pursue this research in more depth. Edna generously modeled the contemporary ASL signs and provided a wealth of information about ASL throughout the development of this work.

Emily collected regional forms of signs from numerous Deaf people across the U.S. She thanks especially Maude Nelson from Alabama, Sara Cardwell Johnston from Indiana, John and Clara Stafford from the Eastern Shore of Maryland, and countless others too numerous to list who have shared their signs and stories with her. The librarians in the Motion Picture and Television Reading Room at the Library of Congress assisted Emily in the retrieval of the ASL films from the turn of the twentieth century and deserve her thanks. Ulf Hedberg and Michael J. Olson at the Gallaudet University Deaf Collections and Archives assisted Emily in locating early documents of the American Deaf community, including early correspondences between Laurent Clerc and Thomas H. Gallaudet and the demographic data concerning the population of students at the American School for the Deaf (ASD). Their dedication to preserving and promoting Gallaudet's legacy is noteworthy.

The majority of the contemporary ASL signs in this dictionary were drawn by our dear friend Carole Marion, a talented Deaf French artist and graduate of the École Nationale des Beaux-Arts (French National College of Art and Architecture). Carole teaches sign language and visual arts in a school for the deaf. Her work was funded by the Centre National de la Recherche Scientifique (CNRS), thanks to Jean-Charles Depaule, director of the Urban Anthropology Lab.

Most of the contemporary Langue des Signes Française (LSF; French Sign Language) signs come from dictionaries produced by the International Visual Theater (IVT). IVT was founded at the end of the 1970s at the prompting of two Americans, Alfredo Corrado (Deaf) and Bill Moody. Today, IVT is directed by the Deaf actress and comedienne, Emmanuelle Laborit. Thanks to her backing, the Éditions IVT authorized the reproduction of a large number of LSF signs from their publications. For that, we thank them.

Pat Mallet (1939–2012) became deaf at the age of nine. He was the author of numerous cartoons published in countless newspapers for children or adults. His hilarious comic strip *The Little Green Men* made him famous. Four collections of his drawings about deafness were published by Éditions du Fox: *As Long as There Are Deaf People*, *Over There Are the Deaf*, *The Hard of Hearing throughout History,* and *Without Words*. Pat was a dear friend. He produced charming illustrations for our dictionary that depict the etymologies of numerous signs much better than lengthy text.

Finally, we wish to thank an anonymous reviewer for helpful feedback regarding our work and Ivey Pittle Wallace from Gallaudet University Press for her patient and enthusiastic support.

INTRODUCTION

American Sign Language (ASL), the language used by signing Deaf people in the United States and Canada, has a rich history.[1] Like spoken languages, sign languages develop as a result of regular and sustained contact between groups of individuals, in this case, individuals who cannot hear. Contrary to popular belief, sign languages are not universal. Each one is shaped by the people who use it, the environment in which it emerges, and the distinct experience of interacting with the world primarily through sight. ASL offers a treasure trove of historical relics from America's past that are stored within the forms and meanings of its signs.

Because Deaf people are most often born into hearing families, the language and culture that develops naturally among them is typically passed down outside the nuclear family.[2] In many ways, the American Deaf community resembles an ethnic minority group. Yet, unlike other minorities, members of the Deaf community are characterized by a shared language and by a disability. As a result, the dichotomy between a cultural view of deafness as an element of identity and a pathological view as a defect that needs to be fixed is ever-present.

The exact number of people who use ASL is difficult to quantify (Mitchell, Young, Bachleda, and Karchmer 2006). Though the U.S. Census collects data on individuals with hearing loss, it does not distinguish between signing and non-signing deaf people. Additionally, many hearing people learn ASL as a first language (children of deaf adults or CODAs) or learn and use it regularly as adults (e.g., family members, friends, teachers, and interpreters). We do know, however, that Deaf people have steadily carved out a space for themselves in the American mainstream so that it is no longer unusual to see them on television, at public events, and in places of employment. They work in all sectors of the economy, attend institutions of higher learning, raise children, and participate in their communities. Many universities and even high schools now include ASL as a foreign language (though it is as indigenous to the U.S. as English). Interpreter Preparation Programs have sprouted all over the country in response to the legally mandated access afforded Deaf and hearing people who need to communicate with each other. With the advent of videophones and federally funded video relay services, Deaf and hearing people are now able to make phone calls to each other through interpreters who use ASL, English, and in some cases, Spanish. As a result, Deaf people have a greater degree of access to the mainstream than ever before and ASL is beginning to be recognized as one part of the diverse linguistic makeup of the U.S.

The increase in access to the mainstream has unavoidably precipitated a shift in the ethos of the Deaf community. Because deafness is a low-incidence disability that affects

---

1. In accordance with convention, we will use "Deaf" to refer to Deaf people who sign and identify themselves with a cultural community and "deaf" to refer to audiological status.

2. Mitchell and Karchmer (2004) found 94–96% of deaf children in the U.S. are born to hearing parents.

only a fraction of a percent of most populations, schools for Deaf children were at one time primarily residential; students boarded during the school year and returned home on weekends and holidays. The physical concentration of Deaf children and adults allowed for the rapid development and transmission of the culture and language. Today, mainstreaming has become the norm, resulting in fewer opportunities for the intergenerational exchange needed to pass down ASL. The profusion of cochlear implant surgeries in young children coupled with the chasm between Deaf adults and non-signing hearing parents has led to fewer children learning ASL. Most Deaf clubs, once the hub of social life for adults, have closed. Remote interactions via videophones and text messaging have allowed for frequent contact in lieu of personal visits.

Many lament these changes as indications of a dying culture, while others view them as a reinvention of what it means to be Deaf in the twenty-first century. The constant is that the community continues to evolve along with its language. While the history of ASL might seem irrelevant to these contemporary transformations, we see it as even more crucial to edifying Deaf people's place in American society. Signs are steeped in history and ASL is a product of American culture—an amalgam of influences both foreign and domestic. By looking deeply into the etymology of this language, we can expose relics of a cultural past that are furtively embedded in contemporary signs.

Signs Have a History

The story of how the Deaf community and ASL came to be usually begins with the founding of the first American school for deaf children in Hartford, Connecticut in 1817. The American Asylum for the Deaf and Dumb (now, American School for the Deaf, henceforth ASD) resulted from the partnership of three men—Mason Fitch Cogswell, a hearing American doctor and father of a deaf child; Thomas Hopkins Gallaudet, a hearing American reverend; and Laurent Clerc, a Deaf French educator. Gallaudet and Clerc's collaboration marked the beginning of formalized deaf education as well as the importation of French Sign Language (Langue des Signes Française or LSF) to this continent. Clerc had attended the historic school in France (now, the Institut National de Jeunes Sourds, henceforth INJS) founded in 1791 to carry on the legacy of Abbé Charles Michel de l'Épée. De l'Épée opened the first school to educate Deaf children using signs, in 1760 in Paris, France, and he is still heralded across the world as the father of deaf education.

Establishing ASD was momentous in many respects, but the one most relevant to this work is that it created a place where Deaf Americans could regularly interact using a sign language, one that happened to be heavily influenced by LSF. Deaf children born into hearing families prior to the establishment of ASD were isolated, had restricted access to communication within their own families, and limited (if any) interactions with other Deaf people. ASD and the other residential schools that followed became a second home where they were able to learn to sign, interact with peers and adults who were also Deaf, and become accustomed to a visually oriented way of life. Some Deaf people had been signing in isolated pockets across the U.S. well before the opening of ASD, but it was not until the founding of this school that ASL as it is known today began to be standardized.

Gallaudet did not know sign language before meeting Clerc, but Clerc was fluent in LSF and taught it to Gallaudet. Very little is known about just what variety of sign language Gallaudet, Clerc, and the first generations of students used; no documents describing signs were published in the U.S. until the late nineteenth century. However, it is in the early nineteenth century where we find the origins, or *etymology*, of much of the language's lexicon. Previous studies of historical change have only scratched the surface of this connection. Now, almost two hundred years later, the history of ASL's lexicon and its link to LSF are finally coming to light.

The Birth of ASL

According to the 1887 Annual Report of the directors of ASD (*Annual Report* 1887), the population of 77 students who attended the school in its first two years came from diverse backgrounds. Most were older than sixteen and had never used sign before. Clerc's historic role in the founding of ASD meant that LSF was both introduced to and used by this nascent Deaf community. We can deduce that Clerc's dialect reflected the areas from which he came, including the municipal community of Paris where he was educated but also regions outside of Paris where he and many of the first students at INJS grew up. His language was also strongly influenced by Signed French, a methodical code that de l'Épée invented to map signs in French grammatical order. A community of Deaf people lived on Martha's Vineyard long before ASD opened, and their language also likely had some influence on ASL's history. Thus, to get a clear picture of what cultural resources were exploited in the development of the signs of early Deaf America, we must consider old LSF and its dialects, the signs used by the first students and teachers at ASD, and cultural practices and ways of life particular to the U.S. and France more than two hundred years ago.

Martha's Vineyard

The first group of settlers came from Massachusetts to the island of Martha's Vineyard in 1644. Originally from England, they continued to move to the island for the next seventy years, and the first deaf person arrived on the island in 1694. For several generations, a disproportionately large number of genetically deaf children were born, raised, and remained on the island, and the entire population of the island used a sign language (Groce 1985).

The first three students from Martha's Vineyard to attend ASD—Mary Smith, Sally Smith, and Lovey Mayhew—were admitted in 1825, seven years after the school opened. No more than four students from Martha's Vineyard were present at ASD at the same time until the 1850s and 1860s, when their attendance peaked at around twelve students (*Annual Report* 1887). Since some of the first generations of ASD students were from the island, it is likely that a number of Martha's Vineyard Sign Language (MVSL) signs were incorporated into ASL, though probably less than is typically assumed. Bahan and Nash (1996) analyzed data collected from Nash's great-grandmother, a hearing resident of the island who knew MVSL. Nash documented approximately 300 signs and found roughly 20 percent of them had cognates in ASL. While it is certainly possible that some of these signs were inherited into ASL from MVSL, without documentation of the signs as they were used before the opening of ASD, there is no way to verify which language transmitted the cognates.

Transmission of old LSF to ASL

Unsurprisingly, the earliest forms of LSF have proved a rich source of data from which to glean information about ASL's history. Many of the students educated under de l'Épée's method, like Clerc, were invited or elected to travel to other countries to propagate it. It is well known that Belgium, Holland, Mexico, Brazil, Switzerland, and Quebec share historical ties to LSF and thus, indirectly, to ASL. In all of these countries, former students of INJS founded schools for the deaf: Joseph Henrion in Belgium, Édouard Huet in Mexico and Brazil, Isaac Chomel in Switzerland, Brother Young in Quebec, and Henri Daniel Guyot, a hearing instructor from INJS, in Holland. Gallaudet and Clerc also carried on de l'Épée's mission soon after the founding of ASD, convincing other U.S. states of the need for similar schools in their areas. From 1817 to 1857, roughly two generations of American students attended twenty residential schools across the East Coast, Midwest, and South that used the sign language from Hartford (Gordon 1892). Many of the students who graduated from ASD moved to these states to be teachers and administrators, thereby assuring the transmission of the method and, more importantly for us, the language used by Clerc, Gallaudet, and their first generations of students. In 1864, Edward Miner Gallaudet (son of Thomas Hopkins Gallaudet), founded the National Deaf-Mute College (now Gallaudet University) in Washington, DC. Many of the students from ASD and other residential schools pursued degrees at the college and became fervent advocates for signed pedagogies.

Oralism and the Milan Congress

As the residential institutions strengthened their roots, a burgeoning movement to eradicate sign language also began to take hold. A philosophical argument materialized between proponents of de l'Épée's method and advocates of the oral method, each attempting to claim success in teaching deaf children (Lane 1984). The first oral schools opened in 1867; by the late 1800s, there were seventy-seven schools for the deaf in the U.S.—eighteen schools used the oral method and fifty-nine used either the manual method (sign) or the "combined" method (sign and speech) (Gordon 1892).

Sustaining the use of sign language as the primary communication method in the schools turned out to be a formidable task in the late nineteenth and early twentieth centuries. Alexander Graham Bell, who was a teacher of the deaf and was fascinated by genetics, became one of the most vociferous and successful advocates for oral education (Lane 1999). The oral versus manual debate quickly distilled into a contest over the superiority of speech or sign. In 1880, a Congress of predominantly hearing educators in Milan, Italy endorsed the exclusive use of the oral method to teach deaf children. They claimed that teaching students to speak was paramount to their integration in a hearing world.

The Milan Congress's edict suppressed the overt use of sign language in almost all schools for the deaf throughout Europe, and especially in France. Deaf children were strictly monitored in their classrooms, playgrounds, and dormitories and were punished for any evidence of signing. French Deaf people continued to sign covertly; however, the result of this policy had a catastrophic effect on the community for a century, particularly in terms of education but also in recording the language. It took one hundred years for the community to reassert ownership of its language and to once again publish documents of LSF during a period now known as the *Réveil sourd* or *Deaf Awakening*.

The Milan Congress also had a negative impact on American Deaf people but less absolutely than in France. While the widespread practice of excluding sign language from classrooms certainly did occur—as did the unjust removal or demotion of most Deaf teachers—the application of that principle took on different forms in each school. Instead of acquiescing to the edict, the American Deaf community united in opposition to it.

Deaf Opposition to Oralism

Three factors contributed to the relative success Deaf Americans experienced in countering the Milan decree. First, the cultural and geographical distance between Europe and the U.S. allowed for some flexibility in the policy's implementation. Americans are wont to pave their own way, even if (and sometimes especially because) it directly contradicts European mores. Far from the watchful gaze of European educators, the Americans interpreted and implemented the mandate according to their own principles. Each state had independent discretion over the operation of its institutions, permitting distinct approaches to and opinions about optimal teaching methods. In most cases, schools implemented dual-track programs where the so-called "bright" students were assigned to oral classrooms and the "dull" students were relegated to manual classrooms where sign language was used (Gannon 2012; Nomeland and Nomeland 2012). Some schools prohibited signing but allowed fingerspelling. Still others completely abolished sign language in the classrooms but disregarded it when students signed in their dormitories (Gannon 2012; Lane 1999).

The second force that fueled the resistance was the healthy number of Deaf people educated in elementary, secondary, and post-secondary institutions founded on signing pedagogies. Gallaudet University had been open for sixteen years while forty-six schools for the Deaf were operating by the time the Milan decree was announced. These institutions educated Deaf children who eventually became successful Deaf adults invested in the preservation of the language for future generations. The National Association of the Deaf (NAD) contributed greatly to the unification of Deaf Americans through a series of films produced between 1910 and 1920. George Veditz, president of the NAD from 1904 to 1910, beautifully conveyed the Deaf community's indignation in the face of oralism's "false prophets." Contrasting the American and French communities, he said,

> For 33 years, the French Deaf have watched, with eyes full of tears, with hearts breaking, as the beautiful language of signs was wiped out of their schools. For 33 years, they have strived, struggled, and fought to reestablish it in their schools. But for 33 years they have been pushed aside. [. . .] The French Deaf look at us American Deaf with jealous eyes. They look at us as a prisoner, locked down with an iron chain about his leg, looks out at those wandering free.[3]

Organizations like the NAD and publications like the *Silent Worker* and the *American Annals of the Deaf* helped to unite geographically dispersed Deaf people behind the common cause.

The third factor to foster Deaf American resistance was the Christian church. Christian groups of various denominations proved instrumental in their critique of oralism. Many leaders and missionaries believed that in order to be saved, Deaf people had to understand the Word of God,

---

3. Translated by Emily Shaw, from *Preservation of the Sign Language* by George Veditz, 1913.

regardless of the medium through which it was conveyed. American religious groups were quick to counteract the Milan edict. Daniel D. Higgins, for example, declared in his dictionary of ASL,

> Do not let the exaggerated propaganda, which claims that all deaf persons are now learning to speak and to read the lips perfectly, deter you from learning this language. Even if those claims were true, the deaf using this language would be with us the rest of our lives. . . . Do not allow slavishness to a method or system, merely mercenary or ambitious motives, or the fear of biased, foolishly proud and sentimental parents lead you to do present or future harm to the pupil spiritually or materially. (Higgins 1942, 1)

Religious men published several dictionaries during the early twentieth century to disseminate across the country, thereby endorsing sign language as a legitimate means of communicating in a social space (Long 1910; Michaels 1923; Higgins 1923, 1942).

The distinct American reaction to the Milan Congress shaped ASL in significant ways. Even at the height of oralism, ASL continued to be used, albeit in a politically charged environment. Deaf individuals were pressed to prove their intelligence and their literacy in English. Consequently, initialized signs and idiomatic expressions borrowed from English became, and remain, characteristic components of ASL. The use of fingerspelled English words and the documentation of ASL signs actually increased after the Milan Congress, unlike in France where it abruptly stopped. Uncovering connections between ASL and LSF is possible today because of the work carried out to maintain ASL's presence in American culture. Though there are many missing pieces in the history of the lexicon, we have a great deal of documentation to mine. We turn next to a discussion of the work of recreating those connections.

Etymology of ASL: Research without Tradition

While the events that transpired during the development of the American Deaf community are well documented, very little is known about the history of its lexicon. William Stokoe's seminal work in 1960 marked the beginning of formal research into the structure of ASL. Stokoe was the first to identify linguistic properties of ASL, spurring a movement to legitimize the language in scholarly circles. Stokoe was also the first to bring attention to ASL's lexicon. In 1965, with Dorothy Casterline and Carl Croneberg, he published the *Dictionary of American Sign Language on Linguistic Principles*, the first text to formally describe the composition of signs and their meanings. The book catalogues over a thousand signs described by three components (or *parameters*): handshape, movement, and location.[4] The authors provide information about regional, gender, and generational variations in many entries as well as in articles in the appendix.

While scholars used this work as a springboard for identifying and describing ASL's phonology, they paid less attention to the important historical information it contained. Given the stigma associated with signing, especially in response to the oral movement, it is not surprising that most of the earliest linguistic studies foregrounded ASL's formal structure—its phonology, morphology, and syntax—over its iconicity to

---

4. Two additional parameters, orientation (Battison 1978) and nonmanual markers (Liddell and Johnson 1986), were later found to be relevant to the structure of signs.

emphasize its parity with spoken language (Taub 2001; Meir 2010).

Nancy Frishberg (1975, 1976) was the first to document how articulatory pressures to ease production, ease perception, and avoid homonymy triggered the diminution of iconicity over time. She developed this argument by drawing data from the NAD film series, the 1918 edition of Long's *Dictionary of the Sign Language*, and Michaels' *A Handbook of the Sign Language of the Deaf* (1923), and then comparing ASL forms with LSF counterparts in Blanchet's (1850) and de l'Épée's (1797) dictionaries.[5] Tracing contemporary ASL signs to their etymons, Frishberg shows that forms become more symmetrical through the assimilation of handshapes and movements. They tend to centralize in the signing space or near the hollow of the neck; two distinct units in compound signs eventually merge into one form; meaningful content performed by the face or body transfers to the hands; and certain parameters, such as handshape and location, become imbued with generic meaning much like sound symbolism in words. These evolutionary tendencies, Frishberg argued, prove that ASL was not pantomime but driven to become as arbitrary as spoken languages.

The early years spent validating ASL's parity with spoken language were not in vain, but they did result in the tendency to discount the importance of imagery in sign language. While no one has gone so far as to identify the origins of the lexicon, scholars have begun to reconsider the role iconicity plays, not just concerning historical evolution (Supalla 2008), but also to help explain phenomena like depiction (Liddell 2003; Dudis 2004), metaphor (Taub 2001; Meir 2010; S. Wilcox 2009; P. Wilcox 2000),

and language processing (Bosworth and Emmorey 2010; Thompson, Vinson, and Vigliocco 2009, 2010; Thompson 2011). For instance, Thompson et al. (2009) have shown that iconicity is so pervasive in sign languages that Deaf signers demonstrate lexical processing advantages for iconicity over hearing people, both signers and nonsigners alike.

Iconicity and metaphor have proved central to uncovering the roots of ASL's lexicon. Historical research documents relics of eras past, but it also contributes to a better understanding of how Deaf people generate signs and convey meaning about their world. For example, the ASL sign STUPID derives from the polysemy (multiple meanings) of the French word *bête,* which can mean "stupid" or "beast." The forked handshape on the forehead from the LSF BÊTE was a loan translation that depicted an animal with horns. The form is both iconic *and* metaphorical. Meir (2010) discusses the emergence of iconicity and metaphor in sign language, both of which require separate mapping processes from source to form in order to be understood (Taub 2001). The concept of a book is mapped to the sign BOOK via select features of the sign (its handshape, point of contact, movement, etc.) that resemble an actual book. Metaphors function similarly. Meir argues that when a form or expression in sign language is both iconic *and* metaphorical (e.g., like the ASL sign STUPID), the double mapping required for each conceptual process to successfully occur must be aligned. Our research demonstrates what happens when the mappings are *not* aligned; that is, when the symbolism behind the forms of signs was lost in transmission or when the cultural context shifted and prompted a reinterpretation of the form. To help explain the process through which Americans made sense of their second-hand forms, we turn to Peircean semiotics.

---

5. Frishberg cites a 1797 edition of de l'Épée's dictionary; however, the authors are aware of only the 1784 edition.

Ordinarily, signs (and words) are conceived of as binary pairs where a form (such as the word *book*) is tied to a meaning (the physical book one reads) through some sort of convention (Saussure 1959). Charles S. Peirce, in his theory of semiotics (1955), provides an alternate account, describing the relation as *tertiary*: a form becomes linked to a meaning via an interpreter's conceptualization of the connection.[6] That is, it is not enough to say that the word *book* is linked to the physical book; in order for the word *book* to exist at all, there must be a person who perceives the word (via sight or sound) and then conceptualizes the object. Though most linguists take for granted that a person generates form-meaning pairs, Peirce maintains that to effectively account for the existence of signs at all, the conceptualization of that association must be a part of the analysis.

Deaf people intrinsically interpret (and reinterpret) symbolism from their lexicon and then map those conceptualizations onto the forms of their signs (much like depicting constructions; Liddell 2003). This is especially evident in the American Deaf community since so many signs were inherited from a different cultural group. Interpreted symbolism is often referred to as *folk etymology*; that is, the explanation of meaning that people derive from their perceptions of a physical form. Once a folk etymology becomes firmly entrenched in a community, a sign's form will often change to suit that symbolism. In this book, we refer to these changes as *reinterpreted* (rather than *folk*) etymologies.

The evolution of the ASL sign WEEK provides a clear example of a reinterpreted etymology. Taub describes "the iconic image represented [in the sign WEEK as] . . . a horizontal row on a calendar" (2001, 135). The four fingers of the left hand are interpreted as representing the four rows of the calendar; the right hand's movement over the left hand is interpreted as the passing of time over the length of a week. Signers can refer to each individual finger as the first, second, third, or fourth week of the month, making the perceived imagery a relevant force behind the grammar of the form. The etymology of the sign, however, in no way represented the rows of the calendar or the passing of time. In the original LSF sign SEMAINE (week), still used as a regional variation in Saint-Laurent-en-Royans, the two hands displayed the French number SEPT (seven) for the seven days of the week, and the right hand crossed over the left hand and rested on the palm. In the French counting system, which uses both hands to represent numbers, DEUX (two) is formed with the right thumb and extended index finger, and CINQ (five) is the open left hand. Americans use the index and middle fingers for the sign TWO, not the thumb and index finger, and an altogether different, one-handed sign for SEVEN. In LSF, the right hand originally exhibited no lateral movement, but once (or, perhaps, because) the symbolism was reinterpreted in the U.S., the right hand moved from right to left across the left palm and the derived meaning of the sign became entrenched.

A Peircean semiotic view of sign creation (including all sorts of symbolic material besides language) is especially germane to this research. The American Deaf community inherited signs from which they generated meaning. Their conceptualizations of the symbolic meanings behind their lexicon tangibly impacted the trajectory of the signs, in effect, accentuating the central role people play in language development. The historical study of ASL is an exercise in uncovering the imagery from which signs derive. With the aid of historical documentation, we apply the phonological processes Frishberg first

---

6. Peirce calls this the *interpretant*. For an accessible reading of Peirce, see also Parmentier (1987).

documented and others expanded upon to uncover the symbolic motivations behind hundreds of signs. The results are compelling on their own but certainly present a new way of analyzing constructions in contemporary sign languages.

An Etymological *and* Historical Dictionary

Once we started reconstructing etymologies from historical texts, we were surprised to discover a wealth of evidence that directly contradicted many of the etymologies even we ourselves believed. Many signs in ASL appear obscure not solely because of articulatory pressures, as has been assumed (Frishberg 1976), but also because of the shifts in the cultural context with which the signs were originally associated.

Laurent Clerc, a product of French culture, brought forms embedded with highly localized cultural meaning to a territory that had a very different culture and that had no knowledge of French Deaf culture. The transmission of the language to American Deaf people automatically resulted in signs losing these French cultural associations. Not surprisingly, LSF contains a myriad of culturally specific signs that we do not have in ASL. For example, the sign AVOCAT (lawyer) depicts the special white collar French lawyers wear in court. It is easy to imagine that many of the signs Clerc brought to the U.S. failed to inspire any associations among the Deaf Americans and consequently dropped out of use.

The unique circumstances surrounding ASL's history provide us with insight into how one group can essentially inherit a ready-made language from another. That Deaf Americans reinterpreted so many of their forms shows the degree to which language users influence the formation of their lexicon. Understanding the cultural groups responsible for the generation of these signs, then, is crucial to accurately document historical developments. Previous studies that compare contemporary ASL and contemporary LSF (e.g., Woodward 1976) only provide an account of where each language ended up. By incorporating the history of each sign in our entries, we provide a richer explanation behind the semantics of the lexicon and show that the forms of signs are always motivated by something, be it an icon, a cultural or material object, an action, a gesture, or a metaphor. Because so many American signs were inherited from a different cultural group, the inextricable link between language and language user is quite clear.

In writing a dictionary that is both etymological *and* historical, we shed light on the progression from etymon to contemporary form as triggered by sociocultural impulses. Before we elucidate our methods, we turn first to summarize the rich historical data unearthed to produce this work.

The Historical Sources

Reconstructing the history of a lexicon is very much like assembling a puzzle with missing pieces. Etymologists work with centuries-old written texts to collect traces of evolutions in forms and meanings of words. Historical texts are the main source through which these researchers reconstruct etymologies. Labov (1972) asserts that these texts

> are produced by a series of historical accidents; amateurs may complain about this predicament, but the sophisticated historian is grateful that anything has survived at all. The great art of the historical linguist is to make the best of this bad data—"bad" in the sense that it may be fragmentary, corrupted, or many times removed from the actual productions of native speakers (100).

Sign languages have had a bleak record of historical documentation largely because they have no written form. Whereas historical linguists of many spoken languages benefit from ancient texts produced by native speakers, historical linguists of sign languages rely on documentation of lexical items (not texts) that are described or illustrated, almost exclusively, by *non*-native users.[7]

The pieces of our etymological puzzle come from three categories of sources. As expected, the first category consists of descriptions and illustrations of French signs from the eighteenth and nineteenth centuries. We collected and scrupulously examined all of the known historical texts of LSF signs: Abbé de l'Épée (1784), Abbé Ferrand (circa 1785), Abbé Sicard (1808), Baron de Gérando (1827), Abbé Jamet (unpublished manuscript, circa 1830, discovered by Yves Delaporte in the archives of a religious congregation), Jean-Baptiste Puybonnieux (1846), Alexandre Blanchet (1850), Brothers of St. Gabriel (1853–1854), Joséphine Brouland (1855), Pierre Pélissier (1856, the only Deaf author in this group), Abbé Lambert (1865) and lastly, Abbé Laveau (1868). These sources provided enough data for Yves Delaporte (2007) to publish the first etymological dictionary of LSF and constitute the missing links between ASL and the old LSF Clerc imported to American soil.

The second category of data consists of American texts and films published in the late nineteenth and early twentieth centuries. In these sources, we typically see signs in the intermediary steps in evolution from the old LSF to contemporary ASL. Jerome S. Brown in Baton Rouge, Louisiana published the earliest known document, *A Vocabulary of Mute Signs*, in 1856. This text contains a collection of English words and rather vague descriptions of signs that Brown felt should be used in the education of Deaf children. The title of Brown's book is misleading since the vast majority of entries are definitions of English words that reveal nothing about the forms of signs. There are a few entries (such as ANIMAL and CONSCIENCE/GUILTY) that provide insight into actual etymologies that can be substantiated by other historical texts. Otherwise, the text has proved less useful.

A far more valuable book, published in 1885, is *The Indian Sign Language* written by anthropologist William Philo Clark. Though focused on documenting the sign languages of the Plains Indians, Clark also compares over 1,000 signs with corollary forms used by "deaf-mutes."[8] Employing ethnographic methodology, Clark describes signs based on years of fieldwork in Plains Indian communities. He did not personally conduct fieldwork in the Deaf community but collected information about ASL from Dr. Philip Gillett, the superintendent of the Illinois School for the Deaf (est. 1846) and Ezra Valentine, an instructor from the Indiana School for the Deaf (est. 1844). Clark describes ASL signs fastidiously and unlike the religious authors of subsequent works, he does not shy away from documenting more secular signs (like COPULATE and BET).

The first book to include photographs of signs, *The Sign Language: A Manual of Signs* by J. Schuyler Long, was not published in its entirety until 1910.[9] In the complete text, Long documents roughly 1,400 signs. A graduate of the Iowa School for the Deaf and

---

7. Pierre Pélissier, a Deaf native signer of LSF, is the only exception in all of our historical sources.

8. It is worth noting, the signs used by Plains Indians are likely not historically related to the signs used by American Deaf people. The two groups did not commingle regularly enough for borrowing to occur. Though Davis (2010) suggests that it is "plausible" signs were introduced to deaf students (24), most of the similarities we have seen (Clark 1885) are between those signs that are already highly iconic.

9. Long published sections of the book in 1908, 1909, and 1910 in the *American Annals of the Deaf*.

Gallaudet College, he served as the principal of the Iowa School for the Deaf (est. 1856) for many years. Long collaborated with Rev. Dr. Philip J. Hasentab of Chicago, who was educated at the Indiana School for the Deaf under, according to Long, the "early masters of the Sign Language who learned it at Hartford." In his introduction, Long explains that his motivation was "to preserve this expressive language, to which the deaf owe so much, in its original purity and beauty, and that it will serve as a standard of comparison in different parts of the country, thereby tending to secure greater uniformity" (1918, 10).

The next text, *How to Talk to the Deaf*, was written by Daniel D. Higgins, a Catholic priest in St. Louis, Missouri, in 1923. Higgins wrote the book for both hearing and oral deaf people who wanted to learn sign. It contains roughly 1,600 entries with text and photographs and includes several annotations that indicate variations in production and meaning. In a later edition (1942), Higgins added explanations of the symbolism behind the signs and appended translations of several prayers, including the Apostles' Creed and the Lord's Prayer.

The last written text we used from the U.S., *A Handbook of the Sign Language of the Deaf*, was also published in 1923 by John Walters Michaels, a missionary. Unlike the previous two authors who hailed from the Midwest, Michaels was from Atlanta, Georgia, and he offers some regional variations from the South not documented elsewhere. Like Long, Michaels associates himself with the "sign masters"; the signs, he says, "are depicted as the author uses them and he claims to be in the third generation from Gallaudet and Clerc, who introduced the language into the United States" (1923, 12). The small dictionary contains illustrations of some signs in addition to brief descriptions of how to produce them.

The third category of data is the film series produced by the NAD between 1910 and 1920 as part of an effort to preserve sign language for future generations. George Veditz, then president of the NAD, organized the films as an act of defiance against the oralist movement. A group of well-known and respected Deaf and hearing leaders were filmed signing sermons, speeches, and stories, thus making the films the only historical source to show signs as they were once used in context. Edward Miner Gallaudet appears on film, as do Robert McGregor and Edward Allen Fay, among others. John B. Hotchkiss, who was a student at ASD from 1859 to 1864, recounts his experience interacting with Laurent Clerc, who had retired but still visited the school. The films are an exceptional rendering of many of the forms we see limited to two dimensions in the dictionaries.

Language Variation

In addition to studying historical texts from France and the U.S. to determine ASL's etymology, we also looked at language variation. Each community in early Deaf America borrowed, adapted, and discarded lexical items to suit their respective ways of life. The geographical expanse of the U.S. is one demographic element that allowed for variation in signs—a factor to which many of the historical authors point, incidentally, as they advocate for standardization through their dictionaries. Due to the cultural relevance of the residential school, it is not surprising that areas around the schools tend to have larger concentrations of Deaf people. We have found many etymons from Deaf people who grew up around the oldest schools on the East Coast, South, and Midwest regions of the U.S.

Ethnic variation has also proved relevant to the history of ASL. Slavery and racial segregation had a significant impact on the language passed down in the African American Deaf community. Residential schools for the deaf in the South were strictly segregated, which gave rise to considerable language variation between African American and white Deaf people (McCaskill, Lucas, Bayley, and Hill 2011; Lucas, Bayley, Reed, and Wulf 2001). Lucas et al. (2001) found that African American signers tend to retain more older forms of signs than their white counterparts. During the process of collecting data for this dictionary, we observed several old signs inherited from LSF in use by African American Deaf people (for example, LIE and WORK) that are not typically used by northern white Deaf people (confirming Lucas et al. 2001). More detailed research of the lexicon of Black ASL may likely reveal more variants with historical ties to LSF.

Traditional variation studies gather data through word lists and elicitation tasks. We have also found etymons in casual interactions. A clear example of this occurred during one conversation Emily Shaw had with a senior citizen from the Indiana School for the Deaf (est. 1844). The woman used a very old variation of the sign BECAUSE (see BECAUSE 4) as she recounted a story about her mother who was frustrated by her (as a child) for repeatedly asking "Why?" Depicting her mother's exasperation, the woman signed the very rare form BECAUSE! just as her mother presumably did in response to her pestering. This variant is not documented in any text, but it provided the missing link that connected the contemporary sign to LSF. When prompted to repeat the sign and explain what it meant, the woman apologized for using the "wrong" sign, judging her old variant as somehow flawed. Countless interactions like this one have revealed some of the rarest and most elusive etymons.

Interestingly, the dictionaries that community members tend to discount as inaccurate often contain variations that tie signs to LSF origins. We consulted several smaller dictionaries published in the 1960s (e.g., Watson 1964; Davis 1966) in addition to Stokoe et al. (1965). Other variants have been found in more recent texts like Shroyer and Shroyer (1984), Riekehof (1987), Costello (1994, 1995, 1999), and Sternberg (1994).

Finally, dialects of LSF have proved a lucrative source of data for documenting the etymology of ASL. Deaf people in several regions of France have maintained old LSF signs that have since disappeared in Paris. These areas include Chambéry, less than 100 kilometers from Clerc's hometown where an all-girls' school retained some older signs that Deaf Americans still use (Delaporte 2012); and Saint-Laurent-en-Royans, whose school for the deaf continued to use sign language covertly during the Silent Century (1880–1980) and where we have found the origins of some of the more obscure ASL signs (like WHY and WEEK). We have consulted contemporary LSF dictionaries published in Paris (IVT 1986, 1990, 1997; Oléron 1974) to serve as references for old signs that remain in the LSF lexicon.

Spoken Language and ASL

The final source of data we have tapped consists of spoken English and French, their written forms, and the gestures that accompany them. Links between a sign and spoken language inevitably occur when written glosses are assigned to translate signs. Uncovering etymological connections, though, is slightly different. For example, traces of English can be found in co-occurring mouth movements (see HAVE and IMPORTANT), initialized signs (like PRINCIPAL and USE/WEAR), and in the semantics and forms of some signs (such as GARBAGE). Because of ASL's connection to old LSF, written French (see STUPID) and even Latin (for example, PROBLEM and SEX/GENDER) are relevant.

Spoken language also has influenced ASL via artificial signed codes. De l'Épée's manual method coupled natural and artificially invented signs to the grammar of written French. He believed that by manually representing the grammar, Deaf students could see and express the written language they could not hear. Methodical signs were largely abandoned by Deaf people in natural conversation. Describing common parlance among American Deaf people, Gordon (1892) states,

> These "methodical" signs, which were never used colloquially, were for words rather than ideas, and were complicated by the addition of manual symbols to indicate the facts and relations of grammatical analysis . . . A practical acquaintance with this De l'Épée-Sicard system has so completely vanished that it is probable that no living teacher can now recite the Lord's Prayer in "methodical" signs. (xlvii)

In the 1960s and 1970s, American schools reintroduced manual codes of English that altered signs to directly map them onto English words. Classroom teachers across the U.S. incorporated invented codes like Seeing Essential English and Signing Exact English. As with de l'Épée's methodical signs, most of the signs from these artificial codes were never incorporated into ASL; however, they were not completely discarded, as some argue (e.g., Supalla 2008). Some initialized lexical items (e.g., LIVE, WINE, AUNT/UNCLE) and invented signs (e.g., FOR, PERSON, and SEX/GENDER) remain a part of ASL unbeknownst to the Deaf people who inherited them from Signed French. In recent years, Deaf Americans have begun to actively reject signs that they perceive to be inherited from these codes even if the etymologies show them to be unrelated (see, for example, OR/THEN and BECAUSE). However, there are lexical items (like SHOES and PRINCIPAL) whose histories were influenced by signed codes and are noted as such.[10]

Emblematic gestures and parts of gestures used by hearing people also factor into the generation of signs in ASL and LSF. It is not surprising that the gestures hearing people use bleed into the local sign language; the primary, meaningful input Deaf people glean from interactions with hearing nonsigners is speech-accompanying (or *co-speech*) gestures. Though we know very little about the historical interactions between hearing and Deaf people (a point Supalla 2008 also makes), daily contact between them certainly occurred. The small percentage of deaf people in any given population guarantees that they will regularly interact with hearing people. Several old signs inherited from LSF (for example, MOCK) were originally borrowed from gestures used by hearing people in France. Parts of gestures are also relevant to the history of signs. For example, the bundled handshape and ring handshape in co-speech gesture (Kendon 2004) convey very similar meaning in ASL and LSF. These data reveal the degree of systematicity exhibited by co-speech gesture. That Deaf people perceive and glean enough meaning from speech-accompanying gestures to incorporate them into their lexicon strongly suggests that gesture is as much a part of spoken language as it is a part of sign (see also Shaw 2013).

The metaphorical significance of places on the body also came from European culture. For example, the heart is the primary location for signs of emotion and personal characteristics, the head is the site of signs for thoughts and knowledge, and the area above

---

10. Future studies might consider why certain invented lexical items are considered acceptable by the Deaf community and become incorporated into the language while others are discarded.

the head tends to be reserved for dreams, theories, and ideas. The nose carries even more specific meaning in LSF—it is the location for sentiments, humor, sexual innuendo, and also negative connotations. We refer to these associations as the sign's *metaphorical meaning*.

Methodology

After the initial contact between old LSF and the signs used by American Deaf people in the early nineteenth century, many ASL signs quickly developed in distinct ways, undergoing either changes in form or meaning, or both. Some signs remained unchanged even after two hundred years. We can group historically related signs according to four general categories: identical forms with identical meanings (e.g., FOR), identical forms whose meanings have changed (e.g., MEANING), altered forms whose meanings have stayed the same (e.g., BROTHER/SISTER), and altered forms whose meanings have also changed (e.g., SEX/GENDER). Because most signs have undergone some kind of change over time, there are often historical links between signs that are today superficially distinct in form, meaning, or both.

We have followed one underlying principle in retracing the trajectory of signs: to propose etymologies based on documentation that can substantiate a change in form and/or meaning. Our process consists of starting with a hypothesis, collecting evidence about a sign, building a proof based on documentation and fieldwork, and providing a conclusive etymology. An example of the method we employed follows.

The sign OLD is produced by pulling the crescent hand downward from the chin into a fist. Americans tend to describe this sign as representing an old man's beard, with the understanding that this metaphorically extends to old women even though they do not have beards. The contemporary LSF sign VIEUX (old) has a slightly different form: the fist taps the underside of the chin. During a trip to Paris, Emily Shaw saw a Deaf person telling a story at a public event, and he signed VIEUX with two fists stacked on top of each other directly under his chin while crouching over like an old person. This depiction revealed the etymology behind the American sign: the hands represent the actual fists of an old person resting his (or her) chin on a cane. Yves Delaporte independently made the same observation in the course of his fieldwork. In France, older people customarily sit outdoors to watch passersby, and they rest their chins on their fists while holding on to their canes. The custom is so widely known in France that when Deaf people embellish the sign VIEUX in a narrative, they are likely to invoke a rendition of that image, *not* an overgrown beard.

The Americans inherited the old LSF sign and adapted it to suit their own cultural associations with older people. John B. Hotchkiss, in his film *Memories of Old Hartford* (1913), also signs OLD with two hands during one of his monologues, only he draws the fists down from his chin. We see here the second step in evolution from the etymon to its contemporary form (where the second hand is no longer a part of the sign). By tracing connections between two contemporary forms with two stylistic variations and historical documents of the sign, we demonstrate not just that the form changed, but also the cultural impetus that triggered it.

The etymologies of many signs (e.g., DANCE, EAT, and TREE) are transparent; we do not document those forms here. However, there are signs whose forms belie their origins (like TIME, which was not originally based on the image of the wristwatch). It is important to note that we do not claim to have found the origins of all signs in ASL; that would be an unconvincing claim for any language. Rather, we are making connections between known records and presenting definitive (and, in some cases, the most plausible) origins for the signs.

Organization of the Dictionary and Conventions

Written glosses represent the languages without orthographies in this book. Some authors of sign language dictionaries have dealt with the limitation of glossing by providing as many homonyms for the English (or French) translations as possible. We have avoided doing so to ease demonstration and have provided the most sweeping translations for signs in as few words as possible. This book is not an instructional text for students of ASL, but it should serve as a resource for those familiar enough with the language to fill in the gaps we intentionally leave. Additionally, we include illustrations of the signs, which should be given as much weight as their glosses. We have tried our best to be clear in our translations of French words for the English reader but this can be difficult considering the number of false homonyms, older meanings of words and signs, and contemporary associations with meanings of words and signs in both languages. In some cases, we include glosses that are less common today because they precisely match the glosses in the historical texts.

Above all, we have tried to create a readable document that follows a logical order. Significant consideration has been given to the order of the entries. In the end, we decided to organize the dictionary alphabetically according to the written glosses. We acknowledge the benefit of organizing a sign language dictionary by handshape or some other feature that does not rely on written language. By assigning glosses and alphabetizing the entries, though, we follow the format of the vast majority of sources from which we gleaned our data, allowing for the easiest means of comparison.

To segment the languages on the page, we have established several conventions. All sign glosses are written in SMALL CAPITALS in English and French. For French signs, we provide an English translation in parentheses immediately following the gloss: — VIN (wine). Emily Shaw translated all of the quotes from French texts. Finally, for theoretical reasons, we intentionally depart from the convention of naming handshapes according to the manual alphabet in lieu of one that describes the forms. We have found that when a handshape is labeled with a letter, that letter can be mistakenly associated with the etymology of the sign. The ASL sign CAREFUL, for example, is commonly referred to as having a K handshape in reference to the English word *keep* (one of the words that can translate this sign). The history of the sign, however, proves that the handshape was motivated by the image of the Devil's pitchfork, one that influenced a slew of signs in ASL and LSF that all relate to notions of caution, danger, hostility, and the worsening of conditions. By describing the handshape as a *fork* handshape, we better capture the sign's metaphorical meaning and we categorically remove reference (be it implicit or explicit) to English-based signing systems. Of course, this is not to say that some signs in ASL and LSF are not initialized; initialized signs are always identified in terms of the letter that represents them. See page xxv for a chart containing our handshape typology.

Illustrations in the Dictionary

This dictionary contains numerous illustrations collected from contemporary and historical sources. Edna Johnston, a Deaf native signer, graduate of the Maryland School for the Deaf, educator, and member of a large Deaf family from the Midwest, South, and East Coast, modeled all of the contemporary ASL signs. Emily Shaw photographed the signs and Carole Marion, a Deaf French illustrator and graduate of the École Nationale des Beaux-Arts (French National College of Art and Architecture), drew them. Marion teaches sign language and visual arts in a school for the deaf in France. In a few instances, Yves Delaporte drew signs. Most of the contemporary LSF signs come from dictionaries produced and copyrighted by the International Visual Theater (IVT), and they are used by permission of IVT.

Two historical works by J. Schuyler Long (1910) and Daniel D. Higgins (1923) are essential sources for the knowledge of ASL's history. The poor quality of the photographs in these texts made it difficult to reproduce them directly in the dictionary. For this reason, Yves Delaporte drew the signs from their originals.

A number of illustrations of LSF signs come from Joséphine Brouland (1855), Pierre Pélissier (1856), Abbé Louis-Marie Lambert (1865), and Abbé François Laveau (1868). Yves Delaporte recently re-edited Lambert's dictionary to make it available to researchers and the general public. Laveau's book has been re-edited by Françoise Bonnal-Vergès in the Éditions Lambert-Lucas (Limoges).

Pat Mallet, a Deaf French illustrator, produced several drawings for this dictionary that clearly depict the etymologies of signs: the image of a typesetter putting type into a stick (PRINT), dueling swordsman (CAN'T and ARGUE), the trumpeter announcing news from Parliament (PUBLICIZE), etc. We also include illustrations of objects and icons from the world that, in the hands of Deaf people, became signs: the hammer that hit the bell to ring the hours (TIME), the horse-driven carriage whose driver took the reins (MANAGE, CONTROL), the globe used in geography courses (EARTH), etc. As much as possible, we have used pictures from the following historical texts for teaching deaf children: Joseph Piroux, *Vocabulaire des sourds-muets* (1830), Abbé Jules Chazottes, *Méthode de Toulouse pour l'instruction des sourds-muets* (1864), Alexandre Blanchet, *Enseignement des sourds-muets* (1864), J. A. Jacobs, *Learning to Spell, to Read, to Write, and to Compose,—All at the Same Time* (1867), and Jérôme Clamaron, *Alphabet dactylologique orné de dessins variés* (1875).

Conclusion

Having undertaken the enormous task of recreating the etymologies of hundreds of ASL signs, we acknowledge the undeniable fact that this work is incomplete. Hundreds, if not thousands, of signs evade explanation simply because we lack enough evidence. While we have many opinions and intuitions about the origins of many signs not included here, we have decidedly resisted the temptation of proposing unsubstantiated claims for fear of perpetuating our own folk etymologies. This work is the first attempt at accumulating all known documentation of the lexicon. It is our fervent hope that more historical documentation of ASL will be found and that more research into the language's etymology will emerge as a consequence of our work. The richness and beauty of this language and its people deserve nothing less.

HANDSHAPE TYPOLOGY

open hand	flat hand	mitten	bent mitten	crescent
small crescent	bundle	rounded bundle	fist	thumb
claw	small claw	double hook	hook	beak
trident	closed trident	right angle	horns	modified horns
little finger	index	paintbrush	fork	key
ring	modified ring	bent middle finger	cupped hand	

Note. Most of the illustrations for these handshapes are from Bill Moody et al, *La langue des signes, dictionnaire bilingue élémentaire*. Paris: Éditions IVT, 1983.

AMERICAN MANUAL ALPHABET

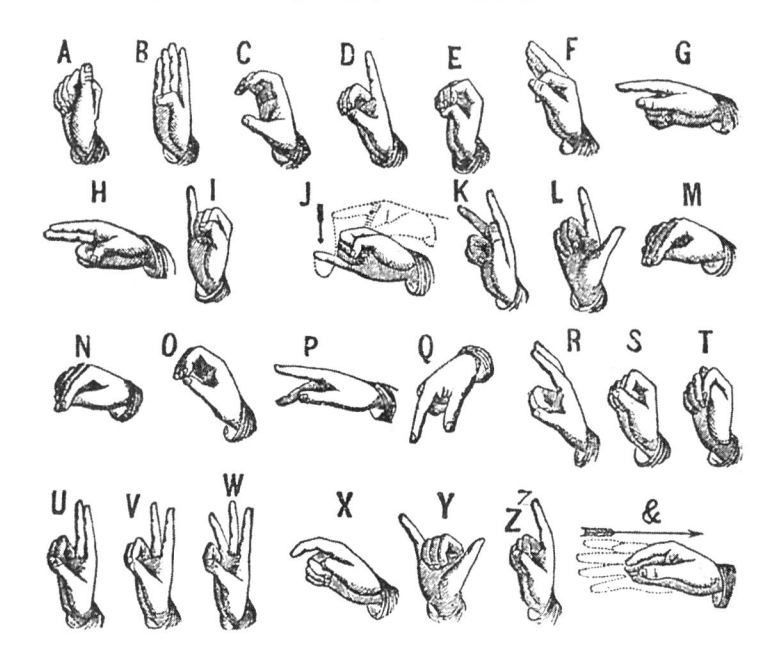

Source: Webster and Campbell, *A Handy Dictionary of the English Language*, 1877.

SYMBOLS AND CONVENTIONS

Symbols

❶ Numbers inside entries indicate variations of a sign that have appeared throughout the course of the evolution of the language.

Conventions

- Small capital letters are used to represent each sign in English and French.
- The meaning of a sign is placed in quotation marks. For example, "right" and "all right" are older meanings of the sign ALL RIGHT.
- Unless otherwise marked, sign illustrations are by Carole Marion. Those marked with the initials "YD" are by Yves Delaporte. The illustrated ASL signs are used throughout the U.S., and the LSF signs are used in Paris, unless otherwise noted. If the illustrations are followed by the phrase "after . . .", then they were drawn from photographs of regional signs in France (Saint-Laurent-en-Royans 1979, Chambéry 1982, Poitiers 1982, Le Puy 1984, Oléron 1974), from photographs in older dictionaries (Long 1910; Higgins 1923; Michaels 1923), from gestures used by hearing people (Wylie 1977), or from other documents listed accordingly.
- On occasion, especially in the case of homonyms, glosses of French signs are translated differently than the original works from which they are cited.
- "Saint-Laurent-en-Royans" is abbreviated as "St-Laurent" in the legends under the illustrations.
- "ALSF" refers to the Académie de la Langue des Signes Française, an association in Paris dedicated to teaching and advancing LSF in French society.
- The expressions "sign used today" and "contemporary sign" refer to signs used since the 1980s, with the understanding that the advent of the Internet has undoubtedly shaped languages in significant ways.
- By convention, the terms *left* and *right* are used to refer to the nondominant and dominant hands, respectively.

A HISTORICAL
AND
ETYMOLOGICAL
DICTIONARY
OF
AMERICAN SIGN
LANGUAGE

✳

A

ABANDON

ABANDON stems from the nineteenth-century French sign ABANDONNER (abandon). The open hands jut outward to express the release of items from one's possession. This sign is also translated by the English word *leave*.

ASL ABANDON

LSF ABANDONNER
(Pélissier 1856)

ABOUT

❶ Kendon (2004) argues that the bundled handshape represents an ensemble of several things (see "The Bundled Handshape," p. 217). The right index finger circumscribes the left, manifesting the meaning of the English word *around* (one of the meanings of *about*). Roth (1948) detected this metaphor and documents it in the entry for ABOUT in his book of basic signs: "the left hand denotes the center core or central idea. The right hand indicates ideas pertaining to the center."

ASL ABOUT 1

❷ This variation of the sign shows the left handshape from ABOUT 1 has assimilated with the right index finger, thus eliminating the metaphorical association with the bundled handshape but retaining the circumscription in the movement.

ASL ABOUT 2

ABSENT

This sign derives from the old LSF sign glossed DISPARAÎTRE (disappear) by Lambert (1865) and means "absent" today. The metaphor behind ABSENT is revealed in the transformation from an open to a bundled hand as the right hand moves below the left hand; the diminution in size ties to the disappearance of something or someone. In ASL, the sign can be used in the literal sense to mean that something disappeared or in the figurative sense that someone passed away.

ASL ABSENT

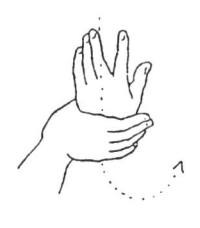

LSF DISPARAÎTRE
(Lambert 1865)

ACCEPT

We see in this sign the act of bringing an object closer to one's body. The transition from open to bundled handshapes reinforces the metaphor of gripping something close to the body (see "The Bundled Handshape," p. 217). This aligns with the literal interpretation of the word *accept*. The same form exists in LSF and is likely the ancestor of the ASL sign.

ASL ACCEPT, LSF ACCEPTER

ADD

The French ancestor of ADD came into existence from the older LSF ENCORE (again; see AGAIN), which also meant "add." The sign is produced when the signer "unite[s] in a bundle the fingers of the right hand and hit[s] it at the center of the palm of the left hand"

ASL ADD

(Lambert 1865).¹ The French sign was imported to the U.S., where it split into two distinct though semantically similar signs: ADD and MORE (see entry). Clark (1885) notes the identical form that we still see in the contemporary LSF sign, where the left hand is held below the right when contact is made. Today, due to assimilation, the hands now draw together in ASL.

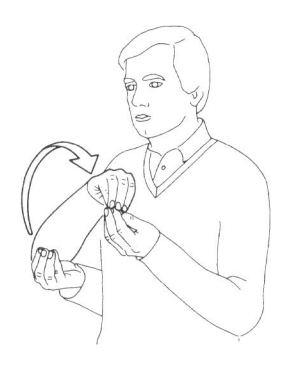

LSF AJOUTER
(IVT 1986)

ADMIT, CONFESS

Described by Higgins (1923) as an "unburdening of the bosom," ADMIT is a gestural metaphor equivalent to "offering one's heart to another," as one does when admitting to or confessing a wrongdoing. A semantically related form is glossed as the sign WILLING (see entry).

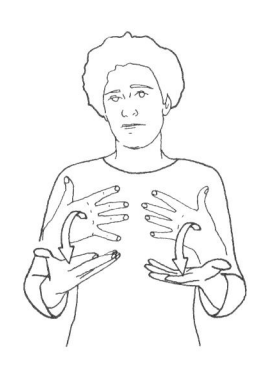

ASL ADMIT, CONFESS

ADVISE

The right bundled hand opens "toward [an] imaginary person . . . as if throwing what it might contain toward the person" (Long 1910). As in the sign INFORM, ADVISE depicts the transmission of information, but it is produced on the back of the left hand instead of the forehead. The back of the left hand also figures in the semantically similar sign WARN, as well as the sign SUMMON (see entries). Tapping the hand is, of course, one way to obtain a Deaf person's attention.

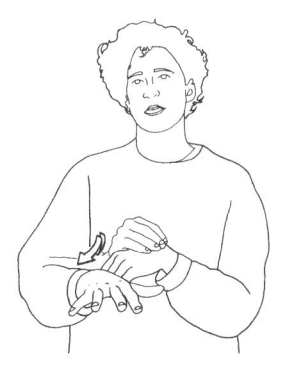

ASL ADVISE

---

1. The quotations from older dictionaries are located in the corresponding entries under the same glosses listed in this dictionary. If an older dictionary glosses a sign differently than in this text, the original gloss will be noted.

AGAIN

This sign is directly inherited from the French ENCORE (again), which Lambert (1865) describes as follows: "unite in a bundle the fingers of the right hand and hit it at the center of the palm of the left hand." In both the ASL and LSF signs, the bundled handshape evolved into a bent mitten hand.

ASL AGAIN

LSF ENCORE
(Brouland 1855)

AGAINST

Inherited from the French sign CONTRE (against), AGAINST is described by Lambert (1865) as follows: "we push back against the object that comes towards the body." The French sign has since been initialized with the letter C, but one variation still widely used in French-speaking Belgium remains uninitialized, like the American sign. The correlation between these two languages, both heavily influenced by LSF, confirms that the original French sign was not initialized.

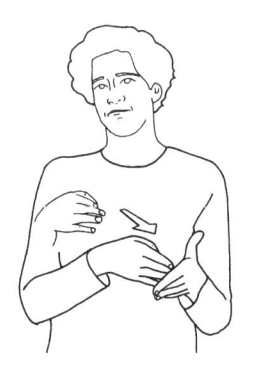

ASL AGAINST

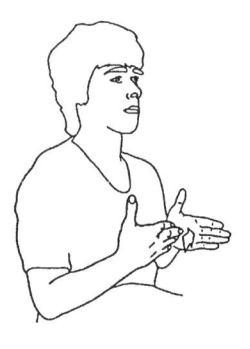

LSF CONTRE (Belgium)
(© CFLSB 1991)

AGREE

❶ In the early twentieth century, the old LSF CONSENTIR (consent) still existed in ASL (Higgins 1923). Lambert (1865) described it as "think or desire same." Long (1910) shows an evolution and reinterpretation of the sign's second part: "bring the other forefinger up alongside parallel to [the left forefinger] but not touching."

ASL AGREE 1
(YD from Long 1910)

❷ Today, the movement of the right index finger is brisk, curved, and downward from near the temple, while the left index finger is initially placed slightly lower than the left shoulder. To denote two parties progressively reaching an agreement, each index finger curves down in sequence without touching. Higgins (1923) translates this sign as "becoming" or "suitable."

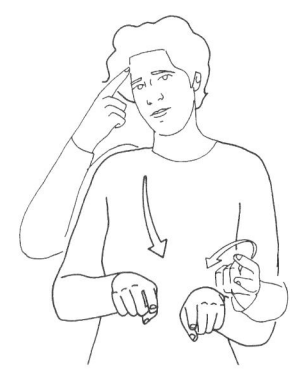

ASL AGREE 2

ALL

❶ The open hands trace the contours of a sphere in space "as if to include the whole" (Long 1910). George Veditz used this sign in *Preservation of the Sign Language* (1913), and it comes from the old French sign TOUT (all): "the right hand, open and above the left hand, has its palm facing downwards and traces a semicircle, the two hands come together at the wrists and the fingers are separated and raised in the air" (Brothers of St. Gabriel 1853–1854).

ASL ALL 2
(YD from Higgins 1923)

❷ The photograph of the sign in Higgins (1923) marks the beginning of the sign's evolution— the right hand moves around the left in a large, circular movement.

❸ Today, the right hand no longer turns fully around the left hand, but rather makes a small circle above before resting on it.

ASL ALL 3

ALL RIGHT

Clark (1885) describes ALL RIGHT under his entry STRAIGHT: "pass lower edge of extended right across palm of extended left, edge touching palm, hands at right angles." This sign was likely inherited from the LSF TOUT DROIT (all right) meaning "follow a straight route." In the earliest records of this sign, the outer edge of the right flat hand traces a straight line across the left palm. In the early twentieth century, this sign could mean "all right," "right," and "correct" (Higgins 1923). We have additional evidence that ALL RIGHT meant "right" or "correct" because of the complementary entry WRONG in Long (1910), where the right hand traces a bent line across the left palm (see FLIP OUT). Today, two unique movements elucidate two alternate meanings of the English word *right*: ALL RIGHT, meaning "okay," is produced with several short concave arcs, while RIGHT, meaning "a privilege to which one is entitled," is produced with a single concave arc. Initialization with the letter *H* results in the sign HONEST.

ASL RIGHT
(YD from Long 1910)

ASL ALL RIGHT

ALLOW

Laurent Clerc brought this sign to the U.S. The two flat hands, palms facing each other, move away from the body as if tracing the edge of a path. Long (1910) glossed the sign MAY, citing that it indicates permission. In France, the etymon of this sign is a gesture used by hearing people to let someone pass but also sarcastically to mean, "Go then, since you want to go there!" (the underlying suggestion being "I think you are wrong"). It is also similar to a gesture where the palms are raised and move around the body, also used sarcastically to mean, "Go ahead, sir." In ASL, initialization with the letters *L* or *P* means LET or PERMIT, respectively.

ASL ALLOW    (Illustration by Pat Mallet)

ALMOST

The tips of the fingers of the right flat hand graze the back of the left hand before contracting into the thumb handshape. Though not documented in historical texts, this sign is possibly an assimilated compound of the signs APPROACH and FIRST, both of which were inherited from LSF.

ASL ALMOST

ASL APPROACH
(YD from Long 1910)

LSF PREMIER
(Lambert 1865)

ALONE

Clark (1885) describes the use of the extended index finger to symbolize a person as a common gesture. The circular movement of the index finger comes from the image of a solitary individual pacing aimlessly.

ASL ALONE

(Illustration by Pat Mallet)

ALWAYS

Lambert (1865) describes the French sign TOUJOURS (always) as "a circle that does not start or finish." Paulmier (1844) describes the sign as "if, with the index, I trace a rapid, circular movement in the air, I cut the wings of time, I describe a circle, the serpent, who is the symbol of eternity in paintings." The circular movement of the hand evokes the never-ending cycle, an image that had been reflected in gestures used by the broader hearing communities (Calbris 2002). In one ASL variation (Higgins 1923), the index finger is held horizontally, pointing away from the signer, identical to the old form documented by Pélissier (1856).

ASL ALWAYS

LSF TOUJOURS
(Pélissier 1856)

ANALYZE

This sign comes from the old LSF CHERCHER (search), where the double hook hand was placed close to the face (Pélissier 1856), and "the movement and expression [resembled] a person who looks from right to left" (Lambert 1865). This sign is not the source of the ASL sign LOOK FOR (see entry for a full explanation). The ASL sign ANALYZE and its French counterpart CHERCHER PARTOUT (search everywhere) depict the act of searching in depth. The double hook handshape is also used in the LSF sign JARDINER (to garden), which transmits the same metaphor behind the word *dig,* whose figurative meaning is to find something through research.

ASL ANALYZE

LSF CHERCHER PARTOUT
(IVT 1997)

AND

The union of the fingers in a bundle symbolizes an ensemble of things (Kendon 2004; see also "The Bundled Handshape," p. 217). The use of the bundled handshape to translate the conjunction *and* manifests the word's meaning in its purest sense. The same sign was once used in Signed French for ET (and), reduced to its final handshape illustrated here.

ASL AND

LSF ET
(Leaflet of a deaf peddler,
19th century.
Above the illustration we
see the symbol & [and])

ANGRY

Higgins (1942) saw the origin of the sign ANGRY as "the old sign of anger, rending of one's garments." In actuality, this sign derives from the French sign COLÈRE (angry), which was originally produced with one hand on the left side of the chest, symbolizing blood boiling in the chest. De Gérando (1827) describes its production as "the open right hand, with open and bent fingers directed toward the heart, executes a rapid and repeated movement from low to high near the heart as if marking the blood agitating." The claw handshape in both LSF and ASL carries metaphorical associations with harsh or mean things (see MAD and SELFISH). Although Long (1910) documents ANGRY as being produced with one hand, it is frequently produced with two hands in contemporary ASL and LSF.

ASL ANGRY

LSF COLÈRE
(Pélissier 1856)

LSF COLÈRE
(IVT 1986)

ANIMAL

The Brothers of St. Gabriel (1853–1854) describe ANIMAL thus: "Sign AIR while batting the hand or with both of the hands forming the letter M pressed against the stomach and following the movement of forced respiration." The LSF letter M is nearly identical to the bent mitten handshape we see in the contemporary ASL sign. Listing qualities of generic concepts was common in old LSF and ASL. Pélissier (1856) cites three signs in his entry ANIMAUX (animals) that correspond to the behaviors characteristic of most animals: "Produce the signs BREATHE, WALK, FLY" followed by the sign ETC. ANIMAL was first documented in the U.S. by Brown

ASL ANIMAL (YD)

(1856) as the sign BREATHE. Clark (1885) similarly describes the production of the sign as "move the hands outwards a few inches, repeating motion to indicate the swelling and contraction of the chest in breathing." The sign has since moved to the area of the upper chest where the fingertips of the bent mitten hands make contact. The original iconic rendering of ANIMAL, then, is completely obscured.

ANY

❶ In the beginning of the twentieth century, the production of this sign involved the extended right thumb jumping along the horizontal axis in small arcs from left to right in front of the signer (Long 1910; Higgins 1923). The root of this sign is the French sign CHAQUE (each), which Lambert (1865) described as "with small jerks of the fist, trace a circular movement in front of the body where only the thumb is raised." The extended right thumb does not represent the letter *A* from the English word *any* as Higgins (1923) suggests, but is from the French sign UN (one) (see "UN (One): The Hidden Number," p. 239). Pélissier (1856) notes that "the closed hand, except for the thumb which appears to be UN, jolts from left to right with successive jumps, as if it wanted to touch or designate each object." This sign also corresponds to the etymology of the French word *chacun*, a compound of *chaque* + *un* (each + one).

❷ In the contemporary sign, the jumping movement has been reduced to a single, outward pivot of the wrist.

ASL ANY 1
(YD from Long 1910)

LSF CHAQUE
(Lambert 1865)

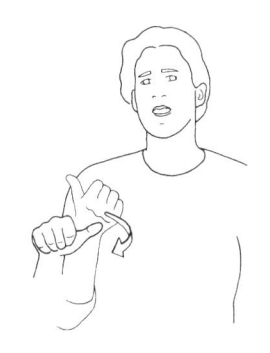

ASL ANY 2

APPLAUSE

The Brothers of St. Gabriel (1853–1854) documented the compound sign FÊTE (feast) as follows: "We clap the palms of the hands against each other and the two hands separate, shaking as with the sign ARBRE [tree]." The first part of the sign, the clap, is the well-known applause gesture used among hearing people. The second part of the sign, where the two hands separate, became the so-called "deaf applause." However, the compound sign remained in use with its meaning of "feast" up until the 1980s in Poitiers, France, which is also the location of the institution run by the Brothers of St. Gabriel. The second part of FÊTE has since diffused throughout France with the meaning "applause." The semantic link between *feast* and *applause* is partly explained by cultural context—in the French residential schools, the only occasion to applaud was during the feast that marked the end of the school year.

ASL APPLAUSE

LSF FÊTE
(YD from Poitiers 1982)

APPLE

There are different regional variations of this sign, but they share a common handshape: a fist that pivots on the cheek representing the apple that one eats. This sign existed in old LSF according to de Gérando (1827), who describes POMME (apple) as "represented by the round form and the action of chewing." Clark (1885) was the first American author to document the ASL sign, which he described as "indicate the size and shape by clasping closed and compressed right with

ASL APPLE

left hand, and then hold closed left hand at mouth, as though eating an entire apple in that way." Noting a slight shift in location, Long (1910) cites the handshape as being placed "at the corner of the mouth," which was likely to allow for a clearer view of the lips for lipreading. Sometime in the first part of the twentieth century, the hooked index finger became the point of contact between the right hand and the cheek. By the 1940s the imagery behind the sign was reinterpreted. For example, Higgins (1942) surmised that the hooked index finger stood for "the depression around the stem." We see, rather, the evolutionary tendency of signs that rotate near the body to eventually make contact on and then center around one point (see WHO 3 for another instance of this phenomenon; see also Delaporte 2008 for examples in LSF).

APPROACH

❶ This sign comes from the old French sign APPROCHER (approach; Lambert 1865) where the back of the right hand moves toward the palm of the left hand (Long 1910). In contemporary ASL, this sign is used in the temporal sense, as in "Memorial Day is drawing near," and also to denote nearing a destination.

❷ Different in form and meaning, APPROACH 2 means "confront" or "meet face-to-face." It is produced by drawing the palms of the two flat hands upwards toward each other.

ASL APPROACH 1
(YD from Long 1910)

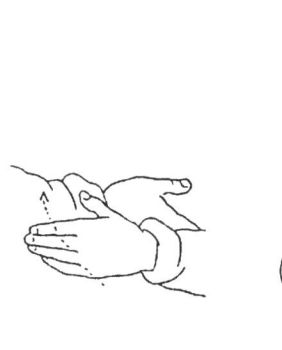

LSF APPROCHER
(Lambert 1865)

ASL APPROACH 2

ARGUE

ARGUE is identical to the LSF sign ENNEMI (enemy), whose etymology Ferrand (circa 1785) described as "men against, swords drawn." Lambert (1865) explained it as "cast the index fingers of each hand across from each other, as two swords." The metaphorical invocation of swords exists in all of the signs semantically related to *discussion* and *dispute* in LSF: DÉBAT (debate), DIALOGUER (dialogue), and SE DISPUTER (argue); and in ASL: ENEMY, OPPOSITE, and STRUGGLE (see entries). Long (1910) saw a different sort of conflict in the sign's symbolism—"let ends of fingers drop, and draw up again, imitating motion of roosters fighting."

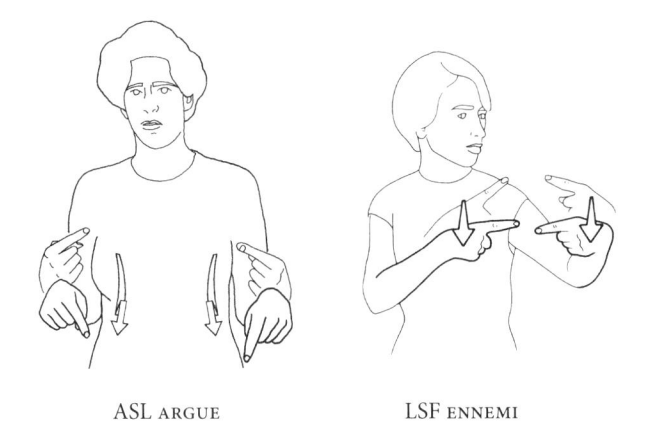

ASL ARGUE

LSF ENNEMI
(IVT 1986)

(Illustration by Pat Mallet)

ARRIVE

Variations of this sign in older texts (Long 1910; Veditz 1913; Higgins 1923) depict the movement of the body (the right hand) as it reaches a destination (the left hand): "1. Drop the back of the right hand in the palm of the left hand. 2. Quickly move both hands out forward in a bouncing manner" (Michaels 1923). Roth (1948) describes the sign slightly differently: "hold the hands before you with the right hand resting in the left hand. Then move both hands forward, lifting the right hand up a little and letting it drop back into the left hand."

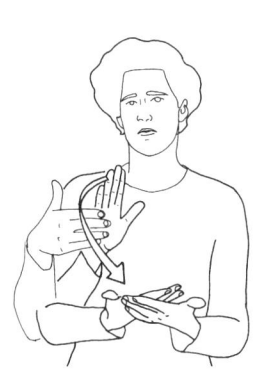

ASL ARRIVE

ASK

Documented first by Brouland (1855), this sign comes from the conventional gesture of clasping the hands to pray. In ASL, the act of praying to God semantically extended to include any request. Today, ASK remains identical to the LSF sign DEMANDER (ask) except in its movement. In LSF, the movement is directed toward the solicited person whereas in ASL the movement is directed toward the signer, foregrounding the solicitor of the request. In contemporary contexts, the sign generally denotes formal requests.

ASL ASK

LSF DEMANDER
(Brouland 1855)

AUTOMATIC

In the most contemporary form, the hooked right index finger slides down the outer edge of the left index finger before quickly rising again. An older variation has the left hand configured in a flat handshape while the right hooked index finger or bent flat hand, traces the outer edge of the left hand. The outer edge of the left hand is implicated in a family of signs linked to skill, precision, and, in this case, automaticity (see entries SKILL and TECHNICAL).

ASL AUTOMATIC

AUTUMN

The symbolism behind this sign is fairly transparent. The raised left arm represents a tree and the right hand represents the falling leaves (Clark 1885). A similar but more iconic sign, AUTOMNE (autumn), exists in LSF, where the open hand depicts a leaf falling from a tree. The brushing contact of the right hand with the left elbow in the ASL sign slightly obscures its root.

ASL AUTUMN 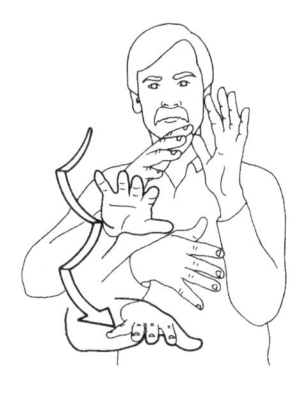   LSF AUTOMNE

AWFUL

❶ The photograph for the sign in Higgins (1923) leaves no doubt as to the origin of the contemporary sign AWFUL—the hair rises on the head as might metaphorically occur in the face of danger. This metaphor appears in English expressions such as "the hair rose on the back of my neck," that describe the experience of encountering a precarious situation. A nearly identical sign exists in Belgium.

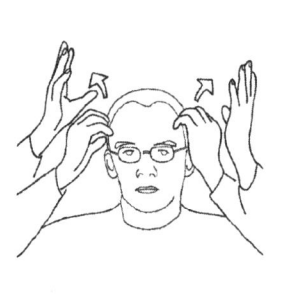

ASL AWFUL 1
(YD from Higgins 1923)

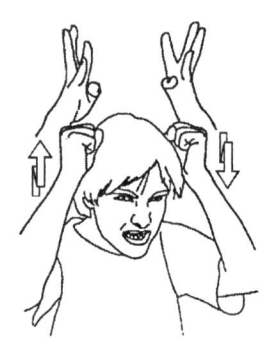

LSF AFFREUX (Belgium)
(CFLSB 1989)

❷ Today, AWFUL is produced in front of the signer with the middle finger flicking outward from the pad of the thumb. It is likely that the shift in location from the head to the front of the signer occurred in the middle of the twentieth century. Watson (1964) notes a variation for AWFUL that he glosses as FEARFUL, which is illustrated like AWFUL 1 but with F handshapes. While it is tempting to interpret the handshape as initialized for *fearful*, it is more likely an intermediary between the

ASL AWFUL 2

18   AUTUMN

older form and the contemporary one. The shift from the ring to the modified ring handshape is common in ASL (see "Handshape Change," p. 148).

AWKWARD

The origin of AWKWARD is the LSF sign PAYSAN (peasant), which depicts the gait of people from the countryside in centuries past. Ferrand (circa 1785) called it a "sign of heavy walking," and Sicard (1808) explained it as showing "the slow and lazy walk of good country folk, their gross habits, badly cut and unkempt." In LSF, the sign also means "impolite." For a detailed account of the etymological relationship between the signs PAYSAN and IMPOLI (impolite) see Delaporte (2007).

ASL AWKWARD

LSF PAYSAN, IMPOLI
(YD from Oléron 1974)

B

BAD

The sign BAD is comprised of two parts. The first is the nineteenth-century French sign BON (good; see GOOD) followed by a form of negation (see DON'T WANT). Clark (1885) also notes BAD as a compound of the sign GOOD and "then turn the hand back down, as it is thrown down to left," a sign of negation. Although there are no texts in France that document the existence of this form in old LSF, a sign identical in form and meaning does exist in Saint-Laurent-en-Royans. There the school for the deaf retained many signs historically similar to ASL, suggesting that this sign for *bad* did exist in old LSF as well.

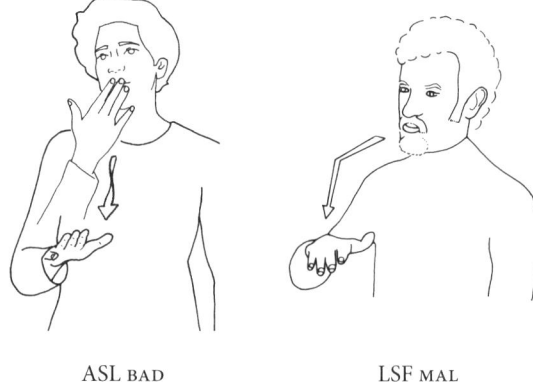

ASL BAD

LSF MAL
(YD from St-Laurent 1979)

BAPTIZE

At one time, this sign was produced as a compound consisting of the sign WATER followed by the extended thumbs "plunged tandem wise down into the water and up again" (Higgins 1923). The handshape is inherited from LSF, where the number 1 as well as *one person* is expressed with the thumb handshape, rather than the index finger. In this case, it most likely stands for *one person* (see "UN (One): The Hidden Number," p. 239).

ASL BAPTIZE

BASEMENT

The thumb hand rotates in a circle beneath the palm of the flat left hand. The extended thumb represents an individual, which can be traced back to the French numbering system where the sign UN (one) can also mean *one person* (see "UN (One): The Hidden Number," p. 239).

ASL BASEMENT

BASKET

❶ The Brothers of St. Gabriel (1853–1854) first described BASKET 1 as "the open right hand, palm turned toward the self is brought to rest on the left elbow and then lifted to the forearm to represent the handle of a basket." The older sign in ASL, as shown by Higgins (1923), shows the intermediary between the original LSF and the contemporary ASL: the right extended index finger crossed over the left forearm, depicting the handle.

ASL BASKET 1
(YD from Higgins 1923)

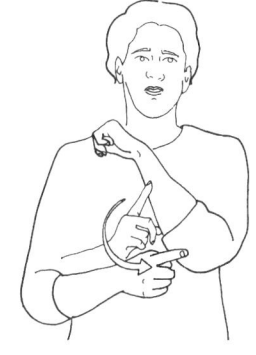

ASL BASKET 2

❷ BASKET 2 had already emerged by the nineteenth century. Clark (1885) describes the shift from an arc on top of the left arm to a convex arc on its underside from wrist to elbow. The pressure to ease production likely motivated the change. BASKET 2 is also commonly used to mean "trash."

(Illustration by Pat Mallet)

BEAUTIFUL

Clark (1885) describes this sign as a compound consisting of outlining the face with the index finger to mean *face* and then "holding extended right hand, palm towards and near face, bring the tips of the fingers and thumb together" to mean *beautiful*. According to Pélissier (1856), the two parts of this sign come from two ancient French signs—JOLI (pretty) and BEAU (beautiful). Once in the U.S., the sign evolved very little. Higgins (1923) wrote that the "right hand finger tips, palm inward, passed down over the face and closed when brought to lips, then ending with a slight upward curve to the right." Blanchet (1850) mentions in his description of the LSF sign BEAU that the open hand at the end of the movement originally represented blowing a kiss. In France, hearing people frequently use a similar gesture to express that something is "splendid" (Wylie 1977). When the sign is reduced to its first part in ASL, it means "pretty." The contemporary ASL form has reduced the two contributing signs by keeping the open handshape of JOLI and then closing it to the first handshape of BEAU.

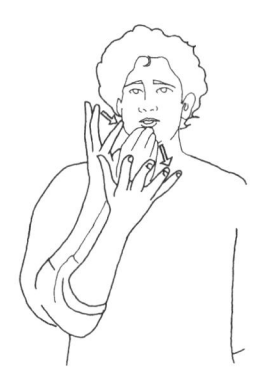

ASL BEAUTIFUL

LSF JOLI
(Pélissier 1856)

LSF BEAU
(Pélissier 1856)

Gesture "splendid" (French hearing people)
(YD from Wylie 1977)

BECAUSE

This highly enigmatic sign contains traces of the LSF C'EST POUR ÇA (that's why), which originally consisted of POUR (for) followed by the letters C and A. The importation of the sign to the U.S. triggered a number of changes, resulting in four variants. Each variant has retained at least one of the three most prominent elements of the old French sign: the index finger of POUR and the letters C and/or A from ÇA.

❶ In the first ASL variant, BECAUSE 1, the index finger glides across the forehead ending with the hand in a thumb handshape. This is the sign POUR followed by the letter A (Long 1910).

❷ In the second variant, BECAUSE 2 (Michaels 1923), we see a remnant of POUR in the initial location of contact, the C in the curved hand that touches the forehead, and the A in the final handshape.

❸ In BECAUSE 3, the orientation of the hand has shifted so that we see only a trace of the sign POUR in the use of the index finger. A remnant of the letter A exists only in the bending of the index finger.

❹ The fourth variant, BECAUSE 4, is an older form used in Indiana and possibly elsewhere (E. Shaw, field observation). To produce this form, BECAUSE 2 is followed by an opening and dropping of the hand away from the body. Here, we see the closest resemblance to the LSF C'EST ÇA (that's it), the most semantically proximal sign to BECAUSE that is also linked to C'EST POUR ÇA.

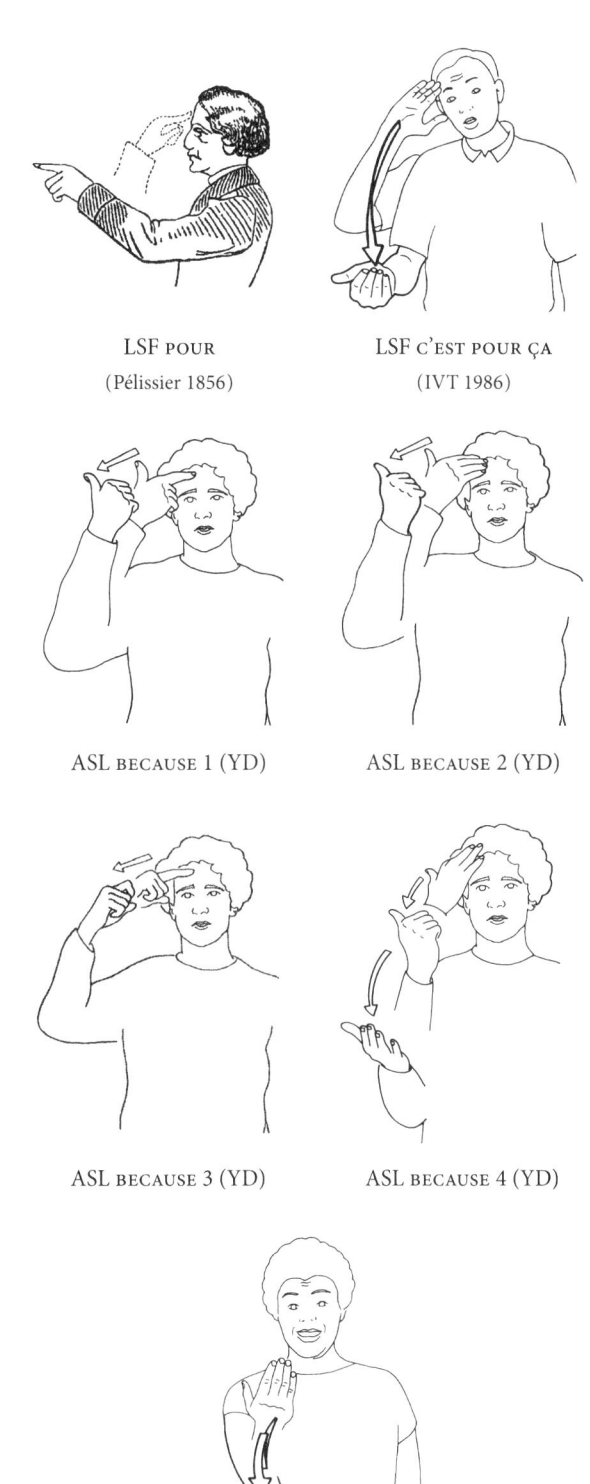

LSF POUR
(Pélissier 1856)

LSF C'EST POUR ÇA
(IVT 1986)

ASL BECAUSE 1 (YD)

ASL BECAUSE 2 (YD)

ASL BECAUSE 3 (YD)

ASL BECAUSE 4 (YD)

LSF C'EST ÇA (IVT 1986)

BEFORE

Abbé de l'Épée (1784) observed that "the deaf and mute, before they come under my tutelage, have come with the idea of the past, the present, and the future.... How did they make it understood that an action had happened in the past? They tossed... the hand over one side of the shoulder." The ASL sign BEFORE conforms to this gesture.

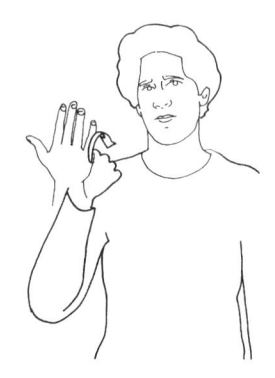

ASL BEFORE

BENEFIT, PROFIT

This sign depicts the act of slipping a small, thin object (i.e., money) into a pocket. An older variation was produced at the hip, whereas the contemporary sign shows the ring handshape positioned at the side of the chest. The same sign has existed for centuries in dialects of LSF outside Paris, especially in Chambéry. Its meaning has since expanded to denote *benefit*, *credit*, and even *points* or *score*.

ASL BENEFIT, PROFIT

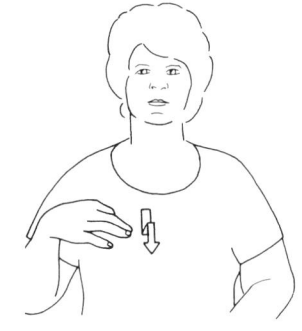

LSF BÉNÉFICE
(YD from Chambéry 1982)

BETTER

This sign is inherited from the compound in LSF mieux (better), which was originally made up of bon (good) followed by premier (first). The sign bon has been in use since the nineteenth century; Blanchet described it as "blow a kiss with the hand" (1850). premier is made by lifting the extended thumb hand (see "un (One): The Hidden Number," p. 239). In ASL, as in the current LSF sign, the two parts of the compound sign good and first have assimilated to become a single unit.

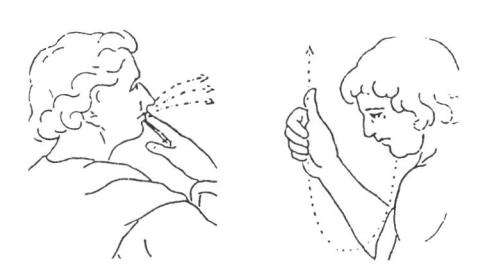

ASL better

LSF bon + premier
(Lambert 1865)

BLACK

Signs for colors tend to become standardized later in the establishment of a lexicon (see red and color). In eighteenth-century France, the sign for the color black was not yet lexicalized; to indicate the color, a signer would merely "show the color black" (Ferrand circa 1785). By the nineteenth century, all of the French authors documented a sign for noir (black) as tracing the eyebrow with the index finger to indicate its color. Clark (1885) states that Deaf people simply "touch the eyebrow with the tip of right index." The contemporary ASL sign has evolved into a slightly higher placement on the forehead and a twisting of the wrist, both of which obscure its origin.

ASL black

LSF noir
(Pélissier 1856)

BLACK 25

BLAME

This sign has a nebulous etymology. BLAME is one member of a lexical family rooted in the old French sign ÉTABLIR (establish) (see "On Common Ground," p. 28), where the left fist symbolized a foundation upon which the right fist established itself (Lambert 1865). The old dictionaries give several forms of the sign in addition to two derived meanings.

❶ In the first American documentation of this sign, Higgins (1923) shows a form much like ÉTABLIR that uses an extended right thumb hand instead of a full fist. This sign remains in use today to establish blame or fault someone. BLAME 1 followed by SELF means "It's my fault."

❷ To assess blame, that is, to blame someone, the right hand is thrust from its resting place on the back of the left hand toward the accused.

LSF ÉTABLIR
(IVT 1986)

ASL BLAME 1
(YD from Higgins 1923)

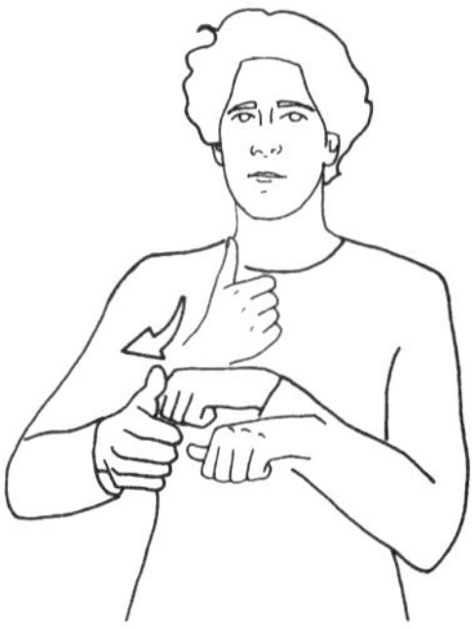

ASL BLAME 2

BLOOD

❶ This is a compound sign first documented in ASL by Clark (1885): "indicate the red color and the flowing." We see the contemporary LSF sign SANG (blood) produced as a similar compound, comprised of ROUGE (red) followed by SE RÉPANDRE (shed).

❷ In the U.S., Deaf people today tend to omit the first part of the compound (RED) or will initiate this sign near the mouth.

ASL BLOOD 1
(YD from Higgins 1923)

LSF SANG
(IVT 1986)

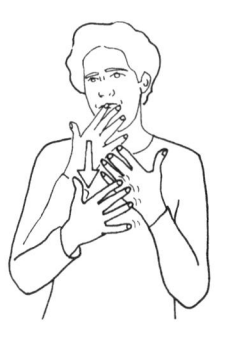

ASL BLOOD 2

BLOW TOP

❶ The right hand, formed in the claw handshape, rises and lowers on top of the left fist. This sign depicts a lid that is thrust open after having held down a pressurized force. We see a similar analogy in the English idioms "blow one's stack" and "he blew a gasket."

❷ Different from the first form, this second sign begins with the right index finger on the forehead, like the sign THINK. This reinforces that the form represents one's inner state of mind.

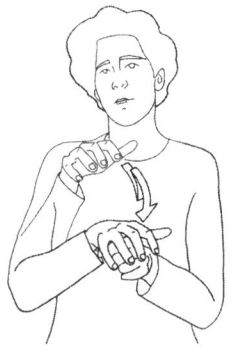

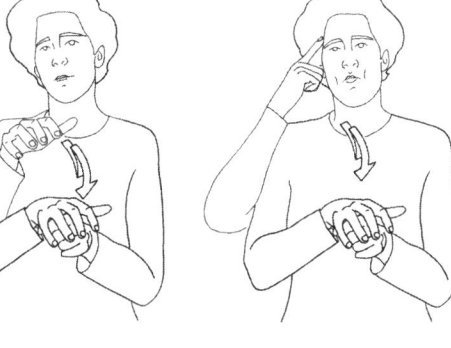

ASL BLOW TOP 1

ASL BLOW TOP 2

BODY

BODY comes from the LSF CORPS (body) described by Lambert (1865): "indicate one's own body by patting the chest, the side, and the thighs with the hands." An evolution of the sign in France and in the U.S. raised the points of contact to the chest and waist. Veditz (1913) uses the sign to indicate a person, not just the body of a person, confirming that CORPS is also the root of the person marker (see PERSON).

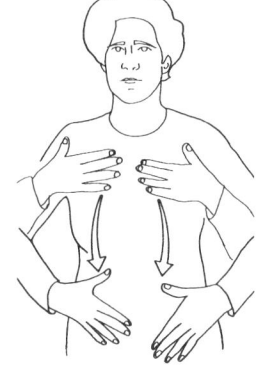

ASL BODY

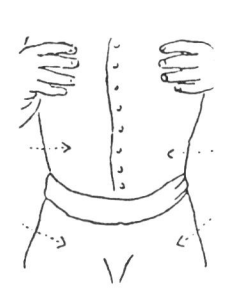

LSF CORPS
(Lambert 1865)

On Common Ground

Several hearing employees at the Institute in Paris (Joseph de Gérando and Alexandre Blanchet, for example) recorded the earliest LSF signs used in the school. These men had an ulterior motive beyond documenting signs: they were linking manual gestures with written forms in French to faithfully execute de l'Épée's method. Because they were well-versed in Latin, like all educated men of that time, their dictionaries contain a considerable number of signs whose forms they created to gesturally represent Latin roots (e.g., GENDER/SEX). Of course, these authors could not absolutely control the signs that Deaf people ultimately used. However, the Deaf community in France eventually adopted several of these invented signs. Over time, the French Deaf community rejected these invented forms, but American signers continue to use some of them unaware that the signs were intended to represent French syntax (e.g., GENDER/SEX, THAN, and PERSON). ASL appears to have retained quite a few more of these invented signs than LSF, partly because the displacement of the language removed all associations that these lexical items had among French Deaf people with Signed French.

It is in this environment that the signs ESTABLISH, INSTITUTION, and BLAME were born. All three signs are founded on the metaphor of a grounded base, represented by the left hand (a fist in LSF and a flat hand in ASL), and an upright entity placed on top of that base (also a fist in LSF and a fist with an extended thumb in ASL).

Both American and French Deaf people extrapolated from iconic forms to create a slew of arbitrary vocabulary. Much like Latin roots reveal concrete associations with English words, these signs are rooted in imagery that can only be explained by referencing all four languages—ASL, LSF, English, and French.

In the LSF signs FONDER (found) and CRÉER (create), the right fist taps the top of the left fist with the palm facing right. Ferrand (circa 1785) describes both as positioning the first stone, and Blanchet (1850) describes them as driving a stake into the ground to mark possession of the terrain. The first step in abstraction from these iconic images occurred in the extension of the meaning of FONDER to name a place. The LSF sign ÉTABLISSEMENT (establishment) is described as "the two hands rest on top of each other, the left hand in the form of the letter S and the right hand in the form of the letter A, which is placed above the left" (Brothers of St. Gabriel 1853–1854, 60). ÉTABLIR (establish) is described by Lambert (1865, 234) as "take with the two hands, as if by the neck, a bottle that was set to the right and set it in front of you."

Normally, establishments and foundations are buildings or entities with institutional power. The association between ÉTABLIR and INSTITUER (institute) in LSF, and then INSTITUTION in ASL, was an easy one to make. Two older texts of LSF (Brothers of St. Gabriel 1853–1854, 60; Ferrand circa 1785, 115) cite an initialized sign that derived from ÉTABLIR to denote *institution*: "Sign the manual letter I and the same sign as establish."

Once transmitted to the U.S., the sign INSTITUTION took on culturally specific meaning. Nearly all of the residential schools in America were called "institutions." The sign for "residential school for the deaf" continues to be INSTITUTION even though these schools are no longer called "institutions" in English. Though the sign existed in older LSF, it fell out of use in the French Deaf community, likely because its initialization indicated such an overt reference to the strongly disliked Signed French.

The final step in abstraction was realized in the sign BLAME. It is likely that the ASL sign derived from the close semantic relationship between the words *establish, institute, found, cause,* and *blame*—all noted synonyms for the sign in the beginning of the twentieth century (Higgins 1923). Higgins (1942, 14) describes the form as the "left hand supporting the right as accepting the burden." He goes further to say that "if this right hand is thrown out towards someone, it means: 'accuse.'" Thus, a distinction based on movement allowed two meanings to emerge: BLAME did not move while ACCUSE moved toward the object of blame. Long (1910) also cites two different forms. In contemporary use, an emphatic version of BLAME meaning "you only have yourself to blame" is essentially a compound of ESTABLISH + YOURSELF. Similar metaphors in English link *blame* with the literal ground on which one stands, as seen in the expression "On what *grounds* do you *base* your argument?"

The juxtaposition of these two classes of signs that differ only in movement is common in ASL (for example, the noun/verb pairs CHAIR/SIT, AIRPLANE/FLY), so it is not unusual that the early sign for BLAME, with a slight modification, functioned as both a noun and a verb. Today, the signs ESTABLISH, INSTITUTION, and BLAME have very different forms, making it difficult to imagine that they are products of the same sign.

BONE

In the nineteenth and early twentieth centuries, BONE was conveyed by tapping the teeth with the hooked index finger (Clark 1885; Long 1910; Higgins 1923). Today, that form is used exclusively for GLASS. Higgins (1923) is the only historical author to cite a different form: "point to prominent knuckles of closed left hand." Today, BONE consists of the double hooked handshapes crossed in front of the signer. A nearly identical sign in LSF means "skeleton" and draws from the image of the skull and crossbones. The double hooked handshape also links BONE to other ASL signs metaphorically associated with hard things (see DIFFICULT, HARD, and PROBLEM).

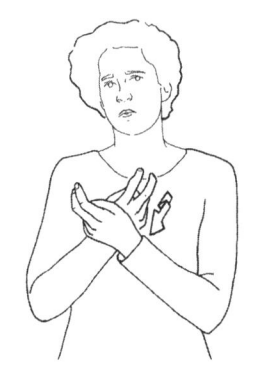

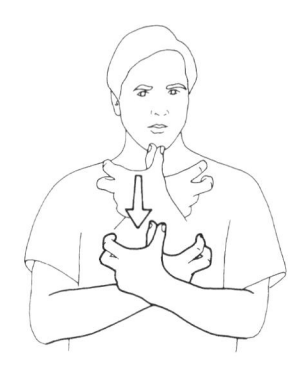

ASL BONE

LSF SQUELETTE
(IVT 1986)

Skull and crossbones
(YD)

BORING

Long (1910) documents a variation of this sign in his entry TEDIOUS: "Place the end of the forefinger on the tip of the nose and press down, bending the head forward slightly as if in obedience to the pressure of the finger." Some may interpret this as a gestural rendition of the English expression "nose to the grindstone." In contemporary contexts, the index finger is placed on the side of the nose and the wrist twists forward, moving the finger off the nose. Though this specific form is not documented in the historical texts, a description of the sign AWL by Clark (1885) might explain the handshape and movement as a play on the double meaning of the English word "boring" which means "dull" but also "drill a hole": "make a boring

ASL BORING

motion with tip of right index, other fingers and thumbs closed, against left palm." The location of BORING is yet another example of the nose evoking negative connotations, also seen in signs like DON'T CARE, LOUSY, and FOOL, JOKE (see entries).

ASL BOSS

BOSS

The sign is inherited from the LSF OFFICIER (officer), which Higgins (1923) recognized as symbolizing "the epaulets on the left arm," the mark of authority for captains in the military. The iconicity behind the sign has slightly diminished as the semantics has expanded; today, the sign refers to all sorts of positions of authority, including *coach*, *captain*, *boss*, and *chairman*.

Illustration of the epaulets of an officer
(Clamaron 1875)

LSF OFFICIER
(Clamaron 1875)

BOTHER

Clark (1885) in his entry COME BETWEEN describes the sign as "lay the lower edge of right hand on curved surface between spread thumb and index of left hand." Translated by Long (1910) as "interrupt, interfere with, come between," this sign is a visual metaphor for what it means to bother someone.

ASL BOTHER

BOY

BOY comes from the LSF sign GARÇON (boy), which was originally a compound of the signs HOMME (man) and JEUNE (young). The second part of the compound has since disappeared. HOMME is described as "taking one's hat to say hello" (Brouland 1855), the "sign of tipping a hat" (Pélissier 1856), and the "sign of lifting and putting a hat back on one's head" (Lambert 1865). Confirming its connection with HOMME, the contemporary ASL sign BOY can also be used to mean "man."

ASL BOY

LSF GARÇON
(Brouland 1855)

Gesture of salutation
(Piroux 1830)

BRAG

This is the repetitive and emphatic form of MYSELF in which the extended thumb, inherited from LSF, carries the value of singularity (see "UN (One): The Hidden Number," p. 239). BRAG is close to the French sign ÉGOÏSME (egotism), which is rooted in the same metaphor as *se vanter* (egotistical) that is, to relate everything to one's self. Lambert (1865) cites the form as "close the right fist and from the back of the thumb, lift and hit the chest two or three times." The lowering of the sign to the hips caused a shift in orientation of the thumbs due to the physical constraint of trying to keep the wrists in the same position, but this obscures the sign's origin.

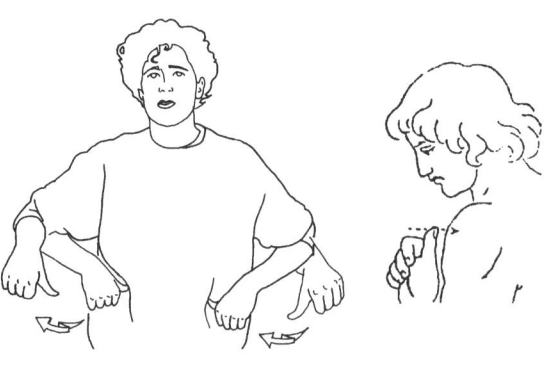

ASL BRAG

LSF MOI-MÊME, ÉGOÏSME
(Lambert 1865)

BRAVE, COURAGE

❶ The older form of BRAVE displays its close ties to the old LSF compound COURAGE (courage). The first part of the LSF sign was a simple pointing to the heart "to show that one is speaking of its force" and the second part was the sign FORT (strong), "produced by bending the arms while closing the fists" (Sicard 1808). Abbé Lambert (1865) glossed the two signs as STRONG HEART. This metaphor also conforms to the etymology of the word *courage*, which comes from the French word *cœur* (heart). The metaphorical influences of *heart* and *strength* are not seen in the early documents of ASL: "taking oneself as if by the lapel of coat and then pulling oneself forward" (Higgins 1923). This description is reinforced by Long (1910), who specifies that the hands are "somewhat open" and initiate at the level of the heart then project away from the chest with force.

❷ Later, BRAVE, COURAGE evolved so that the hands begin on the shoulders rather than the chest, leaving the connection with the heart no longer visible.

ASL BRAVE, COURAGE 1
(YD from Long 1910)

ASL BRAVE, COURAGE 2

BREAD

Both Clark (1885) and Long (1910) characterize the ASL sign as Blanchet (1850) described the LSF sign PAIN (bread): "simulate the action of cutting with the right hand a piece of bread that is held with the left hand." The big loaves of bread of this era were held against the chest with the left hand while the knife sliced through

ASL BREAD, LSF PAIN

the bread towards the left arm. Clark's description is very similar: "holding left hand, back to left, fingers extended and pointing to front . . . make motion of cutting off slices of bread with lower edge of extended right hand, held back to right, parallel to left, and some inches from it" (1885). Thus, in performing the sign, the back of the left hand does not represent a loaf of bread, as is commonly assumed, but rather the hand that held the bread. The migration of the hands toward each other such that the right hand is now in front of the left, obscures the connection with this sign's etymon.

Ancient method of cutting bread
(Nineteenth-century engraving)

BRIDE, BRIDESMAID

Iconic in its origin, this sign represents the way in which a bride carries her bouquet of flowers down the aisle on her wedding day. The sign can also mean "bridesmaid."

ASL BRIDE, BRIDESMAID   (Illustration by Pat Mallet)

BRIDGE

A very old sign that has remained unchanged over the centuries, BRIDGE is cited by Clark (1885) as "make a sign like BASKET, but instead of making the loop under the left arm with the index, make it with first and second fingers." Higgins (1923) saw the symbolism behind the sign as "the four main supports of the bridge."

ASL BRIDGE

BROTHER

❶ This sign is a compound once formed by the signs BOY and SAME (see entries). First documented in ASL by Clark (1885), it derives from the nineteenth-century French sign FRÈRE (brother), which continues to be used in Saint-Laurent-en-Royans. The second part of the contemporary ASL sign has evolved to right angle handshapes.

❷ A variation of BROTHER 1, this sign is the result of a widely recognized process of compounding where two component signs with two different hand configurations (the bundled handshape of BOY and the extended index handshapes of SAME) combine into a sign with a single hand configuration (the right angle handshape in SAME). The modification of the second component, with the thumb extended, has contributed to the divergence from the sign's original form.

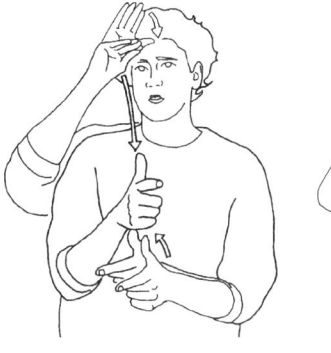

ASL BROTHER 1

LSF FRÈRE
(YD from St-Laurent 1979)

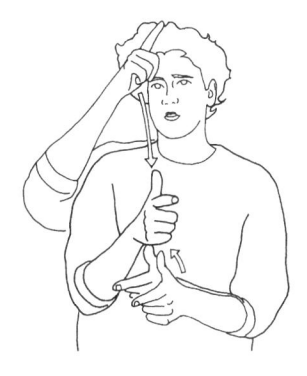

ASL BROTHER 2

BROWN

Historically, most colors were indexed by simply pointing to a nearby object of the same color (see BLACK and RED). BROWN and its variant TAN are the only color signs produced at the cheek. For BROWN, the letter B slides down the side of the cheek. It is possible that the ASL sign derived from an initialization of the old LSF BRUN, MARRON (brown), which Blanchet (1850) describes as "rub the chin with the tips of the four fingers of one hand" to indicate the color of a beard. It is equally possible that the ASL sign emerged independently and refers to brown skin.

ASL BROWN

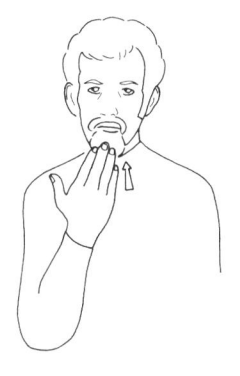

LSF BRUN, MARRON
(YD from St-Laurent 1979)

BUTCHER

This iconic sign, identical in form to the LSF sign, consists of the extended right thumb touching the neck as a butcher's knife might pierce an animal's neck. It capitalizes on the extended thumb as a symbol for something long and thin (see "Meaning of the Thumb," p. 63), which is also seen in the sign DANGEROUS (see entry).

ASL BUTCHER, LSF BOUCHER

BUY

Clark (1885) deconstructs the components of this sign as follows: "make sign for MONEY, for GIVING, and for RECEIVING." The purchase of an object is represented by the payment portion of the transaction, which is the same iconicity found in the LSF sign PAYER (pay) and the ASL sign PAY, identical in form to the LSF sign except with the extended index finger instead of the thumb.

ASL BUY

LSF PAYER
(IVT 1986)

C

CALL

Originally composed of two distinct parts, CALL was documented by Clark (1885) under his entry TELEGRAPH: "tap with tip of curved right index, other fingers and thumb closed, the knuckle of left index finger, and then move the right hand sharply to front." The first part of the sign, then, depicted the visible movement of the telegraph needle, while the second part represented the invisible transmission of pulses through the line. With the advent of the teletypewriter (TTY) in the 1960s and 1970s, the meaning of the sign expanded to "call via TTY." Today, only the second part of the original sign remains. As newer technologies like videophones and texting devices have replaced TTYs, the sign is dropping out of favor, though it is still used, especially when referencing calls made through relay services.

ASL CALL

CAN

This sign matches the French sign POUVOIR (can, power), which conveys a variety of meanings, including "can," "able," "may," and "power" (Pélissier 1856). The sense of power accounts for the hand configurations: "to angle the two arms with closed fists toward the ground to mark power" (Ferrand circa 1785). The sign leverages the symbolism of the fist, which is itself a vehicle of force and ability, though the ASL CAN is not synonymous with power. The movement toward the ground is reminiscent of a command, as in the LSF sign IL FAUT (must) and the ASL sign MUST (see entry).

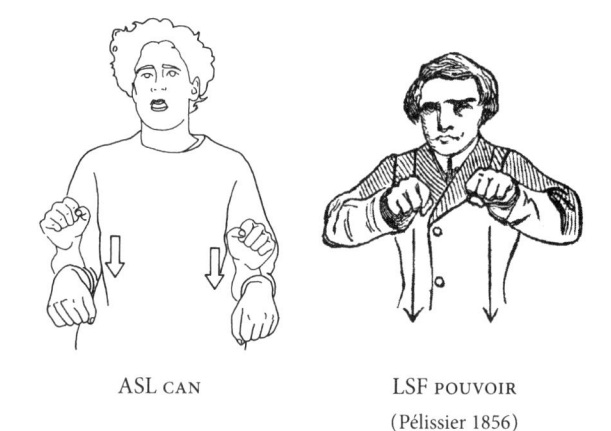

ASL CAN

LSF POUVOIR
(Pélissier 1856)

CANNOT

Found in Clark (1885) under the entry IMPOSSIBLE, as well as in Long (1910) and Veditz (1913), this now ubiquitous sign is identical to the LSF sign INTERDIT (prohibit). In 1853–1854, the Brothers of St. Gabriel described it as IMPOSSIBLE (impossible): "the index of the right hand hits the index of left hand." The fingers may represent a sword fight where one of the adversaries knocks away his opponent's sword (a metaphor also seen in the etymons of ARGUE and ENEMY).

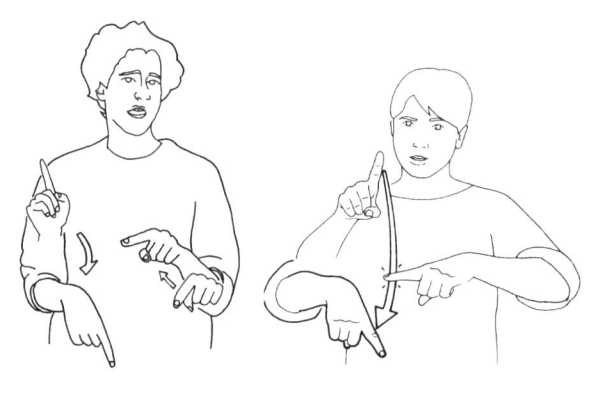

ASL CANNOT

LSF INTERDIT
(IVT 1986)

CAREFUL

The sign is derived from a family of French signs that include MAUVAIS (bad) and DANGER (danger), which are historically linked to a gesture hearing French people used to evoke the Devil (see "The Veiled Devil," p. 176). The American sign CAREFUL can be inflected in a variety of ways by alternating the movement to convey concepts such as "watch over," "take care of," and "keep." Clark (1885) interpreted a secondary image behind the sign—"guarding with double eyes." A similar sign, FAIRE ATTENTION (be careful), continues to exist in LSF.

ASL CAREFUL

ASL WATCH OVER

LSF MAUVAIS
(Pélissier 1856)

LSF DANGER
(IVT 1986)

LSF FAIRE ATTENTION
(IVT 1986)

CARELESS

Clark (1885), Long (1910), and Higgins (1923) all document this sign as one-handed, although today it is frequently produced with both hands. The forked handshape is a trace of the old French sign MAUVAIS (bad; see above), which is borrowed from the gesture used by hearing people in France to signal the Devil. This gesture also contributed to the form seen in the LSF sign DANGER (danger; see HELL and "The Veiled Devil," p. 176).

ASL CARELESS

CAUSE

Long's (1910) documentation of CAUSE reveals a form identical to the French sign ÇA ARRIVE (it happens). A closely related French sign, CAUSER (cause), was used in Paris until the middle of the twentieth century. It consisted of the hands moving away from the signer along the horizontal axis of time, representing the succession of cause and effect (see "Axis of Time," p. 286). The opening of the fists present in all of these signs symbolizes the arrival of something new.

ASL CAUSE

LSF ÇA ARRIVE
(IVT 1986)

LSF CAUSER
(YD from Oléron 1974)

CELEBRATE, ANNIVERSARY

Originating as an iconic sign wherein a signer would be "waving the flag vigorously" in the right hand during celebratory events (Higgins 1942), this sign has since evolved. The left hand now mirrors the right, and both hands have dropped from above the shoulder to in front of the shoulders.

ASL CELEBRATE, ANNIVERSARY

CHALLENGE

The hands in the thumb handshape come together, depicting two opponents confronting each other. The iconicity behind this handshape is the LSF sign UN meaning "one" or "one individual" (see "UN (ONE): The Hidden Number," p. 239). This sign is similar to LSF COMPÉTITION (COMPETITION); it looks like ASL WHICH with the hands a bit closer together and signifies two competitors in a contest. Stokoe et al. (1965) describe CHALLENGE as "meet (in a contest or game)." The ASL sign GAME is semantically proximal to CHALLENGE, but it lacks the initial arched movement of the hands and displays an extra tap.

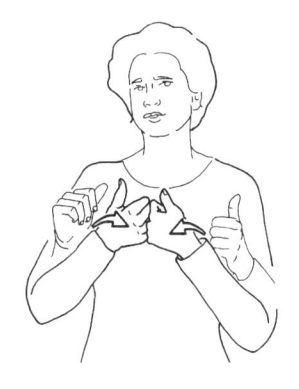

ASL CHALLENGE

CHAMPION

❶ Another meaning of this sign, "crown," reveals its etymology: the right claw handshape lowered on the left index finger represents a crown placed on top of a head. More specifically, CHAMPION 1 depicts the act of putting a crown of laurels on the head of the winner of an athletic event—a tradition inherited from the Olympics of ancient Greece. In an older French sign, in use in Asnières, the left fist represents the human head and is the point of contact instead of the index finger (Shaw has also seen this variant used by some signers in the U.S.). Though most American authors do not mention the imagery behind this sign, Watson (1964) notes in his entry for CROWN that "a champ is being crowned." The sign is common as a

ASL CHAMPION 1

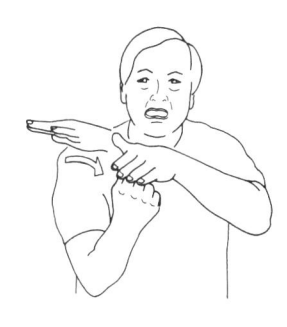

LSF CHAMPION
(regional variant, Asnières, YD)

ASL CHAMPION 2

ASL CHAMPION 3

positive adjective, describing anything of excellent quality.

❷ An older variation of this sign used in Indiana shows a closer etymological relationship to its French origin: the right claw hand is placed near the temple of the signer's head, again, representing the crown of laurels (E. Shaw, field observation).

❸ This form is a reduced variant of CHAMPION 2. The contraction of the little and ring fingers obscures its relationship to the crown.

(Illustration by Pat Mallet)

CHARACTER

In an older version of the sign, the C hand was placed on the signer's heart and then drawn outward from the chest (Long 1910). Today, the sign is produced in the same location but with a small arched movement. In French culture, this area of the chest is the perceived location of personality traits, a belief that finds its roots in numerous metaphors of the heart. There are several nineteenth century LSF examples: a benevolent person was indicated by the signs CŒUR BON (good heart); a capricious person, CŒUR VARIANT (varied heart); a courageous person, CŒUR FORT (strong heart); a depraved person, CŒUR MÉCHANT (mean heart); a proud person, CŒUR GONFLÉ (inflated heart). The location and movement of the sign in ASL has proved especially productive for initialized signs that specify aspects of personal characteristics—ATTITUDE (A hand), LOYAL (L hand), NOBLE (N hand), PERSONAL(ITY) (P hand), and REPUTATION (R hand).

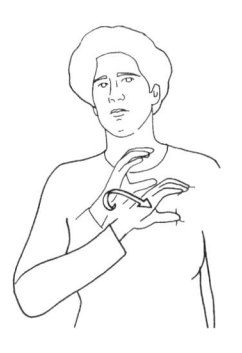

ASL CHARACTER

CHEAT

❶ Stokoe et al. (1965) and Sternberg (1994) characterize this form of the sign as being identical to "mount[ing] a horse." "The derived meaning comes from the use, often dishonestly, of a 'pony' or 'trot' for translating a foreign language; hence the sign in this use is a punning one" (Stokoe et al., 39). (The terms *pony*, *trot*, and *crib* refer to a word-for-word translation of a foreign language, often used to cheat on a test.) In recent forms of the sign, the palm of the left hand faces down to ease production, which obscures the link with HORSEBACK RIDE.

❷ CHEAT 2 likely derives from an older sign documented by Higgins (1923) in his entry ROBBER, where both paintbrush handshapes slide down the sides of the nose. This sign evokes the comic book illustrations of burglars with black masks over their eyes. Over time, the left hand dropped out of use, resulting in the sign THIEF, which also means "cheat" in some regions.

❸ The rubbing together of the little fingers in this regional variation found in Illinois and Florida (Shroyer and Shroyer 1984), draws its meaning from a pejorative gesture widely used in the Mediterranean basin. Rubbing two fingers together symbolizes complicity in undisclosed affairs, most notably in illegitimate sexual relations.

❹ In the handshape of this regional variant seen in New Mexico, Utah, and Wisconsin (Shroyer and Shroyer 1984), the index and little fingers are extended, likely an influence of the metaphor behind the horned handshape (see "The

ASL CHEAT 1

ASL CHEAT 2

(Illustration by Pat Mallet)

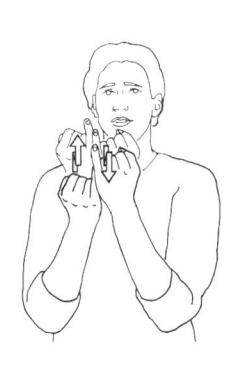

ASL CHEAT 3

ASL CHEAT 4

Veiled Devil," p. 176). It can also be produced with just the extended index finger. The location of the sign is identical to ASL TEMPT (see entry). Cheating and succumbing to temptation are equally negative acts that involve underhandedness and represent a victory for the Devil, the evil tempter. LSF has a sign identical in form to CHEAT 4 that means "spy."

CHEESE

Widely believed to symbolize the process of making cheese by pressing water out of a block, this sign is described by Higgins (1923) as a compound: "Both palms pressed together and pulled apart as if sticky . . . 'Y' shaken at side for 'yellow'." Today, the palms do not separate; instead, the heel of the right hand twists right to left on the left palm, and YELLOW has been dropped. If Higgins' compound was indeed the precursor to this contemporary sign, the only remnant of YELLOW is the twisting movement.

ASL CHEESE

CHOCOLATE

This sign comes from LSF and represents the gesture of grating a piece of chocolate: the left hand stands for the grater while the right hand symbolizes the piece of chocolate. The initialization of the right hand with the letter C breaks the etymological link with its more iconic etymon, but one regional variant seen in Louisiana (Shroyer and Shroyer 1984) maintains the form of the original French sign.

ASL CHOCOLATE

LSF CHOCOLAT
(IVT 1986)

Gestural etymon of CHOCOLATE
(Illustration by Pat Mallet)

CHOOSE

CHOOSE comes from the French sign CHOISIR (choose) that Lambert (1865) compares to the gesture of plucking a flower or to a typesetter picking up characters. The configuration of the ring hand characterizes the small size of the thing that is selected. CHOOSE has since been metaphorically extended to refer to objects of all sizes and abstract concepts. The ASL sign has added the left hand, from which the right hand makes its selection.

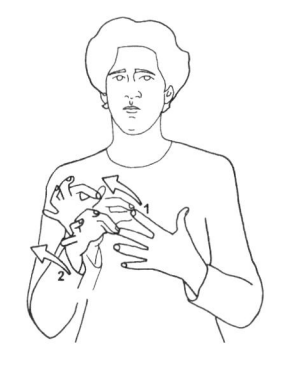

ASL CHOOSE

LSF CHOISIR
(Lambert 1865)

CHRISTMAS

❶ In the beginning of the twentieth century, this sign was formed as a compound consisting of the sign JESUS followed by BIRTH and DAY (Long 1910; Higgins 1923).

❷ The compound has since reduced to a single form, the arm and hand positions come from the last component DAY, and the handshape has been initialized with the letter C. The twisting of the wrist is consistent with the older ASL form of DAY (see entry) where the index finger depicted the progression of the sun from the horizon to the sky.

ASL CHRISTMAS 2

CHURCH

The sign is widely attested, most notably by Higgins (1923), to be a variation of the sign ROCK. The left hand represents the rock, and the right C hand is

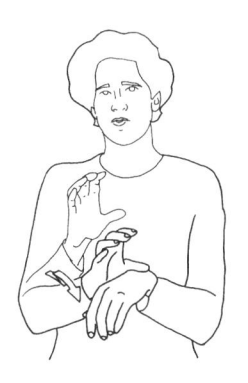

ASL CHURCH

an initialization of *church*. This form references Christ's address to Saint Peter: "You are the Rock and it is on this rock that I will build my Church." From the description in Roth's (1948) dictionary, this sign may be a part of the family of signs linked to ESTABLISH (see "On Common Ground," p. 28).

CLEAN

This sign comes from a gesture meaning "wipe clean" documented in the description of the old French sign PROPRE (clean) by the Brothers of St. Gabriel (1853–1854): "the palm of the right hand sweeps the left hand from the wrist to the tips of the fingers." This is also the sign EFFACE (clear) documented in Brouland (1855). The concrete concept of cleanliness became associated with metaphorical purity as the sign's meaning expanded to include the personality characteristic *nice*.

ASL CLEAN

LSF EFFACE
(Brouland 1855)

CLEAR

❶ The sign described in Higgins (1923) is inherited directly from the French sign CLAIR (clear)—"cross the two fists in front of the forehead and close the eyes then open them suddenly: night passes, the eyes see" (Lambert 1865).

❷ In its current form, the sign has descended to the front of the chest, perhaps for ease of production. It is also used to mean "bright" and "transparent."

ASL CLEAR 1
(YD from Higgins 1923)

ASL CLEAR 2

CLOSE CALL

This sign is not documented in any of the older American texts; however, LSF has an identical sign, PILE, which means "on the dot," "carefully done," "exact," "precise," "impeccable," and "immaculate." In an older variation in Belgium, MINUTIEUX (carefully done), the ring handshape moves from the top of the head rather than the forehead. The Belgian form furnishes the etymology of CLOSE CALL: it is a gestural transposition of the French expression *pile poil* or *au quart de poil* meaning "carefully done, precise." The meaning of the ASL sign seems to stem from the French word *poil* (hair) in that it can also be glossed as "by a hair," and is generally used to mean "just made it" or "that was close."

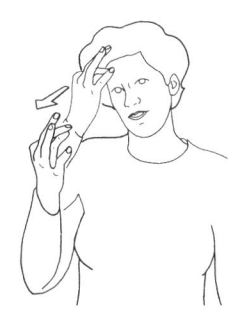

ASL CLOSE CALL

LSF MINUTIEUX (Belgium) (CFLSB 1993)

COLLEGE

This was likely a compound sign at one time composed of SCHOOL (see entry) followed by ABOVE to denote a level beyond regular schooling. Stokoe et al. (1965) note the same symbolism.

ASL COLLEGE

COLOR

In emerging sign languages, it is common to indicate specific colors by pointing to objects of each color. Clark (1885), for example, compared color signs in ASL with those used by Plains Indians: "Deaf-mutes indicate black by touching the eyebrow; red, touch the lips; white, the shirt-bosom; and for the rest, indicate in the same way as with Indians; i.e., point to or touch something possessing the color." In contemporary LSF and ASL, the signs COULEUR (color) and COLOR are produced with the oscillating fingers of the open hand in front of the mouth. The oscillation of the fingers indicates plurality of the colors and may be iconic of their brilliance. Also, the location of these signs is identical to the LSF sign ROUGE (red) and can be explained by the fact that the color red was considered the prototypical color, as evidenced by historical texts. Ferrand (circa 1785) translated *coloris* as "red tint"; Lambert (1865) translated *couleur* as "red paint," and he called the *tricolored sash* (blue, white, and red for France's flag) "red sash." Etymologically, then, COLOR can be deconstructed as meaning "different things like red."

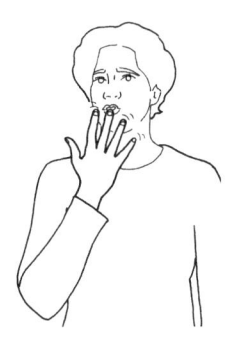

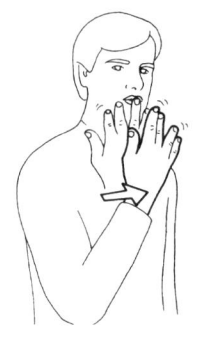

ASL COLOR

LSF COULEUR
(IVT 1986)

COMMUNION

Here, we see the combination of two elements related to the Catholic ritual of taking communion. The ring handshape is iconic, representing the way in which a parishioner holds the communion wafer between the index finger and thumb. This iconicity appears in a similar fashion in the LSF sign COMMUNION. The movement in the ASL sign depicts the sign of the cross that parishioners make after ingesting the wafer.

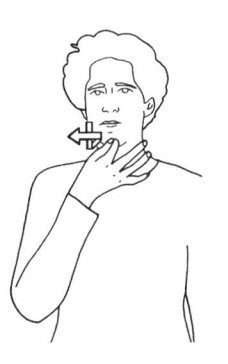

ASL COMMUNION

LSF COMMUNION
(Lambert 1865)

COMMUNISM

This sign represents the Communist hammer and sickle that is seen on the red flag of the former Soviet Union and related territories.

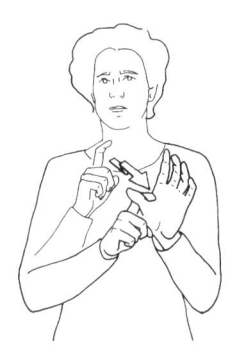

ASL COMMUNISM

(Illustration by Pat Mallet, from a photograph of a Russian soldier planting the Soviet flag on the Reichstag in Berlin in 1945.)

COMPARE

The bent mitten handshapes represent different objects that are compared by bringing them alternately in front of the face. This sign hails directly from the LSF sign COMPARER (compare), which Ferrand (circa 1785) described as "regard the two hands one after another." Long (1910) documents an older ASL variation where one open flat hand is brought next to the other as the signer looks at them. Today, the movement of the arms and head has transferred to the hands.

ASL COMPARE, LSF COMPARER

COMPLAIN

Similar in composition to the sign DISGUSTED (see entry), COMPLAIN is likely based on a visual metaphor of the meaning of the word *complain*: an internal disgruntled feeling from the chest that is made manifest, in this case, with the hand configured as a claw.

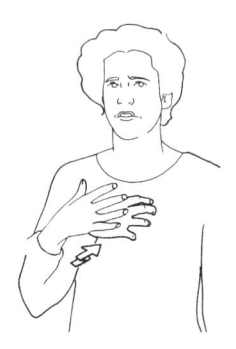

ASL COMPLAIN

COMPLEX

❶ COMPLEX 1 derives from the French sign DIFFICILE (difficult), as recorded by the Abbé Ferrand (circa 1785), where the index fingers were posed on the forehead in the form of a cross. This is almost identical to the old French sign MENSONGE (lie; see LIE) except for the location. The common link between MENSONGE and DIFFICILE—both signed with a cross—is the indication of some kind of obstacle: an obstacle against truth for MENSONGE and against comprehension for DIFFICILE. Today, the cross motif is maintained in the movement of the sign COMPLEX. The sign has lowered to the bottom of the face or directly below it, while the meaning has narrowed to "complex" or "complicated."

ASL COMPLEX 1
(YD)

LSF DIFFICILE
(Illustration reconstructed from Ferrand [circa 1785] by Pat Mallet)

❷ A variant used in Maryland (E. Shaw, field observation), COMPLEX 2 seems to be directly inherited from the LSF DIFFICILE. The only difference is that the sign is produced at the base of the chin instead of the forehead. We see a similar change in the location of the sign LIE (see entry).

ASL COMPLEX 2
(YD)

LSF DIFFICILE
(IVT 1986)

CONCERN

For this sign, the bent middle fingers alternately touch either side of the chest. This handshape is used in the family of signs associated with emotions (see TOUCHED and PITY, and "Handshape Change," p. 148). The location also is consistent with the group of signs associated with personal characteristics and internal states (see CHARACTER).

ASL CONCERN

CONCLUSION

Documented first in 1910 (Long), the ASL sign CONCLUSION is related to the French sign BILAN, DONC (result, conclusion), both of which mean the end of a series of events. BILAN and CONCLUSION share all the same features but handshape, where BILAN is produced with ring handshapes. The LSF sign expresses causation through two metaphors that visually represent the flow of water. The first metaphor represents a plumb line used to measure the depth of water. Lambert (1865) describes DONC (consequently) as follows: "with the thumb and index finger of the left hand, grasp as one might grasp a plumb line that one brings from top to bottom with the thumb and index of the right hand." The second metaphor uses the ring handshapes to depict water as it flows from its source; this metaphor is borrowed from the French word *découler* (ensue), which comes from the word *couler* meaning "running water." Unlike the ASL sign CONCLUSION, which exclusively means the end of something, the contemporary LSF sign BILAN can also mean "leaking water."

ASL CONCLUSION

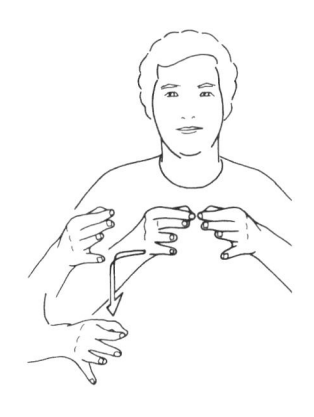

LSF BILAN
(YD, fieldwork)

CONFIDENT

CONFIDENT is identical in form and meaning to the old French sign CONFIANCE (confident), which is described as the "heart drawn toward" by Lambert (1865) and "take from one's heart and give" by Jamet (circa 1830). The moving hands symbolize entrusting one's heart to another person's care. This older LSF form is also maintained in some places in France, such as Le Puy. In ASL, the closing of the hands in the second part of the sign may come from its underlying meaning of seizure: the heart, a symbol of confidence, is held with force.

ASL CONFIDENT

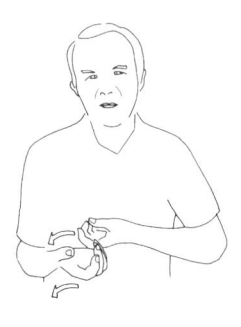

LSF CONFIANCE
(YD from Le Puy 1984)

CONFUSED

This is a compound sign that incorporates the old LSF sign RÉVOLUTION (revolution) that Sicard (1808) described as "trace the orbit of a planet, from its origin and back" (see REVOLVE). The first part is the ASL sign THINK. This compound evokes the sense of swirling, disordered thoughts that one experiences when in a state of confusion.

ASL CONFUSED

CONGRATULATE

Borrowed from a gesture used by hearing people, this sign derives from a form Mitton (1949) described as a "handshake at a distance," such as when a person is congratulated from afar. This sign was already incorporated into LSF's lexicon by the late nineteenth century, as attested in a newspaper article from 1888. Satisfied with a court decision, a sign language interpreter, in front of the courthouse, signs "apparently, giving the handshake, clearly signifying that the three months in prison was at an end and the prisoner was let out to society" (*Le Bon Journal*, 1888). This gesture was intended to be viewed from afar, as it was originally produced higher up in space. In ASL, the sign has lowered to the area in front of the chest.

ASL CONGRATULATE

CONNECT

The ring handshapes join together as a chain might link together two rings. Clark (1885) is the first to document this sign in his entry ALLIANCE. The sign can reference all sorts of connections, both literal and figurative.

ASL CONNECT

CONSCIENCE, GUILTY

To produce this sign, the edge of the extended index finger taps the chest in the area of the heart. This sign can be translated as either "conscience" or "guilty," depending on the context. Because of the proximity in handshape between the extended index finger and the letter G, the sign is frequently assumed to be an initialization of the word *guilty*. However, historical texts in France and the U.S. provide proof that the etymon was not originally initialized. Brown (1856) cites the "forefinger brought up toward body as if reproving." A series of compound signs in nineteenth-century LSF pertained to the domain of conscience or guilt by referencing the heart with the index finger: *cœur juger* (a judged heart/CONSCIENCE), *cœur déchiré* (a torn heart/REMORDS [remorse]), and so on (Lambert 1865).

ASL CONSCIENCE, GUILTY

CONTINUE

CONTINUE belongs to a family of signs in ASL that centers on the symbolic representation of the passage of time (see "Axis of Time," p. 286). This sign is likely inherited from two French signs with similar meaning. The first LSF sign linked to CONTINUE is RESTER (stay), documented by de Gérando (1827) as "the right thumb presses transversally on the left thumb" as if holding it in place; and by Brouland (1855) as "lower the thumbs a bit with a small abrupt movement." The second LSF sign, CONTINUER (continue), shares the same movement as CONTINUE but demonstrates a slightly different configuration and placement of the hands. The semantic proximity of these two LSF signs coupled with the range of forms and associated meanings in ASL, suggests a great deal of flux in the evolution of this sign.

ASL CONTINUE

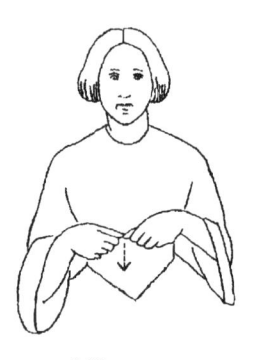

LSF RESTER
(Brouland 1855)

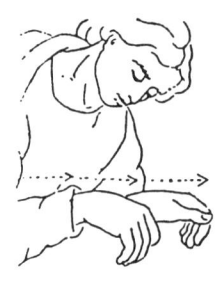

LSF CONTINUER
(Lambert 1865)

COPY

❶ In the early twentieth century, this sign was produced by closing the right open hand into a bundle handshape and placing it on the left palm, as if "taking from one page to put onto another" (Higgins 1942). The older sign, then, was essentially a compound of TAKE and PUT ON PAPER that later changed in form and metaphorical composition such that the sign now includes all sorts of imitation.

ASL COPY 1
(YD from Higgins 1923)

❷ The sequence of movements in the more contemporary COPY 2 is inverted from COPY 1—the open hand first makes contact with the left hand and then pulls outward into a bundled handshape. The depicted act, then, has reversed from recording something from a chalkboard onto paper (Long 1910) to taking something from paper to copy elsewhere.

ASL COPY 2

CORPORAL

In use since the nineteenth century (Pélissier 1856), this sign represents the chevron stripes on military uniforms. In ASL, the sign is produced closer to the shoulder where the stripes are located, as opposed to the wrist in the old LSF sign.

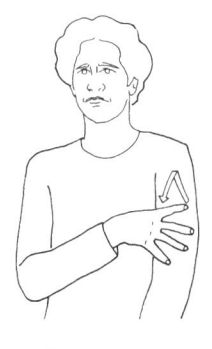

ASL CORPORAL

LSF CORPORAL
(Pélissier 1856)

COST

Inherited from the French sign AMENDE (fee), COST is cited by Higgins (1923) in his entry FINE (charge) as a compound consisting of the sign MONEY followed by the "bent right index, palm in, drawn down left palm" as if drawing money toward the self. In ASL, COST can also mean "fee," "fine," "tax," and "price." While today, the right hooked index finger brushes down the left palm, Long (1910) says the right index finger first moved along the left palm before striking it. The movement is depictive of a blow to the hand, much like the English expression "hit with a big bill." The hooked handshape reinforces the harshness of such a blow (a metaphor also present in the signs TEASE and RUIN).

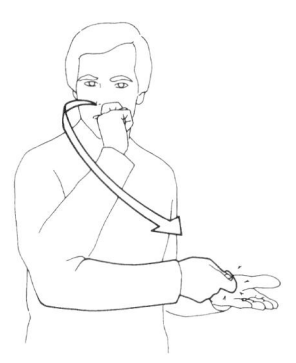

ASL COST

LSF AMENDE
(IVT 1986)

COUNT

This sign is derived from the old French sign CALCULER (calculate), which Lambert (1865) describes "as if grasping a pencil with the right hand, count on the left hand." The ring handshape is common in signs that metaphorically depict the grasping of small or thin objects, like a pencil.

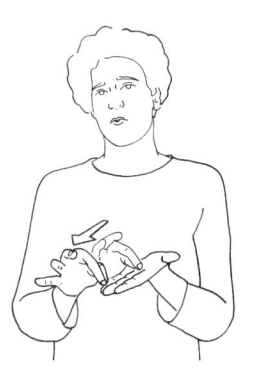

ASL COUNT

COUNTRY

This sign has been interpreted to represent everything from "a tree" and "the land where it grows" (Higgins 1942) to the more recent "elbows of a farm worker" (Sternberg 1994). This form is identical to the French sign CAMPAGNE (countryside) whose etymology, unlike its American counterpart, was documented without ambiguity by the French authors of the nineteenth century: "Simulate the action of cutting wheat with a sickle" (Blanchet 1850); and "harvest" (Lambert 1865). The original LSF sign depicted the action of holding a sheaf of wheat with the left hand and moving the right hand under it as a sickle would cut wheat. The accuracy of this etymology is confirmed by the presence of the same sign in Saint-Laurent-en-Royans, in the southeast of France, as well as in Italy where it is used to mean "August" or "the harvest month" (Radutzky 2001). In the contemporary ASL sign COUNTRY, the movement has reduced to a rotation of the flat handshape on the left elbow, and in LSF the upright left hand has lowered and become inactive. ASL also has a variation with a modified horn handshape, and this is often interpreted as representing the letter Y from the English word *country*.

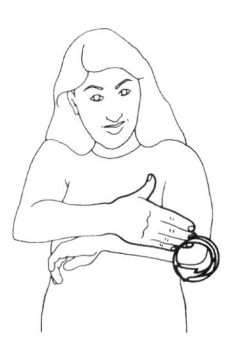

ASL COUNTRY

LSF CAMPAGNE
(IVT 1986)

The Harvest
(YD, from a medieval drawing)

LSF AOÛT
(YD from St-Laurent 1979)

CRAZY ABOUT

This metaphorical sign derives its meaning from a more concrete sign for individuals who are insane. Higgins (1942) documents the form as consisting of the claw handshape moving laterally across the forehead in small, repetitive arcs, showing the "brains are mixed." The contemporary sign involves a single rotation of the wrist across the face with the same hand configuration as its etymon but has adopted a slightly different meaning: "to be crazy about something"—an English expression that denotes extreme affinity for something or someone. The claw handshape often is used to denote negative aspects, and here is likely a trace of the negative association with insanity.

ASL CRAZY ABOUT

CREAM

Often mistaken for an initialized sign, the true etymology of CREAM is quite iconic. The movement of the cupped handshape of the right hand represents the act of skimming off the cream that rises to the top of fresh milk.

❶ Higgins (1923) recognized the iconic origin of this sign, as is seen in his citation: "right inverted 'C' hand moved as if skimming the cream from the surface of the milk." The left hand played no part in the execution of this older sign. Long (1910) describes the transitory phase of this sign's evolution, which would contribute to its diminished iconicity: "making a 'spoon' of the right 'C' hand, make motion of 'skimming' across the back or palm of the left

ASL CREAM 1
(YD from Higgins 1923)

open hand." Here, we see the left hand introduced to represent the surface of the milk, but its orientation has not yet been established; it could appear either palm down or palm up.

❷ By the late twentieth century, the sign underwent two crucial transformations that obscured its iconic roots. First, the left hand became codified as palm up, and second, the right hand evolved from palm down to palm up.

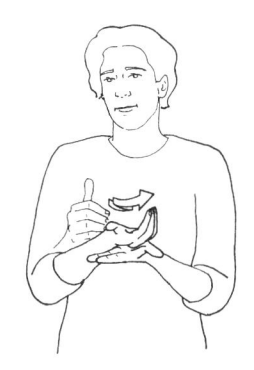

ASL CREAM 2

CURIOUS

This sign is not documented in historical texts and is not related to a French sign. The earliest mention of the sign is found in Stokoe et al. (1965), who cite the key handshape as an alternate configuration of the hand, stating the hand "takes a pinch of skin and shakes." In the most common form, the ring handshape touches the throat as the wrist rotates. In a less common variant, the ring handshape touches the throat, draws away, and then returns.

ASL CURIOUS

CURSE

❶ According to Higgins (1923), the right hand moves "as if taking something from the mouth and throwing it heavenward." Higgins interprets this "something" as throwing the voice or speaking against God. This form of CURSE may derive from an old French sign described by Lambert (1865) as uniquely suited to Deaf parishioners—

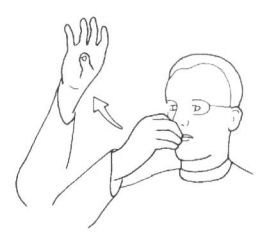

ASL CURSE 1
(YD from Higgins 1923)

"The deaf-mutes who are themselves guilty take the mucous from the nose and throw it up to heaven." This is essentially a directional form of the LSF sign MÉPRISER (despise) aimed at God. Many ASL signs follow this pattern of lowering the hand from the original higher location of LSF signs (see LIE, for example).

❷ The religious undertones of CURSE 1 that are conveyed through the movement toward the sky changed in the contemporary form to projecting the hand away from the mouth and then closing it into a fist. These changes have obscured the iconicity and religious undertones of the older form. However, the claw handshape carries metaphorical associations with harsh or mean things, such as curses.

ASL CURSE 2

CUTE

The sign CUTE derives from the eighteenth century French sign BON, BIEN (good, well), described by Ferrand (circa 1785) as bringing "the index and the middle finger of the right hand to the mouth making the natural sign of a good thing with the lips." In ASL, CUTE has since dropped to the chin. The LSF etymon BON, BIEN produced a family of signs sharing the sense of a "good thing": in LSF, the signs PARFAIT (perfect), EXPERT (expert), and À LA MODE (fashionable); in ASL, the signs CUTE, EXPERT, and SWEET. By metaphorical extension, the sign can also refer to something that is small in size. For example, the ASL sentence I EARN CUTE equates to the English "I didn't earn much."

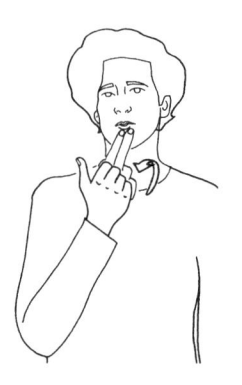

ASL CUTE

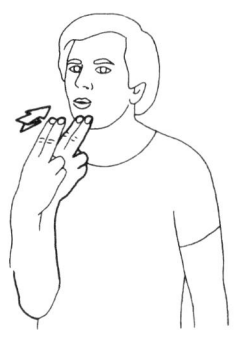

LSF À LA MODE
(IVT 1986)

60   CUTE

D

DAILY

Documented in Long (1910) and Higgins (1923), the ASL sign DAILY is closely related in form and meaning to the LSF sign TOUS LES JOURS (daily). It is also similar to the ASL signs IN A FEW DAYS and TOMORROW (see entry), both of which begin with a thumb hand. Like TOUS LES JOURS, IN A FEW DAYS begins with the thumb brushing the cheek and then moving forward as the fingers open. In all of these signs, the extended thumb represents the LSF number 1 (see "UN (One): The Hidden Number," p. 239). In terms of meaning, the repeated movement in DAILY signals a succession of days, as opposed to the single forward movement of TOMORROW, which signals one day in the future (see "Axis of Time," p. 286).

ASL DAILY

LSF TOUS LES JOURS
(IVT 1986)

DAMAGE

❶ In his NAD film, George Veditz (1913) produces DAMAGE 1 like the French sign EFFACER, ABOLIR (erase, annihilate). The handshape originally represented the letter *A* in LSF, for the first letter of the French word *abolir* (Jamet circa 1830). This handshape was maintained in ASL.

❷ The sign that is used today has undergone two modifications from

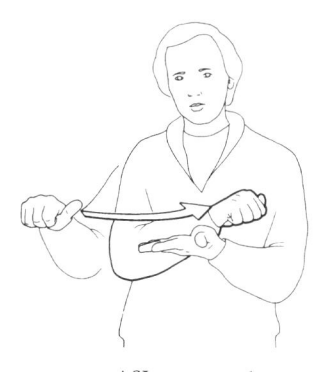

ASL DAMAGE 1,
LSF EFFACER, ABOLIR
(IVT 1990)

ASL DAMAGE 2

DAMAGE 61

the old LSF form: 1) the right hand brushes across the left hand and then moves back to the initial position, and 2) the right hand begins in the shape of a claw before closing into the thumb handshape.

DANGEROUS

In the ASL translation of The Lord's Prayer, A. Clark (1899) and Higgins (1942) document this sign as the equivalent of the English word *trespass*. Clark indicates that the sign is directional. For example, *trespass against me* is signed like the contemporary form, with the right hand moving toward the signer, while for *trespass against you,* the right hand moves away from the signer. In LSF and ASL, the thumb handshape frequently represents one individual, so it is plausible that it symbolizes one person violently attacking another (see "Meaning of the Thumb" p. 63). It is equally plausible that the handshape represents a thrusting knife that is blocked by the back of the left hand since the extended thumb in ASL can also denote a knife (see BUTCHER). Stokoe et al. (1965, 205) note that the sign can be translated into English as *injure* or *danger*. Today, the sign is largely used to mean "danger" or "threat," thus losing an explicit semantic link with a person injuring someone else.

ASL DANGEROUS

The Meaning of the Thumb

In both ASL and LSF, the extended thumb can have several meanings. It can represent an extended, pointy, or thin object such as a knife (ASL BUTCHER, LSF BOUCHER [butcher]), a scalpel (ASL SURGERY, LSF OPÉRER [operate]), a cylinder (ASL SCIENCE, LSF CHIMIE [chemistry]), or the neck of a bottle (ASL POUR, LSF VINAIGRE [vinegar]).

In LSF, the extended thumb also represents the number 1 and, by abstraction, the notions of unity and singularity. This symbolism was transmitted into ASL in several signs, but it is not used for the sign ONE; instead, the ASL ONE is made with an extended index finger (see "UN (One): The Hidden Number," p. 239).

The extended thumb in LSF also depicts the idea of one person in movement, which has carried over to a number of ASL signs. These include —ASSISTANT (one person placed under another), CHASE (one person pursuing another), FAR (one person separated from another), FOLLOW (one person following another), RACE (two people running a race), as well as BEHIND, CHALLENGE, COMMUTE, EACH OTHER, GAME, LIVE APART, and SOCIALIZE. The rupture in the etymological link between the form and its original symbolic meaning allowed for an expansion of its use in ASL to include animate and inanimate objects (for example, a car, a house, or even an abstract concept like work, as in "catch up on my work"). Likewise, as was the case for BEHIND and UNDER, the reference to a person *in movement* eventually became unnecessary. In ASL, then, the extended thumb became a sort of all-purpose tool.

ASL CHALLENGE

ASL SCIENCE

ASL BACKBITE
(YD from Higgins 1923)

The cases where American authors interpret the extended thumb as a person are quite rare. Higgins (1942) recognizes the form in his entry BACKBITE: "right hand is trying to beat the left thumb (a person), down and out of place" (11). Another example is found in Michaels' (1923) entry SWEETHEART (see entry), where he interprets the bending of the thumbs as the bending of heads "like sweethearts do their heads when conversing or courting" (119). But this latter interpretation emerged after transmission to ASL; an altogether different symbolism motivated its French etymon PETIT(E) AMI(E) (sweetheart). The imbued cultural transparency of the LSF extended thumb became lost as the extended index finger slowly replaced it in ASL. That the extended thumb refers to two very heterogeneous categories—"one" and "person in movement"—could only foster its erasure from Americans' consciousness.

DAUGHTER

This form was originally a compound of two signs: GIRL (see entry), which derives from the LSF sign FEMME (woman), and BABY. The contemporary sign exhibits a change in form from its original components. The handshape of GIRL is no longer visible due to assimilation with the flat handshape of BABY. Additionally, the reduplicated movements in GIRL and BABY have been reduced into one sweeping movement of the hand from the cheek to the arm. The male counterpart, SON, is the result of a similar evolution; it began as a compound of BOY (see entry) and BABY, and the handshapes and movement changed. SON is similar in form to DAUGHTER, except that the first part of the sign contacts the forehead rather than the cheek.

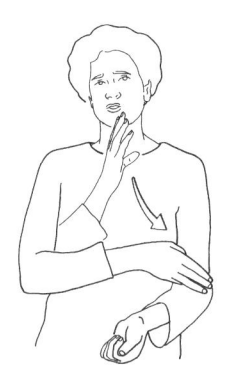

ASL DAUGHTER

DAY

This sign first appears in Ferrand (circa 1785). He describes the movement as "tracing the index finger following the course of the sun's movement across the sky from rising to setting." Clark (1885) first documented this sign in the U.S., saying that it indicated the "path of the sun in the heavens." In the contemporary form, the movement has been truncated to a quarter circle that shows only part of the sun's course. This change has reduced the iconicity of the original LSF sign.

ASL DAY

LSF JOUR
(Pélissier 1856)

DEAF

The form and meaning of this sign hails directly from LSF. Blanchet, the doctor at the school for the deaf in Paris, cited its use in his 1850 dictionary, where he described it as the extended index finger pointing to the ear and then the mouth. This sign likely emerged from a gesture Deaf people used to quickly identify themselves by pointing to their ear and mouth while shaking their heads to indicate they could not hear or speak. In France it is still culturally acceptable to use the term "deaf-mute," which is also a direct translation of the sign's original meaning. However, American Deaf people consider the term outdated and offensive, even though the ASL sign maintains the original reference to "mute" by touching the index finger near the mouth. ASL has two additional variants of this sign—in one, the direction of movement is reversed, and in the other, only the upper cheek is touched (Lucas 1995).

ASL DEAF

LSF SOURD-MUET
(Lambert 1865)

DECEIVE, FOOL

❶ This sign is one of many derived from the evil eye gesture used by hearing people in the Mediterranean region to project injury or ill will on another person (see CHEAT, IRONIC, MOCK, and WRONG). The gesture consists of pointing the horn handshape toward an adversary. In nineteenth-century France, the right hand was placed over the left hand to produce the sign TROMPER (deceive, wrong). Clark (1885) describes it in his entry CHEAT

ASL DECEIVE 1

as "an underhanded exchange." In a similar variant used in Colorado, the right hand passes under the left hand (Shroyer and Shroyer 1984).

❷ In this variant, the index finger of the left hand represents the person who is being deceived. In old LSF, the sign TROMPER could be directed toward the location of a person who was wrong. The directional movement of DECEIVE 2 is the sole remnant of the LSF etymon.

LSF TROMPER
(Pélissier 1856)

ASL DECEIVE 2

DECIDE

The etymology of the contemporary sign is clarified by Long's (1910) description of a compound, where the signer first produces THINK and then, "after balancing hands as in [JUDGE], bring them to an abrupt stop exactly opposite." This is very similar in form to the semantically related ASL sign JUSTICE (see entry), which itself derives from the LSF sign BALANCE (scales). The motivation behind this contemporary form and LSF BALANCE draws from the metaphor "thoughts are objects," particularly ones that are to be "weighed" before a decision is made. Today, the only trace of JUDGE or JUSTICE is in the ring handshapes.

ASL DECIDE

DEFEAT

Here the fist, a symbol of force and power (see CAN, TRY, and BRAVE), thrusts towards an adversary to defeat it. Long documented this ASL sign in 1910 and it is very similar in form to the French sign VAINCRE (defeat). The distinction between the LSF and ASL forms is in the difference in movement and left hand configuration. VAINCRE bends at the elbow while touching the left fist, whereas DEFEAT bends at the wrist while touching the left extended index finger. The ASL sign, then, appears to be a reduced form of the LSF sign. Both contemporary signs can be directed away from or toward the signer, depending on who experiences the defeat.

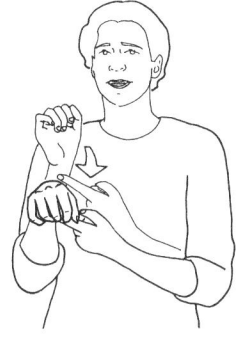

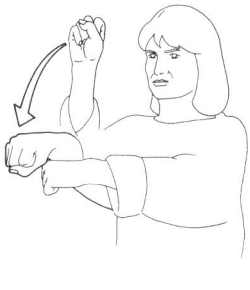

ASL DEFEAT

LSF VAINCRE
(IVT 1986)

DEFEND

Early documentation of this sign in France describes the form as being iconic, representing a knight's or soldier's shield. The signer would depict the action, and "put the left hand on the chest of the [signer] like a shield, and with the other push away the enemy" (Ferrand circa 1785). Later, the two hands assimilated, adopting the same movement and handshape, so that now both fists push away from the body. Although this sign is no longer used in France, it was transmitted to Belgium and the U.S., where the form remains unchanged to this day.

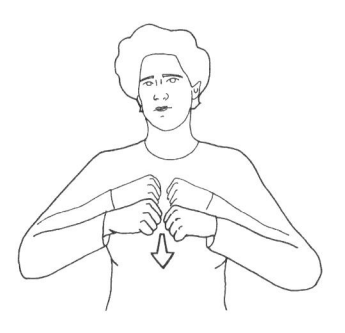

ASL DEFEND

LSF DÉFENDRE
(Belgium; CFLSB 1989)

DELICIOUS

❶ In this very iconic sign, signers "draw extremity of right tips across the lips as if licking them one after the other" (Higgins 1923). The sign was inherited from the LSF DÉLICIEUX (delicious; Lambert 1865), in which the signer must "pass the tips of the fingers of the left hand over the lips as if licking them" (de Gérando 1827). This form and meaning is maintained in contemporary LSF.

LSF DÉLICIEUX, ASL DELICIOUS 1
(Lambert 1865)

❷ The sign's evolution reduced the movement to a single contact on the lower lip with the right middle finger (the same handshape used to indicate TASTE and TOUCH, see entries), followed by the sign SMOOTH (where the thumb glides along the fingertips of the bundled hand, from little finger to index). The two components further reduced into a new sign in which the thumb and index finger of the modified ring handshape contact the mouth and fingers then close into a fist. The movement away from the mouth is the sole trace of SMOOTH, the second part of the original compound.

ASL DELICIOUS 2

DEMAND

According to Long (1910) and Higgins (1923), DEMAND was once produced as an emphatic form of OWE, which came from the LSF sign DEVOIR, DETTE (owe, debt; see OWE 1). The movement was directed toward the signer to indicate that one was owed something. Eventually, DEMAND became a distinct ASL sign independent from its etymon. The subsequent evolution of OWE 2 (see

ASL DEMAND

entry), where the tip of the index finger taps the left palm, facilitated this separation of DEMAND and OWE and allowed them to become two different signs.

DENY

An emphatic version of NOT (see entry), which comes from the LSF RIEN (nothing), DENY is produced with both hands. Because of its etymon, this contemporary sign could be literally translated as "not, not," a forceful denial of an accusation.

ASL DENY

DEPEND

We find the etymology of DEPEND rooted in the form documented by Sicard (1808), who describes the sign DÉPENDENCE (dependence) as "feigning the attachment of one thing on another thing that is higher than the thing being attached." Higgins (1923) confirms the link in his entry, explaining DEPEND as the "left hand pointing outward, palm rightward, and then right bent index hanging on upper edge of left hand." This sign, then, is an iconic rendering of "hang on," which corresponds to the etymology of the word *depend* from the Latin verb *pendere*, meaning "to hang from." Over time the handshape of the right index finger (originally bent) assimilated to match that of the left, and the movement of both hands became the same, obscuring the iconicity that had originally motivated this form.

ASL DEPEND

DETERIORATE

❶ This sign is motivated by the metaphor "down is bad." Using the arm to represent a measuring tool, the right flat hand makes successive jumps down the left arm, an action that Higgins (1942) interprets as the "downward stages of degeneration." The sign's antonym is produced with the reverse movement, and is glossed as IMPROVE (see entry).

❷ In an altogether different form with the same meaning, both hands in the thumb handshape are brought down to signal the deterioration of states experienced by an individual. The raised thumbs are inherited from the French number UN (one), which is commonly used to stand for individuals (see "UN (One): The Hidden Number," p. 239). The movement of the hands employs the spatial metaphor "down is bad," which is common in both French and American cultures.

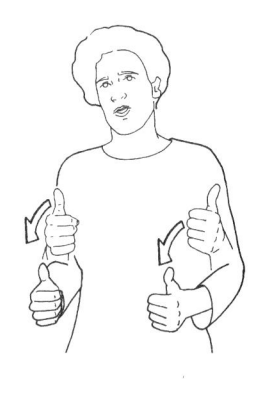

ASL DETERIORATE 1

ASL DETERIORATE 2

DIE

Sharing the same meaning and very similar in form to the LSF sign MORT (die), this ASL sign has been documented as both one-handed (Clark 1885; Long 1910; Higgins 1923) and two-handed (Higgins 1923). Today, the two-handed variant is the most commonly used form. In the early ASL sign, both hands began with palms up and then turned over. Today, the sign begins with the right hand palm up and the left hand palm down, and then the hands turn over so that they reverse their respective orientations. Clark (1885)

ASL DIE

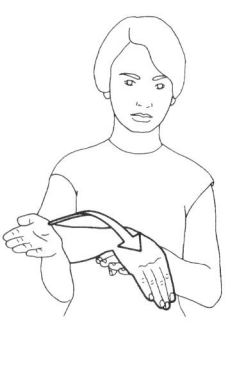

LSF MORT
(IVT 1986)

describes the image behind the sign as a living entity being "knocked over, such as the sudden falling of an animal on being shot."

DIFFERENT, BUT

This sign derives from the old LSF CONTRAIRE, DIFFÉRENT (contrary, different), which Lambert (1865) describes as "unite the two index fingers then curtly separate them drawing them away from each other." In ASL, this sign has taken on the additional meaning of the English conjunction *but*, allowing it to introduce something new to the discourse.

ASL DIFFERENT, BUT

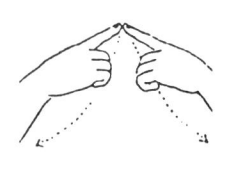

LSF CONTRAIRE, DIFFÉRENT
(Lambert 1865)

DIFFICULT

The double hooked handshape is used in a family of signs to convey notions of hardness, both physical and mental (see BONE, HARD, and PROBLEM). Long (1910) characterizes the form as symbolizing the "effort to push each beyond the other," and translates it "Struggle, indicating trying to overcome obstacles." Higgins (1923) reinforces this link in his entry for HARD, where he lists possible English synonyms as *difficult, scarcely, reverses, obstacle,* and *stone*. ASL DIFFICULT is almost identical to the LSF sign PIERRE (stone), which comes from the old LSF DUR (hard; Brouland 1855). Both the contemporary LSF and ASL signs use the double hooked handshape as a metaphorical symbol of hardness.

ASL DIFFICULT

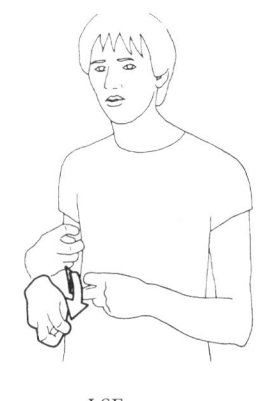

LSF PIERRE
(IVT 1986)

LSF DUR
(Brouland 1855)

DIRTY

This is the French sign SALE (dirty), which is semantically related to COCHON (pig). It is produced as follows: "place the fingers of the right hand, symbolizing the head of the hog, under the chin and lightly move them as if searching in front of itself" (Lambert 1865). In their entries for SALE, Sicard (1808) and Blanchet (1850) both refer the reader to COCHON. Pélissier (1856) has a similar description in his entries SALE and COCHON. Both the LSF SALE and the ASL DIRTY reflect the stereotype that pigs are dirty animals.

ASL DIRTY

LSF SALE, COCHON
(Pélissier 1856)

DISAPPOINTED

The French sign DÉÇU (disappointed) is the etymon of the ASL sign DISAPPOINTED. The contemporary form of DÉÇU is a compound consisting of GOÛT (taste) where the index finger touches the mouth, followed by a form of negation where the open hands drop in front of the chest, literally meaning "taste not." If this form ever existed in ASL, the negation has since disappeared and been replaced by a facial expression. As with many other signs (DRY and TASTE, for example), the point of contact in DISAPPOINTED has lowered from the mouth to the chin, and the movement is now in the opposite direction.

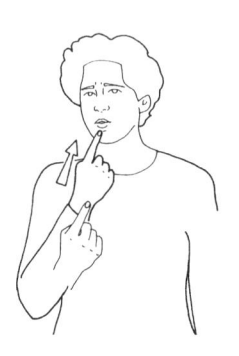

ASL DISAPPOINTED

LSF DÉÇU
(IVT 1986)

DISCUSS, DEBATE

Higgins (1923) describes the sign DEBATE as the "right index struck several times onto the left supine palm and then left index struck several times onto the right supine palm." This form is still used in some contexts today especially when referencing formal debates or extensive discussions between two parties. While his text states that the index finger strikes the palm, Higgins's illustration shows only the tip of each finger touching the respective palms. Long (1910) characterizes this sign as being used when "one often emphasizes his points." Over time, the edge of the index finger, rather than the fingertip, became the point of contact with the palm, and the alternating movement from one hand to the other was dropped.

ASL DISCUSS, DEBATE

DISGUSTED

To produce this sign, the claw handshape moves in a circle on the chest and the signer's face is contorted, which often co-occurs with internal feelings of anger or disgust, either literal or figurative. The claw handshape is a metaphorical association with harsh feelings (see ANGRY, COMPLAIN, and MAD). When ME is added after the sign, it conveys the figurative sense of being disgusted with oneself, as in "I should have thought of that before."

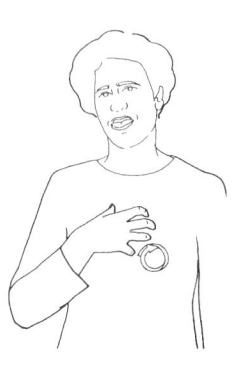

ASL DISGUSTED

DIVIDE

❶ According to Higgins (1923), this sign originally was a compound. In the first part, the right flat hand cut the left palm in half, and in the second part, both hands traced "in the air the two right angles placed at either side of the dividend" (Long 1910).

❷ Today, the two parts of the sign have been consolidated into a single fluid movement.

ASL DIVIDE 1
(YD from Higgins 1923)

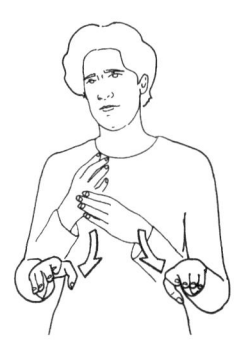

ASL DIVIDE 2

DO, ACTION

Blanchet (1850) described the old French sign FAIRE (do), which referred to manual activities, as "the fingers of the two, slightly bent hands, agitate in front of the body from right to left." Clark (1885) was the first to document this sign in the U.S., stating that signers "indicate action by horizontal motion of hands to front." In contemporary LSF and ASL, the sign has expanded its meaning to include the concept of "work" and "action" specifically in cases where the labor is manual in nature.

ASL DO, ACTION

LSF FAIRE
(Lambert 1865)

LSF FAIRE
(YD from Chambéry 1982)

DOCTOR

This sign derives from the French sign MÉDECIN (doctor), which is described as "check[ing] the pulse" (Ferrand circa 1785). In ASL, the sign has several initialized forms to express different medical professions, such as N for NURSE, D for DOCTOR, and P for an older form of PSYCHIATRIST. Some older signers continue to use the M handshape, inherited from the initialized form in LSF.

ASL DOCTOR

ASL NURSE

The gestural etymon of DOCTOR
(Goust 1954)

DOLL

❶ Michaels (1923) clarifies the etymology of this sign by describing it as "draw the hooked index finger from your forehead down over your nose and chin and sign BABY." The first part of the sign signifies the profile of the face, like in the old LSF sign IMAGE (picture) (Pélissier 1856; see PICTURE). DOLL is one of many signs in an important lexical family in LSF where the bent index finger or the extended thumb traces the profile of the face. Other contemporary LSF signs that incorporate this feature include PORTUGAL (whose form references the country's shape, see PICTURE); MUSÉE (museum), where portraits and statues are collected; DESSIN (drawing), symbolizing the profile of drawn faces; LUNE (moon), which is popularly associated with the human face; and TIMBRE (postage stamp), which in France used to feature the profile of the Greek goddess Cérès.

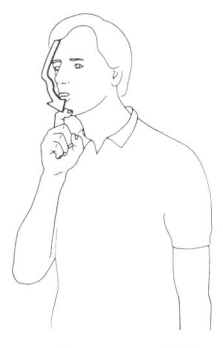

ASL DOLL 1, LSF PORTUGAL (IVT 1990)

LSF MUSÉE (IVT 1986)

❷ Today in ASL, the hooked index finger brushes the length of the nose. The original long movement has been

ASL DOLL 2

reduced into a shorter, redoubled one. At the same time, the second part of the compound, BABY, has been deleted.

DOLLAR

Essentially unchanged since the early twentieth century, this sign was once executed by having the fingertips of the right crescent hand dragged along the length of the left palm from the base of the thumb to the tips of the fingers; this movement highlights the rectangular shape of the American dollar (Long 1910; Higgins 1923). At some point, the orientation of the left hand changed to palm in, and the right fingertips traced the length of the left index finger. In another variation, the right hand grasps the tips of the left fingers and then pulls away, closing to a bundled handshape, thereby obscuring the link with its more iconic root.

ASL DOLLAR

DON'T CARE

❶ Higgins (1923) explains that this sign moves away from the forehead, representing the removal of thoughts from the head. This action is based on the metaphor "ideas are objects." As such, objects can be shared with others (for example, INFORM) or, as in this case, removed and thrown away. Long (1910) notes that the sign moves out either from the forehead or "the end of the nose"; however, he says that the latter "is a rather objectional [*sic*]

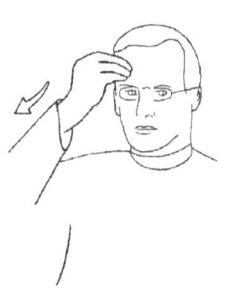

ASL DON'T CARE 1
(YD from Higgins 1923)

slang sign but much used to designate lack of interest."

❷ The contemporary sign evolved from Long's second variant, and it is identical in form to the old LSF sign MÉPRISER (despise). Lambert describes MÉPRISER as "wip[ing] one's nose with the fingers and throw it in the face of an object" (1865). This twisting motion of the hand is a form of negation found in a number of ASL signs (for example, DON'T KNOW, DON'T WANT, and DON'T MIND). When French Deaf people direct this form upwards or "toward the heavens," it is glossed as MALÉDICTION (curse; see CURSE).

ASL DON'T CARE 2

DON'T MIND

The extended index finger moves away from the nose in this sign, which is likely a negated form of THINK (meaning "mind") that was simply lowered to the nose. Interestingly, Long (1910) lists this form as a synonym for DON'T CARE, which may have been used interchangeably during his time. Today, though, DON'T MIND is exclusively used in positive contexts, particularly when asking a favor or responding in the affirmative as in "I don't mind." The same form exists in the LSF sign NE PAS CROIRE (don't believe), which is frequently produced at the nose when used to mean "guess," "feel," and "sense."

ASL DON'T MIND

LSF NE PAS CROIRE
(IVT 1986)

DON'T WANT

This is the sign WANT flung outward to convey negation. This method of negation is visible in several contemporary ASL signs (see DON'T CARE and DON'T MIND). The same sign exists in LSF except that the hands are in double hook shapes, an artifact of the letter V for the French word *vouloir* (want).

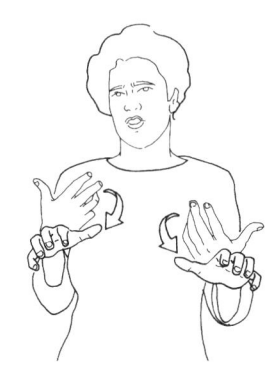

ASL DON'T WANT

DOUBT

Long (1910) states that DOUBT means to "express incredulity," and Higgins (1923) describes its production as "scratching the eyelids or pulling them down." DOUBT appears to be composed of the sign SEE followed by a trace of negation in the bent fingers, indicating something that is not seen. This sign's etymon is found in two gestural metaphors inherited from France. First, the hook handshape often conveys negative meaning in LSF, a feature that is well adapted to the notion of refusing to believe. Second, several LSF signs that express uncertainty or a refusal to believe are located near or on the nose. This particular association with the nose comes from the double meaning of the French word *sentir*, which literally means "to smell" or "to sense," and figuratively means "to have a feeling that." Examples include DEVINER (guess), SOUPÇONNER (suspect), and a variant of NE PAS CROIRE (don't believe).

ASL DOUBT

DRY

Historically, the sign was made by drawing the index finger across the lips, as if wiping the mouth after taking a drink. According to Clark (1885) the sign "indicate[s] that a person is dry by holding crooked index across mouth"; whereas Higgins describes it more concisely as "lips are dry" (1942). The sign has since lowered to the chin, and the extended index finger flexes into the hook handshape as it draws across the chin. This evolution in location also has occurred in the signs LIE and TASTE (see entries).

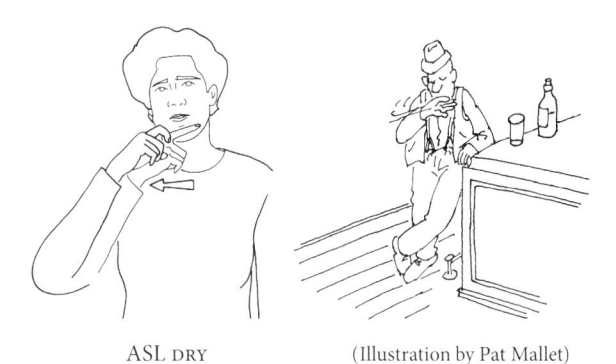

ASL DRY

(Illustration by Pat Mallet)

DUMB

In France, tapping the head with the fist can signify that a person is hard-headed or has an empty head. This gesture is accompanied by spoken phrases like "It rings hollow!" or "It echoes in there!" In both cases, the gesture is a declaration of another person's lack of intelligence. This gesture is equally potent in the U.S.—both Long (1910) and Higgins (1923) gloss the sign as DUNCE. But, rather than characterizing the head as empty, Higgins (1942) explains that "the skull is thick and hard, knowledge is unable to penetrate."

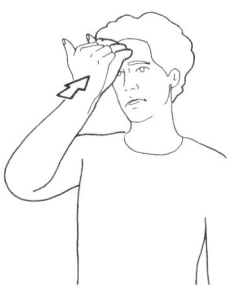

ASL DUMB

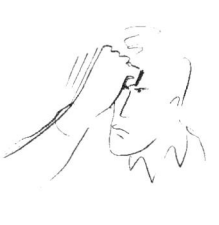

Gesture "hard-headed"
(France, hearing;
illustration by Zaü)

DURING

Here, the two hands trace a straight line away from the signer's body along the axis of time (see "Axis of Time," p. 286). This sign derives from the French sign PENDANT (during), which itself comes from the old LSF sign TEMPS (time) used by Abbé de l'Épée. Sicard (1808) states that "the sign for TEMPS, by the movement of the right hand [. . .], traces a straight line, to indicate the duration of time." An initialized version of PENDANT appeared later in LSF. The contemporary American sign is not initialized but instead uses two extended index fingers placed parallel to one another. Early on, the meaning expanded to include *meanwhile* and *while*, particularly when used to compare two things (Higgins 1923).

ASL DURING

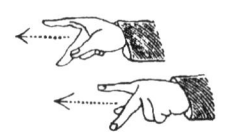

LSF PENDANT
(Pélissier 1856)

E

EACH

EACH descends directly from the LSF CHAQUE (each), which is also glossed as CHACUN (every) and is of the same origin as the ASL sign ANY (see entry). Pélissier describes CHAQUE as produced with "the closed hand, except for the thumb which appears to be UN (one), jolts from left to right with successive jumps, as if it wanted to touch or designate each object" (1856).

❶ In the early twentieth century (Long 1910; Higgins 1923), EACH was produced with both hands in the thumb handshape. The outer edge of the right hand moved down the inner edge of the left hand while moving from right to left. Higgins describes it as the "right hand repeatedly struck down onto left as thumbs point in various directions from right to left." The lateral movement and handshape are both traces of the LSF etymon.

❷ In the contemporary form of EACH, the movement has significantly reduced, and the lateral movement has disappeared.

LSF CHAQUE
(Lambert 1865)

ASL EACH 2

EARTH, GEOGRAPHY

❶ The fingertips of the right thumb and middle finger straddle the back of the left fist, which pivots. This form, documented in Long (1910) and Higgins (1923), leaves no doubt as to the iconicity of the sign—the thumb and the middle finger represent the metal axis of a globe that deaf children would have had in their classrooms, while the left fist represents the globe itself. This etymology of the form explains the expansion of its meaning to include "geography."

ASL EARTH 1
(YD from Long 1910)

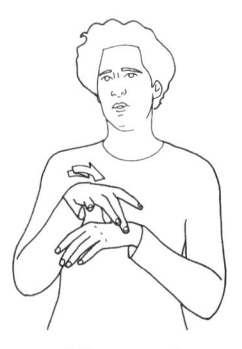

ASL EARTH 2

❷ Today, the thumb and the middle finger no longer encircle the left fist but instead are posed on the back of the open hand. In a break from the sign's original iconicity, the left hand stays immobile while the right hand rocks back and forth.

(Illustration by Pat Mallet)

EASY

Perhaps deriving from one meaning of the word *easy* as something that is pliable or lenient, the right hand brushes the fingers of the left hand, bending them to demonstrate the ease with which they move. Higgins (1942) describes the action as "light, not heavy, the yielding left fingers are easily lifted." The concept behind the sign, then, is the association between something that yields as also being *easy*.

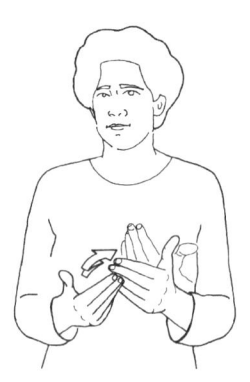

ASL EASY

EGG

The Brothers of St. Gabriel (1853–1854) provide the first, rather lengthy, description of this sign. The Brothers explain that "the thumb and first two fingers of the left hand touch at their tips, assuming the shape of an egg, the right hand forms the letter H, the palm is turned toward the body diagonally, and taps the thumb and index of the left hand on the side near the nail simulating the action of cracking an egg, then the fingers of both hands turn towards the ground to imitate emptying a cracked egg." Clark (1885), Long (1910), and Higgins (1923) all describe the sign with both hands configured in the paintbrush handshape but as maintaining the movement of the old LSF sign. The assimilation of the left hand to the shape of the right, along with the downward movement of both, slightly obscures the imagery behind this sign.

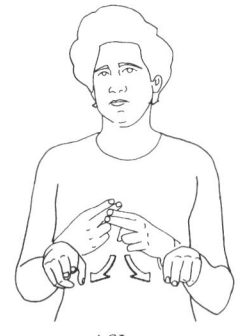

ASL EGG

(Illustration by Pat Mallet)

ELECT, VOTE

This sign is a gestural representation of the act of placing a candidate's written name on a ballot into the voting box. Sicard (1808) was the first to describe this sign under his entry ÉLECTEUR (elector, voter) in which the signer would "imitate the action of one who chooses and elects the most honest and virtuous person to place in the public sphere, by writing their name and throwing it in the urn."

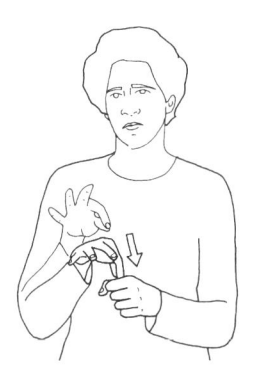

ASL ELECT, VOTE

ELECTRICITY

This sign derives from the French sign ÉLECTRICITÉ (electricity). Long (1910) first documented the ASL sign and remarked that it was still "not uniform," suggesting other variations existed at that time. The tapping of the two hooked index fingers represents the contact between two wires to create an electrical charge. Some older signers use double hooked handshapes to produce this sign (E. Shaw, field observation); this variation may be a trace of the sign's lack of uniformity to which Long referred.

ASL ELECTRICITY

(Illustration by Pat Mallet)

EMBARRASS

EMBARRASS is documented as having four different forms: 1) the open hands rise along both sides of the face (Higgins 1923); 2) the open hands remain in place on the face (Long 1910); 3) the hands are closed in the beginning of the sign and then raise up along the sides of the face into an open hand; and 4) the open hands rise in a curved movement in front of the face (Riekehof 1987). Regardless, all of these forms convey the same metaphorical meaning as the signs SHAME, SHY, and PROSTITUTE (see entries), in which the color red takes over the face as if one is blushing. These ASL signs all derive from the original French sign HONTE (shame) where the back of both bent mitten hands rotated outward from the cheeks. Ferrand (circa 1785) described the sign as "pass the back of the two hands on the two cheeks to indicate the redness that reveals this emotion." Long

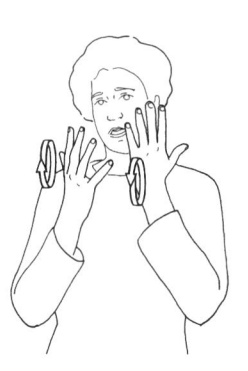

ASL EMBARRASS

84 ELECTRICITY

(1910) establishes the link when he notes that the ASL sign originally began with RED, but this component of the sign has since been dropped.

EMPTY

Higgins (1923) documents an older variation of this sign in his entry BALD, which he also glosses as NAKED. To produce the sign, the "right palm moved over back of left closed prone hand." This sign likely derived from the semantically related French sign NU (naked), where the right hand rubbed over the back of the left hand (Lambert 1865). The handshape of the ASL form has since evolved into a bent middle finger that sweeps across the back of the left hand. This phonological change is apparent in a number of signs in LSF (for example, TARD, RETARD [late]) and in ASL (for example, FORGET, PITY, and SICK), where the flat hand has evolved into a bent middle finger (see "Handshape Change," p. 148). In ASL, EMPTY has proved highly prolific in its meaning; it can be translated by "bald," "nude," "naked," "blank," and, in some regions, "bare feet." When the movement across the back of the left hand is repeated, the sign means "available" (as in, "Is this seat available?").

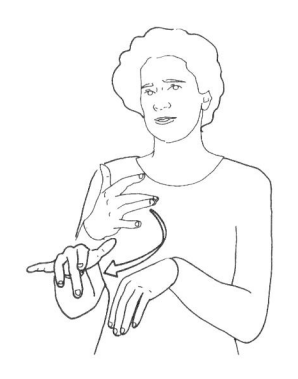

ASL EMPTY

ENEMY, OPPOSITE

This sign is well documented in LSF as ENNEMI (enemy), which is also the source of the ASL sign ARGUE (see entry). Ferrand (circa 1785) described ENNEMI as "men against, swords drawn." The Brothers of St. Gabriel (1853–1854) wrote that "the index fingers touch each other at the tips and quickly separate." The extended index fingers pointing at each other are iconic representations of two swords drawn during a duel. Lambert (1865) also notes this iconicity, explaining that the signer must "cast the index fingers of each hand across from each other, as two swords." Once transmitted to the U.S., the overt reference to swords was lost. Clark (1885) documents the same form that Higgins (1923) describes as a compound that began with the sign FRIEND followed by the hands tearing "apart to remain at the sides pointing at each other threateningly." Today, the ASL sign maintains only the second part of that compound, making it closer to the old LSF sign. When the person marker is added, the meaning becomes "enemy." The contemporary form can also mean "opposite," "oppose," or "contrast."

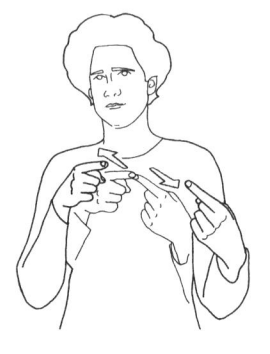

ASL ENEMY, OPPOSITE

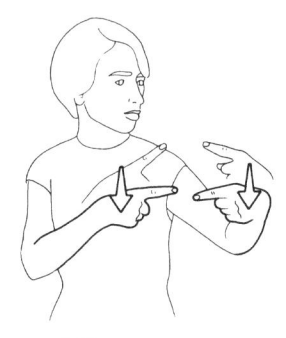

LSF ENNEMI
(IVT 1986)

ENGLISH

The origin of this sign is explained in Clark's (1885) entry BRITISH: "cross the hands over the abdomen to indicate an Englishman." Originating from American stereotypes of British people as being prim and proper, this characterization accounts for why the early

ASL ENGLISH

twentieth-century documents show the hands first folded before being drawn toward the body (Long 1910; Higgins 1923). Today, there is no movement toward the body; instead, the focus has shifted to the contact made between the two hands. Additionally, the sign's meaning has expanded to include the English language (spoken and written), as well as England and its people.

ENJOY

The sign comes from the old LSF sign CONTENT (glad, pleased), which Pélissier (1856) illustrated with the flat hand circling the heart. Higgins (1923) cites the translation "pleasure" in his entry PLEASE, where one hand rubs the chest in a circular movement. At some point, the ASL sign split into two distinct forms with two different meanings. When both flat hands rub the chest and stomach in alternating circles, the sign is ENJOY, while the one-handed form is PLEASE. The extension of the sign's meaning likely occurred as a result of the polysemy of the word *please*, which can be used to mean "cause one to feel pleasure" and also to initiate a polite request.

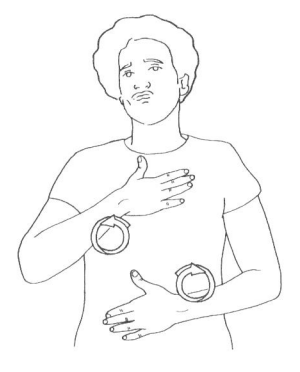

ASL ENJOY

LSF CONTENT
(Pélissier 1856)

ENTHUSIASTIC

Rubbing the hands together is a gesture used by hearing people in France to mean "rejoice" or "I can't wait." It can also be used sarcastically to mean "this is going to be good" when one intends to inflict harm on an adversary. The ASL sign has assumed a more limited meaning than that of the gesture. Long (1910) describes it as "giving the idea of enthusiasm manifested toward object at hand." The sign can also express the synonyms *motivated* and *ambitious*.

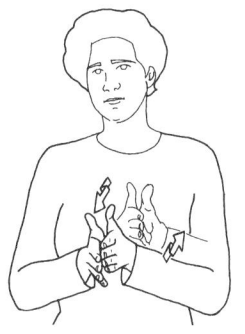

ASL ENTHUSIASTIC    (Illustration by Pat Mallet)

ESTABLISH

This sign is related to the LSF sign ÉTABLIR (establish), which itself is an iconic representation of an object being placed on the ground (see "On Common Ground," p. 28). It differs only slightly from the French form in handshape and movement. The shift from the fist to the thumb handshape may be a metaphorical reference to the concept of one unit being placed on the ground (see article "UN (One): The Hidden Number," p. 239).

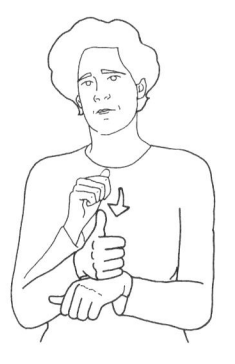

ASL ESTABLISH 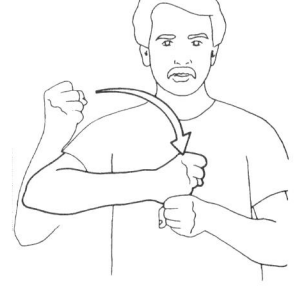   LSF ÉTABLIR
                       (IVT 1986)

ET CETERA, ETC

This form appears to derive from the old French sign ET CETERA, which Lambert (1865) glossed as DIFFÉRENT, DIFFÉRENT, DIFFÉRENT. In ASL, instead of three iterations of the sign DIFFERENT, the hands draw away from each other while the index fingers wiggle.

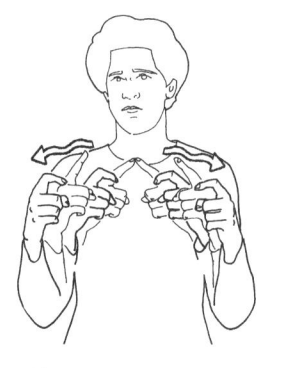

ASL ET CETERA, ETC.   LSF CONTRAIRE, DIFFÉRENT
                       (Lambert 1865)

EXACT

ASL EXACT comes directly from the old LSF sign that Lambert (1865) described as "unite the thumb and index of the right hand and hit the exact center of the palm of the left hand." The sign represented an arrow hitting the center of a target. In ASL, both hands assumed the key handshape, but the sign can also be produced with two ring handshapes, retaining the original configuration of the right hand in the old LSF sign. When the sign is made with two P hands, it means "perfect."

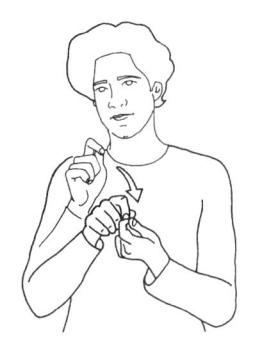

ASL EXACT

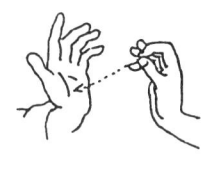

LSF EXACT
(Lambert 1865)

EXAGGERATE

❶ Long (1910) and Higgins (1923) describe EXAGGERATE 1 as deriving from the ASL sign MORE (see entry), which itself was inherited from the LSF sign AJOUTER (add). Higgins (1942) characterizes the meaning as "thinking and making it more and more from various angles." AJOUTER still exists in contemporary LSF.

❷ Derived from the meaning of STRETCH, as in "stretch the truth," the movement of the right fist in EXAGGERATE 2 consists of short, successive jumps (Sternberg 1994) or a single jump (Costello 1994) away from the left fist. This form is depictive in that the fist handshapes preserve the imagery of grasping a pliable object to stretch it, both literally and figuratively.

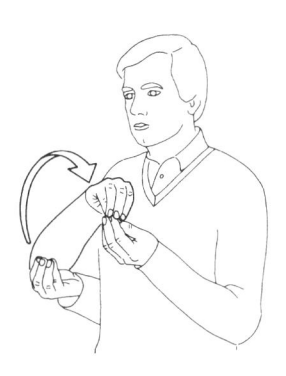

ASL EXAGGERATE 1,
LSF AJOUTER (IVT 1986)

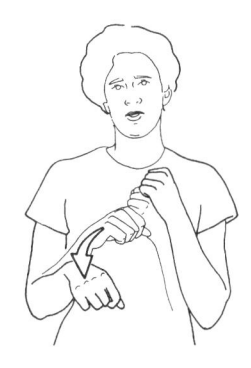

ASL EXAGGERATE 2

EXCITED

EXCITED is identical to the two-handed emphatic form of the LSF sign INTÉRESSANT (interesting), which, in certain contexts, means "exciting." The one-handed form of INTÉRESSANT is identical to the semantically related ASL sign FEEL. Long (1910) notes that this sign is produced while "assuming a nervous manner," but today it is used exclusively to denote a positive sense of excitement. To produce EXCITED, the left and right bent middle fingers alternately brush up and off the chest in upward circles. The handshape and location are consistent with a family of signs related to physical and emotional sensations (see CONCERN, FAVORITE, PITY, and TOUCHED). When the hands are configured with the letter E, the sign is EMOTION.

ASL EXCITED

EXCUSE

This sign comes from LSF PARDON (excuse), which Ferrand (circa 1785) described as "all is erased by wiping the palms of the hands to show that nothing remains." Lambert (1865) preceded this sign with FAUTE (fault), so that "fault [was] erased, by passing the right hand over the palm of the left hand." EXCUSE, then, was what Deaf people used to ask to erase a mistake. Like so many signs, the meaning has expanded to include forgiving a mistake and also to excuse an interruption.

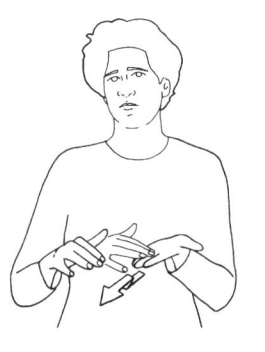

ASL EXCUSE

LSF PARDON
(Lambert 1865)

EXPENSIVE

Originally a compound, this sign once consisted of MONEY (see MONEY 2) followed by shaking the hand to indicate intensity. Today, EXPENSIVE retains only a trace of the first part of the compound, the bundled handshape, and instead of laying the right hand in the left palm, today only the fingertips contact the palm, further obscuring its origin.

ASL EXPENSIVE

EXPERIENCE

❶ In the film *Preservation of the Sign Language*, Veditz (1913) signs EXPERIENCE with both hands in the bundled handshape held slightly above his head. He then opens his hands as they move toward his face. The form symbolizes the sum of knowledge being cast into the brain, creating the foundation of an experience. Some Deaf people in the U.S. still use EXPERIENCE 1 (e.g., Alabama; E. Shaw, field observation). This sign is a directional form of the old French sign ENSEIGNER (teach; see TEACH), where the sum of knowledge is directed toward the signer.

ASL EXPERIENCE 1
(Regional variation, Alabama. YD)

❷ Today, the sign begins with the open fingers of the right hand on the cheek, and then they close into a bundle handshape while dropping twice just below the jaw. The order of opening and closing the hands has reversed from EXPERIENCE 1, and the location of the sign lowered and moved closer to the body. These changes break the etymological link entirely.

ASL EXPERIENCE 2

EXPERT

This sign is related to the old French sign BON, BIEN (good, well), which is formed by bringing "the index and the middle finger of the right hand to the middle of the mouth" (Ferrand circa 1785; see CUTE). In LSF, this sign gave rise to the contemporary sign À LA MODE, EXPERT (fashionable, expert), which has since lowered to the chin. In ASL, the sign's positive connotation has been reinforced by the shift in handshape from the paintbrush to the ring, a configuration that carries the metaphorical meaning of precision and detail in ASL and also is a common gesture among hearing people (see EXACT). Calbris (2002), for example, observes that French words such as *précis* (precise), *exact* (exact), and *rigoureux* (rigorous) are often accompanied by gestures with the ring handshape. Kendon (2004) also documents the ring handshape as a gesture that co-occurs with spoken phrases denoting precision. In ASL, EXPERT is used to describe exceptional capability in some regard, not just "I am an expert," but more broadly "I can do that extremely well."

ASL EXPERT

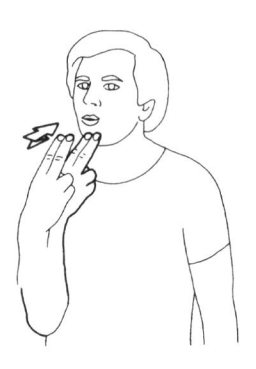

LSF À LA MODE, EXPERT
(IVT 1986)

EXPLAIN, TELL A STORY

❶ This old sign originates in the LSF EXPLIQUER (explain), and has remained unchanged since the eighteenth century. Abbé Ferrand (circa 1785) provides its etymology, explaining that the form represents "remov[ing] the folds with both thumbs and index fingers as is done to make a roll of ribbons." Higgins was not far from this original etymology when he described the ASL sign as "pulling apart of shreds" (1923), and later as "untangle the tangle" (1942).

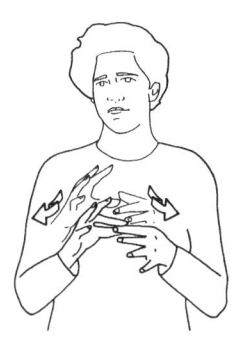

ASL EXPLAIN, TELL A STORY 1

LSF EXPLIQUER (Lambert 1865)

❷ This variation of EXPLAIN, TELL A STORY 1 differs only in movement. Instead of repeatedly coming together and separating, each hand moves front to back, and the hands no longer come in contact. In LSF, this variation continues to be used in a regional dialect in Saint-Laurent-en-Royans.

LSF EXPLIQUER (IVT 1986)

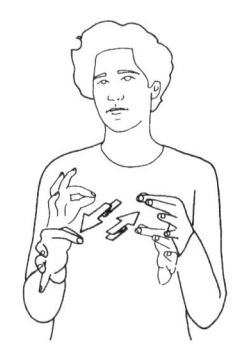

ASL EXPLAIN 2

F

FAIL

Long's description of FAIL reveals the iconic etymology of the contemporary sign: "Stand V on the palm; suddenly throw out the ends, and let the V fall on the palm" (1910). The sign iconically depicts a fall to represent a setback or failure. Today, the forked handshape is retained, but the back of the right hand glides from the wrist to the fingertips of the left palm, thus obscuring the more literal origin.

ASL FAIL

FAITH

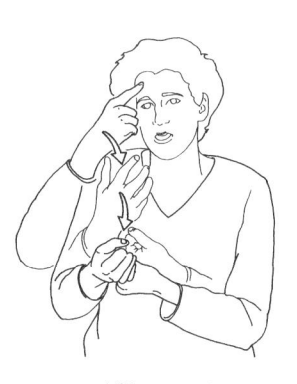

❶ FAITH 1 is a compound sign comprised of the signs THINK and CONFIDENT (see entry). Jamet (circa 1830) described the old French sign CONFIANCE (confident), the etymon of CONFIDENT, as "take from one's heart and give." The structure of FAITH is similar to that of the old LSF sign CROIRE (believe, have faith), a sign that Abbé de l'Épée invented. He first pointed to the forehead and then the heart to signify submitting to God with the mind and the heart.

ASL FAITH 1

❶ FAITH 2 is the more commonly used form in contemporary ASL. It is an initialization of FAITH 1, which obscures the sign's origin.

ASL FAITH 2

FALSE

❶ In nineteenth-century LSF, the index handshape, with the palm down, passing in front of the mouth meant both "false" and "lie." The polysemy of this sign appears in old ASL as well; Long (1910) translated FALSE 1 as "false, a lie."

ASL FALSE 1, LSF MENTEUR
(Pélissier 1856)

❷ In a second variation of the sign, Long describes a slightly different form where the index finger points vertically instead of horizontally. This slight change in composition, Long explains, indicates "a less heinous falsehood, a fib, or softens the accusation, and is used in preference to LIE when speaking of imitations or false material" (1910). Higgins (1923) also describes this variation—"right vertical index palm leftward pushed across the lips from right to left." By the early twentieth century, then, with Long's distinction we see the first documented evidence of a bifurcation in form and meaning for two distinct signs FALSE and LIE (see entry).

ASL FALSE 2
(YD from Higgins 1923)

❸ Today, the location has shifted to the front of the nose. The movement of the sign away from the mouth and toward the nose conforms to several LSF and ASL signs that express the sense of uncertainty or a refusal to believe (see DON'T CARE and DOUBT). LIE has since evolved into a distinct sign that is produced at the chin (see entry).

ASL FALSE 3

FAMOUS

Clark (1885) gives the origin of this sign under his entry FAME, in which he states that "deaf-mutes make their sign for TALK with both hands, moving the hands well out to right and left, one's words spread out over the country." The sign, then, was originally a compound of TALK (see entry) followed by an indication of the expanse over which that talk spread. Today, the only trace of the first part of that compound is the index fingers departing from the chin. The successive arcs of the index fingers moving away from the signer are remnants of the words being spread about the object of fame.

ASL FAMOUS

FANCY

Like FINE (see entry), FANCY comes from the old French sign JABOT (ruffles), which depicts the lace or cloth ruffles on the front of shirts in the eighteenth century. The small movement of the hand toward the chest represents the layers of lace, which Higgins (1942) documents in his description. In contrast to the tapping motion in the sign FINE, the circular movement in FANCY serves an emphatic function that is even more exaggerated when the sign is produced with both hands moving in alternating circles.

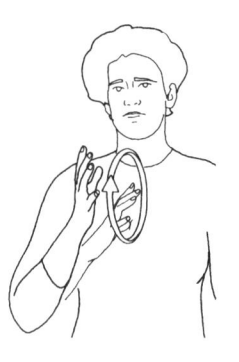

ASL FANCY

FASCINATED

❶ This is an older sign that is also the etymon for INTERESTING (see entry). Higgins (1923) explains that the signer places the right ring handshape "before the face and as if to take hold of the nose, and the left before the chest. Both hands drawn frontward, and body showing an inclination to follow." This form is rooted in the expression to be "pulled along by nose and heart" (Higgins 1923, 1942). Long (1910) describes this sign as "giving the idea of drawing the attention out." In the upper part of the sign we see the French sign ÊTRE DÉÇU, SE FAIRE AVOIR (be taken or fooled), also founded in the same metaphor: "take the nose away from the body" (Lambert 1865).

❷ In the contemporary sign, both hands in claw handshapes move away from the center of the face and close into fists. This location preserves the representation of one's face or nose being drawn toward an object of interest.

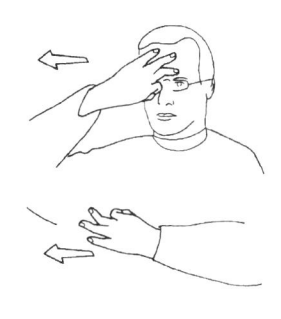

ASL FASCINATED 1
(YD from Higgins 1923)

LSF ÊTRE DÉÇU, SE FAIRE AVOIR (IVT 1986)

ASL FASCINATED 2

FAST

This sign symbolizes the act of abstaining from food during the Catholic season of Lent. It is similar to the old ASL sign PATIENCE, which Higgins (1923) defined as "fast from food" (see PATIENCE 1), and LSF SACRIFICE (sacrifice). The ring handshape used in this sign may have come from one of two sources—either by initialization for the English word *fast* or from the sign COMMUNION (see entry), where the

ASL FAST

handshape symbolizes the shape of the host. The ASL sign LENT is the same as FAST except that it is initialized with the letter *L*.

FATHER

FATHER is semantically related to an old French sign for *man* (see MAN 1), where the thumb of the open hand touches the forehead and then the chest. FATHER preserves only the first part of this compound. The demarcation between MAN 1 and FATHER appears to have occurred before Laurent Clerc's departure for the U.S. because one LSF sign for PÈRE (father) is identical to the ASL sign, and it is still used in Auvergne, France (Y. Delaporte, field observation). The ASL sign has two variations: the thumb can tap the forehead or the thumb can rest on the forehead while the fingers wiggle.

ASL FATHER
(YD)

LSF PÈRE
(Auvergne, France; YD, fieldwork)

FAVORITE

FAVORITE is likely the result of a metaphorical extension of the sign TASTE (see entry), which itself is inherited from LSF GOÛT. Something thought or known to taste good often becomes favored or preferred. The bent middle finger handshape used in this sign corresponds to several semantically related signs in ASL, all of which convey physical or emotional sensations (see CONCERN, EXCITED, and TOUCHED).

ASL FAVORITE

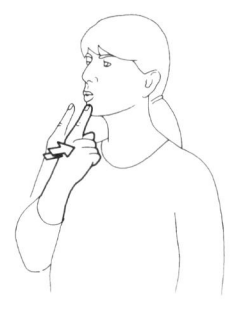

LSF GOÛT
(IVT 1986)

FEAR

❶ The palms of the hands face out as they wave downward, depicting the action of protecting oneself from danger. This same movement has also been described as distancing oneself from danger (Higgins 1923) or the body recoiling from danger (Clark 1885; Long 1910).

❷ In FEAR 2, the palms of the open hands face in and move toward each other as if grabbing the body. This same gesture exists among hearing people in France (Calbris and Montredon 1986).

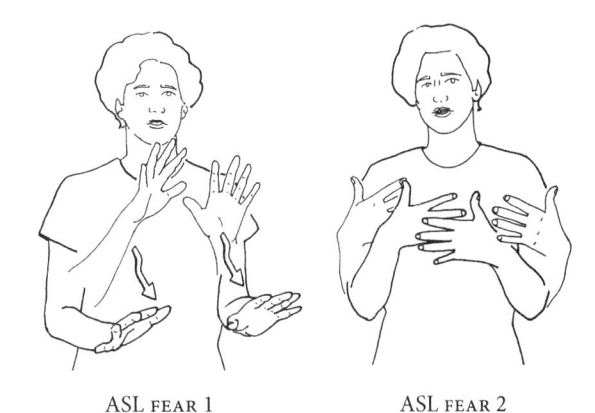

ASL FEAR 1

ASL FEAR 2

FEMININE

This sign is inherited from the polysemous LSF sign ÉLÉGANT that, depending on context, can be translated as *chic* (style), *efféminé* (effeminate), *élégant* (elegant), *mademoiselle* (young lady), *maniaque* (finicky), or *méticuleux* (meticulous). In ASL, this sign's meaning has become restricted to describing someone who is feminine or effeminate. The small circular movements of the two hands in the LSF sign come from a gesture used by hearing people in France to convey a chic or effeminate demeanor. The ring handshape is used in a number of gestures in Europe and the U.S. to express both delicateness and precision (Kendon 2004; see CLOSE CALL and EXACT). Hearing Americans do not use this gesture to depict femininity, thus it is not surprising that Costello (1992) reinterpreted the form as symbolizing "an effeminate way of walking."

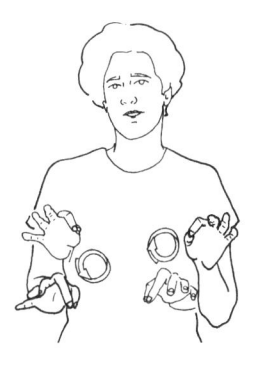

ASL FEMININE

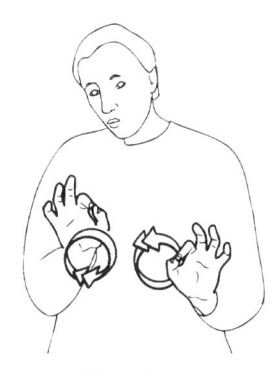

LSF ÉLÉGANT
(IVT 1997)

FEW, SEVERAL

The old LSF sign PLUSIEURS (several) was first noted in 1808 by Sicard, who stated that the signer must show "all of the fingers of the hand as if one were counting without giving enough time to determine an exact number." The successive extension of the fingers originally followed the French counting system, which begins with the thumb as the number 1 (see "UN (One): The Hidden Number," p. 239). The ASL sign quickly evolved to accommodate the American counting system in which the index finger represents the number 1. Clark (1885) describes the American form as "hold closed right hand, back down, in front of body, extending fingers one after the other, commencing with index." In addition, the sign's meaning expanded to either "few" or "several," depending on the co-occurring facial expressions.

ASL FEW, SEVERAL

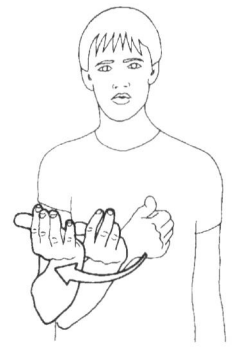

LSF PLUSIEURS
(IVT 1986)

FILE, APPLY

Watson (1964) reveals the iconic origin of this sign in his illustration of a spindle, which used to be the way clerks filed business papers. A clerk would punch each piece of paper on a metal spindle and later "run a piece of string through the holes [to] tie up the bundle" (Lubar 1992). Today, the sign can be used in the literal sense to indicate filing papers and also to appeal a ruling or apply concepts in an abstract way.

ASL FILE, APPLY

FINALLY, SUCCEED

The etymon of this sign is most likely the French sign ALLER (go), where the two extended index fingers rotate alternatively as they move away from the body. Long (1910) describes an earlier form of the ASL sign in his entry SUCCEED that suggests this link with ALLER: "with the extended index fingers raise the hands, revolving the fingers around each other." Higgins (1923) illustrates the sign as originating with the index fingers pointed down and ending pointed up near the signer's temples. Today, when used to mean "finally," the sign is commonly glossed as PAH and is co-expressed with a nonmanual marker where the mouth opens resembling the articulation of the English syllable *pa*.

ASL FINALLY, SUCCEED

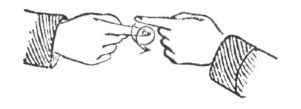

LSF ALLER
(Pélissier 1856)

FINE

This sign, like FANCY (see entry), comes from the old French sign JABOT (ruffles), which depicts the lace or cloth ruffles on the front of the shirts of the upper class in the eighteenth century. FINE was incorporated into both MONSIEUR and MADAME (depending on whether MALE or FEMALE preceded it; see FATHER, MAN, and WOMAN). The small movement of the hand toward the chest represents the layers of lace. Though the etymological link between JABOT and its contemporary derivatives has been lost in modern France, the link has remained intact in the consciousness of Americans. Several authors, old and new, explicitly refer to the connection. Higgins (1942)

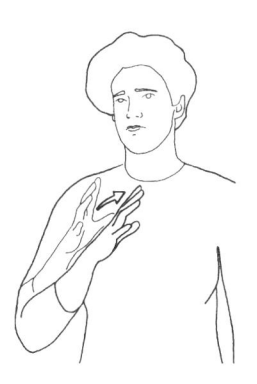

ASL FINE

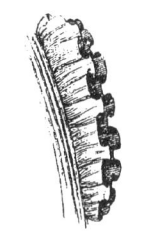

Ruffles on a shirt
(Piroux 1830)

describes the sign as "indicating the fancy ruffles and laces formerly affected by so-called gentleman and ladies"; and Costello (1994) says the sign shows "the ruffles on the front of a fine, old-fashioned shirt." A recent change consists of wiggling the fingers to mean "cool" or "neat."

FIRST

This contemporary form of FIRST maintains its etymological connection to LSF through the use of the extended thumb to signal the number 1 (see "UN (One): The Hidden Number," p. 239). Either because of pressures to accommodate to the U.S. system of counting or assimilation, FIRST is sometimes produced with an extended left index finger instead of the thumb, distancing it from UN.

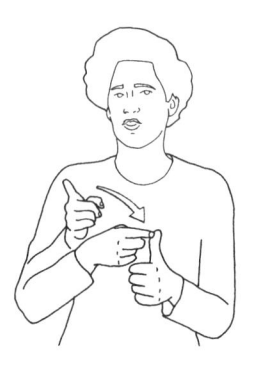

ASL FIRST

FIT

This sign is nearly identical to the LSF ADAPTÉ (fitted), except that the hands assume claw handshapes rather than keys. The hands represent two small objects that are fitted together. Ferrand equates the "fitting" of the two hands to the hinged lid of a snuffbox (circa 1785). In ASL, the hands are configured in loose claws and the fingers come together and interlock. This gives the impression of fitting together two grooved objects, like cogs on a wheel.

ASL FIT

FLATTER

The extended left index finger is caressed by the right hand, conforming to the etymology of the corresponding English verb. *Flatter* comes from the French *flatter*, meaning "stroke or caress." Though this sign is not documented in historical texts, the extended index finger is often used to represent a person, an iconic use that appears in several ASL signs, including CHAMPION, PICK ON, RECRUIT, and SITUATION (see entries).

ASL FLATTER

FLIP OUT

Long (1910) illustrated this sign with the outer edge of the right hand oscillating over the left hand to depict a wavy line, and it meant "wrong." For its antonym, RIGHT, he showed the right hand moving in a straight line across the left palm. The contemporary sign FLIP OUT is an extension of the original meaning of "wrong," such that one who is *flipping out* is perceived as *wrong in the head*. The movement has changed so that the right hand moves down from the forehead to the left palm and slides from the heel to the fingertips before abruptly bending. This movement is closely related to the older ASL form by representing a straight mental path that then bends or breaks. Davis (1966) describes it as "veering off the main course." Stokoe et al. (1965) identify the sign as both *wrong* and *unsound*, reinforcing the shift in meaning from the generic *wrong* to the more specific *flip out*.

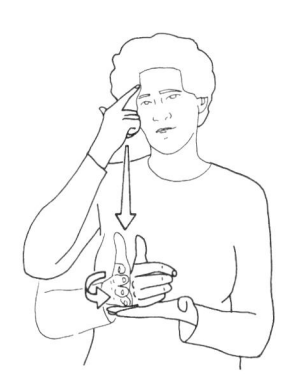

ASL FLIP OUT

ASL WRONG
(YD from Long 1910)

ASL RIGHT
(YD from Long 1910)

FLIRT

The oscillating fingers used in this sign convey the metaphorical meaning of "shiny things," which we also see in the origins of the signs COLOR and FRIENDLY (see entries). The short movement of the hands away from the signer's body gives the impression that the signer is transmitting flattering words to another individual. Higgins (1942) describes FLIRT as "just words from the lips towards the person flattered," indicating that the sign may have originally started at the mouth but has since lowered to the chest.

ASL FLIRT

FLOWER

This sign derives from the old French sign FLEUR (flower), which depicted the "action of taking a thing in the hand, bringing it to the nose several times to smell it" (Blanchet 1850). Clark (1885) describes an earlier form of the ASL sign FLOWER as a compound, where the signer first gestured to indicate a flower stem and then "place[d] the right hand near nostrils, as though inhaling the perfume." The first part of the compound has since disappeared, and only the bundled handshape remains to perform the depictive action of grasping a flower and bringing it up to each nostril.

ASL FLOWER

FOOL, JOKE

Higgins (1923) documents this sign with the English translations "fool," "joke," and "hoax." He describes its production as the "right bent index of 'X' hand hooked over the nose to pull down with a slight jerk." The contemporary ASL form can be produced with either a key (X) or ring handshape and is commonly used to mean "fool," but can also mean "fake" in sports contexts to describe when a player throws off the opposition (E. Shaw, field observation). The form with the ring handshape matches the LSF sign être déçu, se faire avoir (be taken or fooled), where the signer pulls down his nose with the ring handshape. Lambert (1865) noted the metaphor as "take the nose away from the body." In French culture, representations of trickery and deception tend to be invoked by the word *nez* (nose). For example, the expression *faire un long nez* means "be deceived" and *se faire mener par le bout du nez* means "be led by the nose," as a naive person might be. Higgins (1923) confirms this interpretation by characterizing JOKE as "pulled by the nose." The semantic derivation from *naive, duped, deceived* to *fool, joke* is evidenced by the polysemy of the English words *fool* and *joke*; in this case, it refers to the verbs.

ASL FOOL, JOKE

LSF ÊTRE DÉÇU, SE FAIRE AVOIR
(IVT 1986)

FOR

This is the same form and meaning as the LSF sign POUR (for), which was described for the first time by Abbé de l'Épée (1784) and may have been invented by him. Lambert (1865) later described the same form as produced by "touch[ing] the index finger on the forehead (thought) then thrust[ing] it in front of the body (directed towards)." With a short and repeated movement, the ASL sign also functions as a question meaning "What for?"

ASL FOR

LSF POUR
(Pélissier 1856)

FOREVER, LONG TIME

This sign derives from the very old LSF JUSQU'A (until, from one moment until another), documented since the eighteenth century as being made with the French manual letter J, which is also the modified horn handshape (Ferrand circa 1784; Blanchet 1850; Lambert 1865). According to Lambert (1865), the hand draws away from the body: "advance to the front the manual letter J, from one point to another." This particular contemporary variation, where the thumb of the modified horn handshape contacts the temple then moves directly away from the face, has not been found in older texts, but it is widely used in both ASL and LSF. When produced with one short movement and the mouth shaped in a circle, the sign means "a long time," as in "I waited in line forever." When produced with repeated circles extending from the temple, it means "a prolonged period of time." When the LSF sign is repeated, it also means "a long time." The upward

ASL FOREVER, LONG TIME

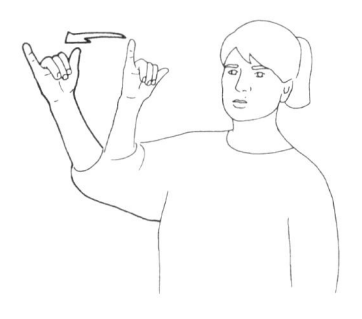

LSF JUSQU'A, C'EST LONG
(IVT 1986)

migration of the hand in both ASL and LSF may be due to the location of the sign FUTURE, WILL (see entry).

FORGET

FORGET comes from an old LSF sign meaning "forget" that has since disappeared. De Gérando (1827) described the form as "rapidly pass the hand over the forehead." Ferrand (circa 1785) states that the signer must "bring the hand over the forehead and throw it behind the head with a look in the eyes and face that I don't remember anymore." This stems from the metaphor "ideas are objects," and the action depicts the signer removing objects (ideas or memories) from the mind. This form was first documented in the U.S. by Clark (1885), who describes how the fingertips of the right flat hand swipe the forehead and then close. A contemporary variation of ASL FORGET consists of the bent middle finger handshape sliding across the forehead. This form is typically reserved to denote forgetting specific things like a topic to discuss (for example, "My mind has gone blank"). This handshape is commonly used in ASL to indicate blank or empty spaces, as in the signs BALD and EMPTY (see entries).

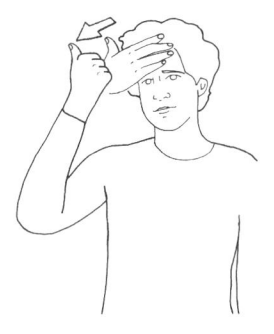

ASL FORGET

FORK

This sign was originally produced as a compound in LSF (Pélissier 1856), in which the right fork handshape first contacted the mouth and then the left palm. The contemporary ASL form retains the second part of the compound to show the tines of a fork pressed into food. This newer form was first documented in the early twentieth century by Long (1910) and represents the most literal interpretation of the handshape. A myriad of LSF and ASL signs with metaphorical relationships to forked entities incorporate this handshape (see CAREFUL, HELL, and WORSE).

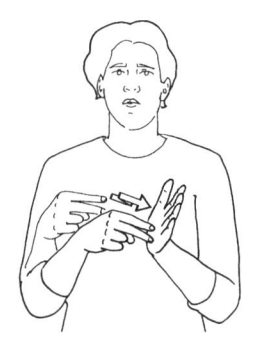

ASL FORK

LSF FOURCHETTE
(Pélissier 1856)

FRIEND

The sign FRIEND comes directly from the French sign AMI (friend). Lambert (1856) described it as "unit[ing] the two indexes in a ring." In the ASL sign, the index fingers hook together, one palm down and the other palm up, and then "the hands change their relative position" (Long 1910). This is an iconic representation of the link between two people and the reciprocity inherent in friendship.

ASL FRIEND

LSF AMI
(Lambert 1865)

FRIENDLY

Long (1910) describes this sign in his entry CHEERFUL as "'beams of joy' radiating from the face." Oscillating fingers symbolize shiny things in several signs (see COLOR and FLIRT). The etymology of this sign may also derive from the polysemy of the English word *pleasant*. Roth's (1941) description states that the sign "come[s] from pleasant weather. The sign indicates pleasant breezes blowing against the face. We use this sign to indicate a person who is of a pleasant disposition." LSF has a similar sign—FRAIS (cool)—that originated as a gesture centuries ago. This sign represents a breeze of fresh air, "the act of waving oneself with one or both hands" (Lambert 1865). The ASL sign COOL is exactly the same. The extrapolation of a concrete sensory experience to a gesture also occurred in the development of signs like FAVORITE (see entry). While FRIENDLY may come from the same root as FRAIS, it no longer has a literal association with a cool breeze and the reduplicated movement has disappeared.

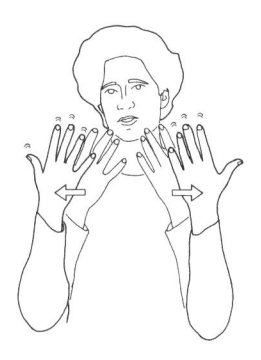

ASL FRIENDLY

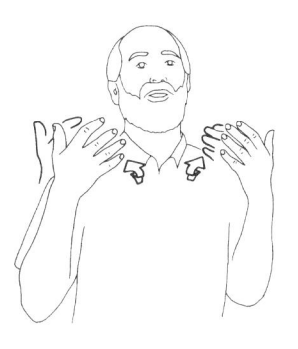

LSF FRAIS
(IVT 1986)

FROM

The origin of FROM is the old Signed French DE (from), which Sicard described in 1808 as follows: "take back the hand that one had directed towards a goal, and trace the hand, in the air, in a straight line from the point in space where it was directed." The right index touches the left at the beginning of the sign, like the ASL GOAL (see entry), then draws away into a hooked

ASL FROM

LSF DE
(Laveau 1868)

handshape. Higgins (1942) interpreted the sign as "something drawn away from under left index." Unlike most Signed French signs, the one-handed variant of DE (Laveau 1868) continues to be used by Deaf people in France; the index finger also draws toward the signer into a hooked handshape.

FRUIT

Identical to the contemporary LSF sign FRUIT (fruit), this sign likely represents the grasping of a small piece of fruit brought toward the mouth. Ferrand (circa 1785) indicated that the signer moves the hand toward a tree "as if picking an apple and bringing it to the mouth" in his entry FRUIT. The sign is now initialized with the letter *F* in both ASL and LSF.

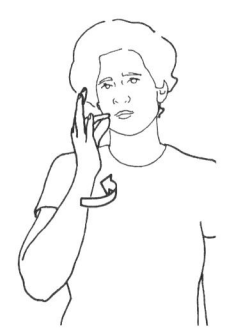

ASL FRUIT

FRUSTRATED

FRUSTRATED is an iconic representation of a door closing in one's face, meaning encountering an obstacle that is out of one's control. A similar sign in LSF can be translated as "hurl oneself against a wall," another common French and English idiom used to describe the feeling of being frustrated. When FRUSTRATED is made with both hands alternating in movement, the sign conveys repeated frustration.

ASL FRUSTRATED

ASL FRUSTRATED (emphatic)

FUN

This is a hybridized compound of the signs FUNNY and STAY (see entries), both of which are very old signs in ASL and LSF. FUN can be translated literally as "an enjoyable experience that lasts," and it retains only part of each of its components. The reduplicated movement of FUNNY has disappeared while the handshape of STAY has assimilated with the paintbrush handshape of FUNNY.

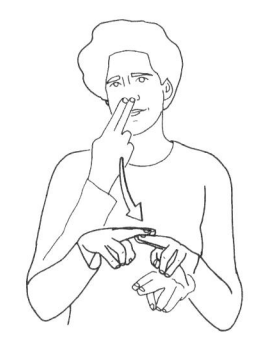

ASL FUN

FUNNY

Though we have not found documentation of this sign in old LSF, the resemblance between the contemporary LSF sign HUMOUR (humor) and the American form strongly suggests that FUNNY is of French origin. Long (1910) cites the sign in his entry FUNNY, HUMOROUS: "Rub the nose downward with the ends of the fore and middle fingers two or three times and look funny." The location of the sign on the nose reinforces the symbolic link between the nose and humor. The French word *nez* (nose) and English word *nose* both derive from the Latin *nasus*, which can be translated as "nose" or "mockery." In Europe, the nose is perceived as a comical feature (for example, Cyrano de Bergerac and the red nose clowns wear). The configuration of the hand as a paintbrush is likely an initialization of the word *humor* in English and *humour* in French.

ASL FUNNY

LSF HUMOUR
(IVT 1986)

FUTURE, WILL

This sign was inherited from the very old LSF sign FUTUR (future), which Pélissier illustrated in 1856. The flat hand is placed at the height of the shoulder and moves away from the signer along the axis of time, "indicating future" (Long 1910; see "Axis of Time," p. 286). A recent evolution in the U.S. has resulted in the derived form WILL, which consists of a shortened movement away from the signer after the thumb makes brief contact with the cheek; this change in form indicates the very near future.

ASL FUTURE

LSF FUTUR
(Pélissier 1856)

ASL WILL

G

GET

❶ In the older form of GET, the right hand executed a capturing movement over the immobile left fist (Long 1910; Higgins 1923). This is similar to the ASL sign WIN (see entry), which is a cognate of the LSF sign GAGNER (win). GAGNER has two meanings in French: *gagner un prix* (win an award) and *gagner quelque chose* (get or gain something). In ASL, two distinct forms—GET and WIN—evolved, possibly because their English translations have distinct meanings.

❷ In GET 2, both claw hands close and pull in toward the body.

ASL GET 1
(YD from Higgins 1923)

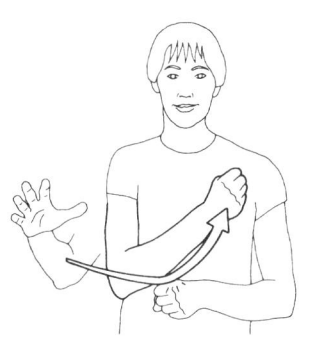

LSF GAGNER
(IVT 1986)

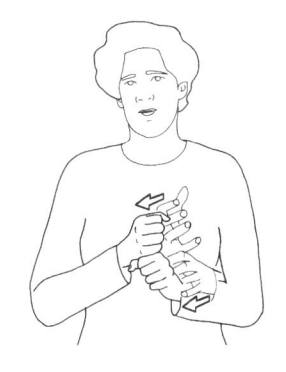

ASL GET 2

GET GOING, LEAVE

This sign was inherited from the LSF SE SAUVER (escape). It has been translated into English by words like *fast* (Roth 1941), *scram* (Stokoe et al. 1965), and *leave clandestinely* (Long 1910). Because the primary movement is carried out by the right hand, which begins beneath the left, the sign metaphorically links to something secret or discreet—one additional trace of its French etymon. Today, the sign is used not so much to convey a secret departure as a quick one.

ASL GET GOING, LEAVE

LSF SE SAUVER
(IVT 1986)

GIRL

This sign comes directly from the French sign FEMME (woman), which has been noted since Abbé de l'Épée's time. At least two French authors (Puybonnieux 1846; Lambert 1865) indicate the unambiguous, iconic origin of this sign in their descriptions: the thumb traces the length of the cheek to represent the drawstrings of the bonnets that girls once wore. In GIRL, the movement is now one or two short strokes on the lower chin.

ASL GIRL

LSF FEMME
(Brouland 1855)

Girl's bonnet
(France, 19th century)

GIVE UP

This sign is a gestural metaphor that corresponds to the literal meaning of "surrender." The open hands extend above the shoulders symbolizing that one no longer bears arms and abandons combat.

ASL GIVE UP

(Illustration by Pat Mallet)

GLASS

This is the same sign used for centuries by Trappist monks (*Us des Cistercians* 1890) and French Deaf people (with the middle finger instead of the index). Tapping the teeth is an analogy for the strength of glass. Over time, due to pressures of centralization that we also see in signs like DRY, RED, and TASTE (see entries), GLASS is now most frequently produced on the chin instead of on the teeth.

ASL GLASS

LSF VERRE
(IVT 1986)

GO

❶ This is one of several ASL signs (see FINALLY and TRIP 1) that stem from the French sign ALLER (go): "roll the index fingers one over the other" (Sicard 1808), "like a wheel that rolls away" (Lambert 1865). The sign remained unchanged for a long time in ASL. Michaels (1923) described it as "move the fingers forward revolving one over the other as you make the movement," and it continues to be used in formal contexts as well as by some older signers.

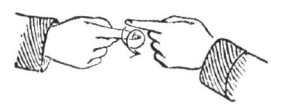

ASL GO 1, LSF ALLER
(Pélissier 1856)

❷ This contemporary sign displays a rectilinear movement of both index fingers away from the body. An intermediary form also exists where the sign moves forward in a circular movement (Sternberg 1994; Costello 1999).

ASL GO 2

GOAL

The French sign BUT (goal) is identical in form and meaning to the ASL sign GOAL. Lambert (1865) described BUT as "place the right index finger on the forehead and then direct it towards the left, raised index finger a short distance from the body: thoughts directed towards." Closely linked to the sign FOR (see entry), GOAL differs only in the use of the left index finger to represent the target to which the right index is directed.

ASL GOAL

LSF BUT
(IVT 1986)

GOAT

The sign comes from the French sign BOUC (billy goat; Pélissier 1856), and it also was used by the Plains Indians (Clark 1885). In these iconic variants, the hand assumes the bundled shape on the chin and then moves up to the forehead, where the fingers of the double hooked hand flick up, thus representing the beard and the horns of a goat. In the contemporary form, the hand is configured in a fist when it contacts the chin and forehead, and the fingers flick up immediately after each contact. Here, we see an assimilation of handshape and orientation at each point of contact, in addition to an extra flick that was not evidenced in older forms.

ASL GOAT

LSF BOUC
(Pélissier 1856)

GOD

❶ The sign GOD comes from the old LSF SAINT (holy), which represents the Holy Spirit or, as Lambert (1865) described, the breath of God that spills "from the forehead to the heart."

❷ Two old signs for GOD combined three signs from LSF in two different ways: DIEU (God; point to the sky), CROIRE (believe; point to the heart), and SAINT (holy; point to the sky then the heart). Michaels' (1923) description states, "point the index finger […] heavenward […] move the hand down before your face slowly, spread out the fingers as you do so," which conforms to the LSF SAINT. His illustration, though, begins with the LSF DIEU and ends at the heart as in LSF CROIRE. The same form is cited by Clark (1885). Higgins (1923) reveals a shift in the pragmatics of the signs GOD 1 and GOD 2 in his entry: "Some merely point the index toward heaven, but this seems to be better used only when we refer to God as angry with sin."

ASL GOD 1

LSF SAINT
(YD, fieldwork)

ASL GOD 2
(Michaels 1923)

LSF DIEU
(Abbé de l'Épée)

GOLD

The sign GOLD originated as a compound of the old French sign OR (gold), described as "sign earring" (Ferrand circa 1785), and JAUNE (yellow; the same sign as the ASL YELLOW). GOLD is now a single form that can begin with either the index or bent middle finger touching the ear rather than grasping it. The sign is also used for CALIFORNIA, so named for the California Gold Rush of the mid-1800s.

ASL GOLD

LSF OR
(Lambert 1865)

GOOD

Inherited from the nineteenth-century LSF sign BON (good), this sign was described by Blanchet (1850) as: "Send a kiss with the hand." Clark (1885) describes the same form produced with two hands for *good-day*, *good-bye*, and *thank you*. Long (1910) noted that GOODBYE was "used indiscriminately to greet one, thank one, and bid farewell." In LSF BONJOUR (hello) and MERCI (thank you) are similar homonyms.

ASL GOOD

LSF BON
(Lambert 1865)

GOSSIP

This is the old French sign BAVARDER (gossip), first illustrated by Pélissier (1856) and described by Blanchet (1850) as "the right hand in front of the mouth […], quickly open and close the thumb from the other fingers to simulate the movement of the lips." The form depicts the covert transmission of the spoken word metaphorically extended to sign language. The current configuration of the hands is often interpreted to be the letter G for *gossip*, but Long (1910) saw the iconic motivation behind it when he wrote that the hands "imitate the movement of the lips in talking."

ASL GOSSIP

LSF BAVARDER
(Pélissier 1856)

GOVERNMENT

The older ASL dictionaries describe the movement of GOVERNOR as the index finger tracing a circle in proximity to the temple (Michaels 1923), or posing on the temple then tracing a circle in the air only to return to its point of origin (Long 1910; Higgins 1923). Roth (1941) interpreted the sign to represent "the people as a whole, and by touching the temple, indicated that they are of one mind." Contemporary authors propose links to the double meaning of the English word *head*—the physical head ties to the metaphorical head of a state (Sternberg 1994; Costello 1999). These etymologies are alluring but do not explain the circular movement that occurs at the temple. The origin of GOVERNMENT is in fact the French sign RÉPUBLIQUE (republic), which is an iconic representation of the tricolored badges worn on the hats of republicans during the French Revolution. The movement today has been reduced to a contraction and extension of the index finger, in addition to a reduced rotation of the wrist that nearly eliminates the original circle. When the sign is made with a P handshape, it means POLITICS.

ASL GOVERNMENT

ASL GOVERNOR
(Michaels 1923)

Cap worn during the French Revolution

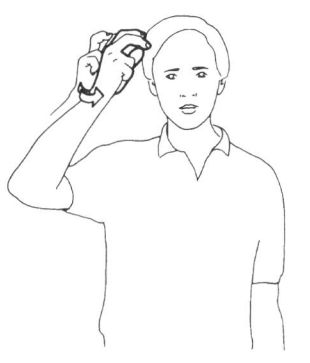

LSF RÉPUBLIQUE
(IVT 1990)

GRAB A CHANCE

This comes from the old LSF sign GAGNER (win) described by Jamet (circa 1830) as "throw the die, take them." The semantic derivation of *grab a chance* from *win* is explained by the etymology of the French sign, which represents the action of tossing dice. The LSF sign HASARD (chance) is identical in form to

GRAB A CHANCE but it is produced with different facial expressions: "HASARD: sign for playing dice, sign can mean to win or to lose" (Ferrand circa 1785). The ASL sign always has a positive connotation, and it almost exclusively means "take a chance" or "grab the opportunity." Thus, we see a metaphorical extension of the sign's meaning from the literal act of taking a chance when playing dice to the abstracted chance with intangible experiences.

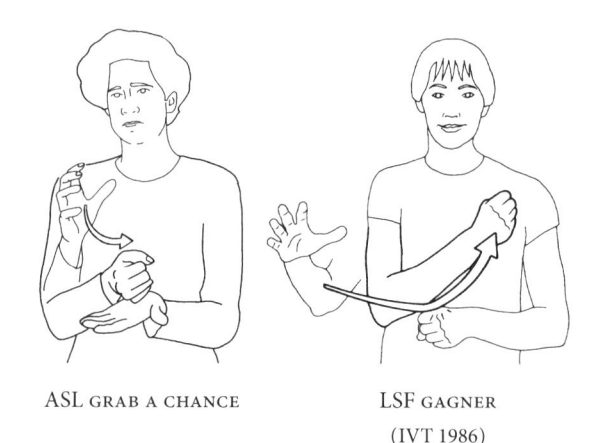

ASL GRAB A CHANCE

LSF GAGNER
(IVT 1986)

GRADUATE

❶ Long (1910) and Higgins (1923) describe a form they interpreted to be a compound of "indicating paper with a seal" (Long) followed by the sign LEAVE (see entry). The etymology of the first part of the compound is likely related to the French sign JUSQU'AU BOUT (right to the end) where the circular movement of the fist represents a temporal cycle.

❷ The subsequent evolution of the sign is the result of two noticeable changes: the reduction of the large circular movement of the first part of GRADUATE 1 to a much smaller rotation of the wrist, and the elimination of the second part of the compound (LEAVE). In GRADUATE 2 the edge of the right fist hits the left palm, suggesting that the sign represents the seal that sanctions a degree. The link to the original form is now obscured by the initialization of the sign with the letter G.

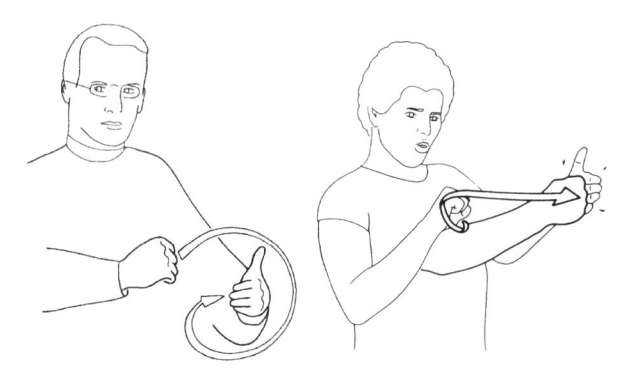

ASL GRADUATE 1
(first part of compound)
(YD from Higgins 1923)

LSF JUSQU'AU BOUT
(IVT 1997)

ASL GRADUATE 2

120   GRADUATE

GRADUATE SCHOOL

The back of the right fork hand makes contact with the heel of the open left hand to represent the additional years of study required for an advanced degree. At one time, Gallaudet University had a preparatory year that preceded the traditional four years of undergraduate study, which accounts for the use of the left open handshape for the number FIVE instead of FOUR. The right hand then represents the two years after undergraduate study, the standard length for American master's degree programs. The structure of this sign, showing the number 5 with one hand and the number 2 with the other to indicate seven years, is identical to the etymology of the sign WEEK (see entry), where the right hand was the French number 2 and the left hand the number 5, indicating seven days.

ASL GRADUATE SCHOOL

GRANDPARENTS

This is a compound of GRANDFATHER and GRANDMOTHER. Extrapolating from the semantic pairs FATHER/MAN and MOTHER/WOMAN (see entries) these two individual signs exhibit a movement that symbolizes the passing of generations. In older variations (Clark 1885; Long 1910), both hands mirrored each other but at a location slightly lower and in front of the signer's chest.

ASL GRANDFATHER   ASL GRANDMOTHER

GRASS

❶ Describing GRASS 1, a sign that is no longer used, Clark (1885) writes that Deaf people sign GREEN "then make their sign for GROW, and indicate stalk with extended index finger."

❷ It is possible that this sign evolved from the old sign for HAY. Long (1910) is the only historical author to document this form, which is similar to his description of HAY: "Push the right '4' hand upward in front of or against the mouth." The raised fingers, then, likely symbolized the tall stalks of grass from which hay is made. Today, the placement of the hand under the chin suggests an evolution that allowed for the mouth to be more visible for ease in lipreading (a similar fate of many signs such as FAVORITE, GLASS, and LIE).

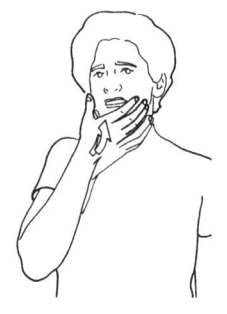

ASL GRASS 2

GRAY

All the historical authors document this sign as a compound of BLACK followed by WHITE and then MIX (Clark 1885; Long 1910; Higgins 1923). Today, GRAY retains only the location of the last part of the original compound. In the contemporary form, the open, spread fingers of both hands alternate passing back and forth through each other. This movement represents the mixing of two different things, in this case the colors black and white.

ASL GRAY

GREASE

Also used to mean *gravy*, this sign was first described by Clark (1885) as "denote the dripping" from meat. The mitten handshape of the left hand is also employed in the sign MEAT (see entry), thus creating a semantic connection between the two signs. GREASE originally was produced with the right index finger and thumb making contact with the left hand, whereas today the middle finger and thumb execute the movement. The shift in point of contact from the right index to the middle finger is common in ASL, as documented in several signs, such as LIKE, TELL A STORY, and INTERESTING (see "Handshape Change," p. 148).

ASL GREASE

GREEN

This sign is likely inherited from the old French sign VERT (green). VERT was originally produced with the letter *V* "stretching horizontally a bit down" representing "the color of the grass, turf, prairie" (Pélissier 1856). Clerc and Gallaudet may have replaced the V handshape with the letter *G* to represent the English equivalent *green*. Its contemporary location and movement matches that of several other color signs, such as YELLOW (see entry), BLUE, and PURPLE, all of which are initialized.

ASL GREEN

LSF VERT
(Pélissier 1856)

GRIEF

This sign is a gestural metaphor depicting the action of a heart breaking or being crushed. This same idea also exists in the French expression *cœur brisé* (crushed heart, broken heart). Higgins (1923) shows both fists twisting over each other. Today, the sign can also be produced with both hands in the claw handshape and the right hand slightly above the left near the heart; the right hand descends as both hands turn into fists and twist. The twisting movement makes the metaphor of a broken heart palpably clear.

ASL GRIEF

GUESS

Higgins (1923) lists this sign under his entry ORIGINAL, where the signer first points to the temple for THINK then grasps the air in front of the forehead. Many older Deaf people still produce the sign here, which is likely a gestural metaphor for "ideas are objects." Sternberg (1994) posed this meaning in his description: "To snatch an idea, a thought is grasped." The sign no longer begins with THINK and the location has lowered to the area in front of the signer's nose, thus obscuring its origin as a compound and making it a homonym of the sign MISS (as in "I missed the bus").

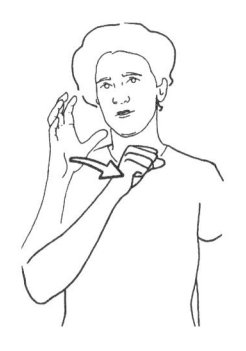

ASL GUESS

GULP, MAKE A MISTAKE

The right claw handshape is drawn away from the signer's throat while it simultaneously closes into a fist. Colloquially glossed as GULP due to its location at the throat, the sign's closest English translation is the expression "egg on one's face," which means that someone has made a mistake and is embarrassed by it. The initial claw handshape reinforces the sign's negative connotation, as is also seen in MAD, ANGRY, and COMPLAIN (see entries). Although this sign is not documented in historical texts, its proximity in form to the semantically related sign WITHHOLD, SUPPRESS makes it possible that the two share an etymological link. In WITHHOLD, SUPPRESS, the claw hands drag down the length of the signer's body and close into fists, representing the metaphor "the heart is the center of emotion" and showing that the signer suppresses emotions by grabbing them from the chest and moving them into the gut. Stokoe et al. (1965) note the same connection between the two forms, which they translate as "restrain one's feelings, repress" (180, 192).

ASL GULP, MAKE A MISTAKE

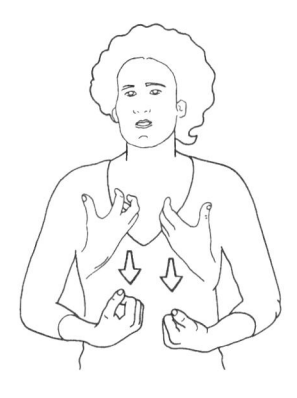

ASL WITHHOLD, SUPPRESS

H

HABIT

This is the old French sign EMMENOTÉ (shackled), which shows the hands in chains to symbolically convey "contracting bad habits" (Lambert 1865). This idea is found in both French and English, most notably in the expression *slave to habit*. Long (1910) identified the symbolism early on as "mental slavery." Both Long and Higgins (1923) document the sign as a compound that began by pointing to the forehead for THINK, thus confirming the metaphor of an imprisoned mind or spirit. Initialization has produced two variations of this sign: U for USED TO and T for TRADITION.

ASL HABIT

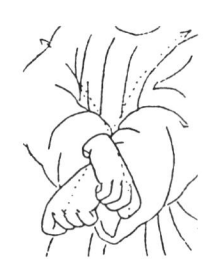

LSF EMMENOTÉ
(Lambert 1865)

HALF HOUR

This sign derives from the old French sign CADRAN (dial), which Lambert (1865) described as "act as if holding a pocket watch, place the right thumb in the center of the left and with the index open like a compass, indicate the hours by the circumference." The contemporary sign HALF HOUR depicts the path of the compass needle around the dial or face of a watch with the right flat hand. This sign is a cognate of LATER (see entry).

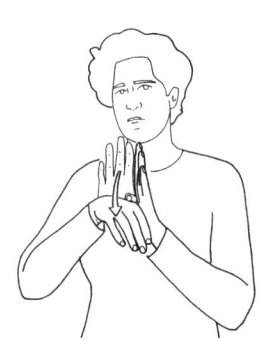

ASL HALF HOUR

HAPPEN

The origin of this ASL sign is uncovered in the close relationship between the French verbs *venir* (come) and *arriver* (arrive). The French phrase *Qu'est-ce qui est arrivé?* can be translated into English as "What arrived?" or "What happened?" Ferrand (circa 1785) first noted the use of the LSF signs ARRIVER and VENIR for announcing an event that recently happened: "Same sign as VENIR, then quickly pass the right hand perpendicularly in front of the left hand with the fingers and the palm turned toward the face." Sicard (1808) similarly observed that "the sign of an event that recently happened is made by representing the action or feat of something by signing ARRIVER which is originally the sign VENIR." Clark (1885) is the first American author to record the sign, which he included in his entry ACCIDENT: "the index fingers alone extended and held about horizontally, and pointing about to front; by wrist action suddenly turn the hands, backs towards each other." In his entry HISTORY, he also describes a sign glossed as HAPPENINGS—"hold the hands in front of shoulders, backs up, index fingers only extended" and pointing toward each other after which the wrists rotate and drop down, like the sign COME. George Veditz (1913) uses an intermediary form of HAPPEN in his film *Preservation of the Sign Language*, where the sign is directed toward the signer, like in COME. In another example of HAPPEN's link to COME, Edward Allen Fay signs the contemporary form HAPPEN in his film *Dom Pedro's Visit to Gallaudet College* (1913). Neither Long (1910) nor Higgins (1923) saw the association between HAPPEN and

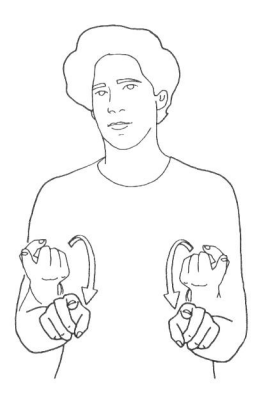

ASL HAPPEN

LSF VENIR
(Lambert 1865)

COME or ARRIVE. According to Higgins (1942), the sign meant something "falls out." Over time, the sign has greatly expanded in meaning to include *event*, *accident*, and *history*, as well as to introduce a narrative (as in, "Let me tell you what happened").

HAPPY

The sign is closely related to the LSF AVANTAGE (advantage). The hand moving upward as it taps the center of the chest is indicative of the metaphors "the heart/chest is the center of emotion" and "up is good." These metaphors explain Lambert's description of the sign as a "lifted heart" (1865). LSF AVANTAGE has several translations, all of which connote positivity: *avantage* (advantage), *avoir un coup de chance* (be lucky), and *être assez heureux pour* (be fortunate, be happy for). Clark (1885) notes two forms of HAPPY. He explains that when tapped over the heart, it meant "pleasure" and when moved circularly, it meant "happy," "pleased," and "glad." In ASL, as in LSF, the location of the contemporary sign has since moved to the middle of the chest.

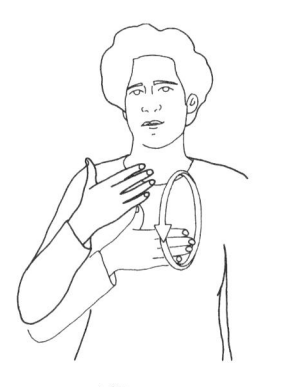

ASL HAPPY

LSF AVANTAGE
(Lambert 1865)

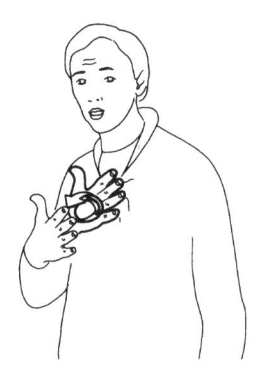

LSF AVANTAGE
(IVT 1997)

HARD

This sign originates from the LSF DUR (hard): "Hit the back of the left hand with the back of the bent index finger of the right hand as one would do if resonating a vase" (Blanchet 1850). Cistercian monks also have used the sign for centuries: "Hit the back of the hand with the joint of the middle finger" (*Us des Cisterciens* 1890). Hearing people use a similar handshape when knocking on a hard object like a door. The change to a double hooked handshape occurred in tandem in LSF and ASL. In addition, the phonological process of assimilation occurred in ASL so that the left hand frequently assumes the same handshape as the right.

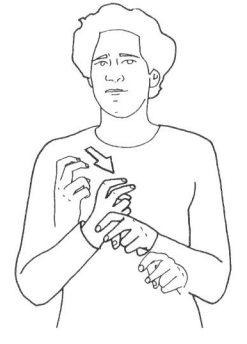

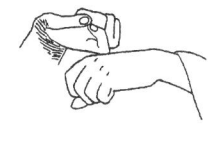

ASL HARD

LSF DUR
(Brouland 1855)

HATE

We see in this sign the flicking movement associated with reprimands or rejection. The middle finger is held down by the thumb and then briskly flicks open. This same gesture has been documented in France since the nineteenth century. The form standardized as a sign in LSF, and was then passed on to ASL, taking on the meaning "hate" and more recently "reject."

ASL HATE

LSF HATE
(YD from Oléron 1974)

HAVE

❶ This very old sign comes from the old LSF AVOIR (have) described as "open the two hands and bring them towards the self in a half-circle" (Ferrand circa 1785), and "the idea of possession" (Pélissier 1856). Long (1910), Veditz (1913), Roth (1941), and Watson (1964) all documented that

ASL HAVE 1
(YD from Long 1910)

LSF AVOIR
(Pélissier 1856)

possession was signaled by bringing the palms of both hands to the chest.

❷ Over time, the form has changed significantly, so that now the tips of the bent mitten hands touch the chest. Even so, the American form HAVE 2 is closer to its etymon than the contemporary LSF sign, which has evolved quite differently and is exclusively produced with one hand. It is possible a similar fate awaits HAVE 2 as it is also produced with only one hand in certain contexts. Signers frequently accompany the manual component by slightly biting the bottom lip, an abbreviated articulation of the English word *have*. The nonmanual signal has become so ubiquitous that signers can produce the labiodental gesture alone and still be understood as signing HAVE (Shaw 2013).

LSF AVOIR
(Lambert 1865)

ASL HAVE 2

HEARING

This sign shares the same form and meaning with the sign used in France since the nineteenth century. The rotation of the index finger in front of the mouth meant PARLER (speak) in all of the works written by French Deaf people of this era. Hearing people were referred to as *parlants* (speakers; Berthier 1868) or *entendants-parlants* (hearing-speakers; Richardin 1834). In this case, Deaf people primarily characterized hearing people by their ability to speak, rather than their ability to hear, reinforcing Deaf people's proclivity for attending to visible movements over invisible sounds.

ASL HEARING

LSF PARLANT
(Pélissier 1856)

HEAVEN

Clark (1885) describes HEAVEN as "the arch with both hands held curved, backs up, above head" followed by the sign ENTER, indicating that it was a compound. Today, only a trace of the sign ENTER remains, and it precedes the depiction of the sky rather than following it.

ASL HEAVEN

HEIGHT

The edge of the right index finger taps the top of the head twice, symbolizing the horizontal rod used to measure height on a doctor's scale. The LSF sign TAILLE (height) is the same, except for the use of the flat hand instead of the index finger.

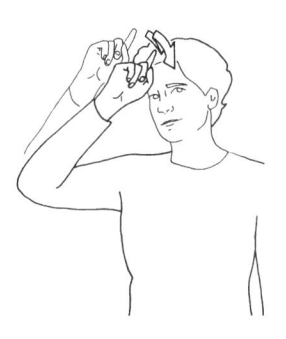

ASL HEIGHT

LSF TAILLE
(IVT 1986)

Measuring the height of the students
(Pastouriaux and Régnier 1954)

HELL

In the sign HELL, we see remnants of a gestured curse used in Europe for centuries. The gesture is produced with the forked handshape symbolizing the Devil's pitchfork, which is thrown toward the ground in the direction of hell. In the thirteenth century, the gesture was sculpted on the door of the Bamberg Cathedral in Germany, and it is still used in rural France (Y. Delaporte, field observation). Long (1910) notes that the sign originated as a compound of DEVIL followed by letting the index finger "descend as far as it can." In the contemporary ASL sign, the etymological link with the pitchfork has been obscured by the closing of the index and middle fingers to form the letter H, the result of initialization for the English word *hell* (see "The Veiled Devil," p. 176).

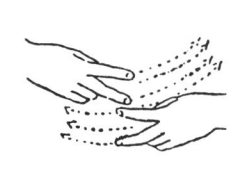

ASL HELL

LSF DIABLE
(Lambert 1856)

The damned at Bamberg Cathedral
(YD from Schmitt 1995)

HELP

This sign derives from the old French sign AIDER (help): "slightly lift the left arm with the right" (Brouland 1855). HELP was first documented in the U.S. by Clark (1885), who described the palm of the right hand lifting the elbow of the left hand to indicate the physical act of providing assistance. The sign has since evolved so that now the palm of the left hand lifts the right raised thumb hand.

ASL HELP

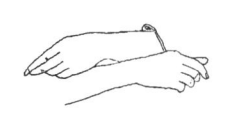

LSF AIDER
(Brouland 1855)

HIS, HERS, ITS, THEIR

This sign comes directly from the old French sign SON that can be translated by any of the contextually appropriate possessive pronouns *his*, *hers*, *its*, or *their*. Though the sign has since been initialized in LSF, the original variant continues to be used in areas outside Paris. In addition, Deaf people in both the U.S. and France refer to typical characteristics of a person or group of people through this form. The sign for the international conference Deaf Way, for example, is DEAF + THEIR. The seemingly banal possessive pronoun, then, experienced a semantic shift from "this is his (hers, its, etc.)" to something like "this behavior is *typical* of him (her, it, etc.)." In both ASL and LSF, the expression is accompanied by the mouth movement *pih,* an abbreviated mouthing of the syllable *pi* in the French word *typique* (typical).

ASL HIS, HERS, ITS, THEIR

LSF SON
(Pélissier 1856)

HOME

From an old LSF sign no longer used in France, HOME was first described by Ferrand (circa 1785) under HABITER (inhabit, reside) as "sign HOUSE, EAT, SLEEP." Clark (1885) cites the exact same sequence of signs: "for HOME make sign for HOUSE, EAT, and SLEEP or BED." Michaels (1923) describes the ASL form without HOUSE: "make the sign for EAT. Lean the side of the head in the palm of the hand. Close the eyes as if to sleep." The sign eventually transformed as a result of the well-documented process of compounding, where two different handshapes—here the bundled

ASL HOME

ASL EAT

ASL SLEEP

handshape of EAT and the flat hand of SLEEP—evolved into one handshape, the bundled handshape of EAT.

HONEST

The right H hand moves in a straight line from the heel to the fingertips of the left palm. The movement of the right hand is a symbolic translation of the metaphor "straight is good," which is also found in the related signs RIGHT and STRAIGHT and indicates moral integrity. Higgins (1923) lists the words *just* and *fair* as English synonyms of the ASL sign HONEST, whereas today its meaning is restricted to the semantically related concepts of *honesty*, *truth*, and *integrity*.

ASL HONEST

ASL RIGHT
(YD from Long 1910)

HONEY

Both Long (1910) and Higgins (1923) document this sign under the entry MOLASSES, while Stokoe et al. (1965) add the English translation "syrup." The ASL sign is likely inherited from the French sign CRÈME (cream), which has the identical form of the index finger drawing the length of the chin and then twisting away from the mouth as if having been licked. French desserts are often accompanied by a thick, sweet cream. This type of cream was traditionally stored in pots—like honey or molasses—and surreptitiously tasted by dessert lovers who dipped their fingers in to taste.

ASL HONEY, LSF CRÈME

HONOR, RESPECT

This sign derives from the old LSF POLITESSE, RESPECT (politeness, respect): "take the hand, held horizontally and prone, and apply the outer edge to the forehead; lower the hand and the head while tracing a half circle and an upward movement" (Blanchet 1850). Initialized with the H handshape, this is the contemporary ASL sign HONOR, and when produced with the R handshape, it is the ASL sign RESPECT. In ASL and LSF, both hands are now used, suggesting that the two signs must stem from the same etymon. In ASL, the sign is directional, so that the hands can move toward the signer from neutral sign space to express the meanings "you honor me" or "you respect me."

ASL HONOR, RESPECT

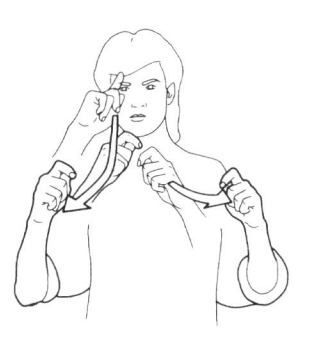

LSF POLITESSE, RESPECT
(IVT 1997)

Gesture of respectful salutation
(Illustration by Le Rallic in De Bardy 1937)

HOPE, EXPECT

From the old French sign ESPÉRER (hope), HOPE, EXPECT was originally indistinguishable from the LSF ATTENDRE (wait; see WAIT) except for the orientation of the palms. Both signs express the same metaphorical meaning of pulling something towards the body for which one waits or hopes. Paulmier (1844) expressed this meaning quite lyrically as "the heart drawing near the one thing that it seems to aspire to by taking the two hands in front as if to pull that thing close." Lambert (1865) mentions the same metaphor in his description—"Imprint on the hands the movement of COME, COME, COME." In the nineteenth century, the forearms were brought toward the body. Clark

ASL HOPE, EXPECT

LSF ESPÉRER
(Lambert 1865)

(1885) describes this sign in his entry ANXIOUS, which is identical in form to the LSF ESPÉRER, with the addition of "an upward look with the eyes, with an intense or expectant expression of countenance." Much later, in LSF and in ASL, the arms immobilized and the movement transferred to the fingers that now bend. In LSF, the dominant hand is placed close to the forehead and the hands face each other. This form likely transferred to ASL since we see both hands elevated above the shoulders close to the head where hopes are metaphorically thought to reside.

LSF ATTENDRE
(Pélissier 1856)

LSF ESPÉRER
(IVT 1986)

HOT

Blanchet (1850) described the French sign CHAUD (hot) as "the open hand, palm placed in front of the mouth; simulate the action of warming it with one's breath." Clark (1885) recognized the image behind the sign in his entry for HOT: "Suddenly throw the hand out, and extending the fingers, at same time make motion with mouth as though the hand was blown on by the breath." Later in both ASL and LSF, the sign evolved so that the hand now twists away from the mouth, a shift that Higgins noted as early as 1923 in his description to move the hand away "as if to drop the hot article."

ASL HOT

LSF CHAUD
(Pélissier 1856)

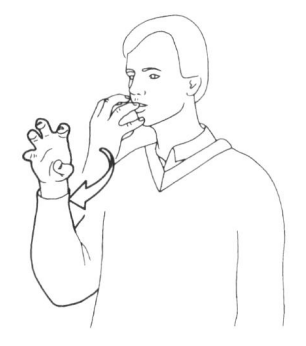

LSF CHAUD
(IVT 1986)

HOW

❶ The etymon of HOW 1 is the old French sign COMMENT (how) documented by de l'Épée (1784), Ferrand (circa 1785), Sicard (1808), and Blanchet (1850). Ferrand cites the same sign as meaning *manière* (manner) and *manier* (handle): "With the right hand handle [i.e., rub] in any direction over the left." Blanchet's description reveals that the sign had simplified with time: "Pass the palm of the hand over the back of the other hand one time" (1850). The polysemy of the sign MANIÈRE/MANIER is founded on the etymologies of the French words *manière* and *manier*, both of which come from *main* (hand), as well as the first meaning of *manier* (touch with the hand). Long (1910) and Higgins (1923) both document this sign in ASL, which at the time, also was used to mean "manner" (Higgins 1942). The semantic relationship between *manner* and *how* is seen in the definition of *manner* as "a way of doing something": "he explained the manner in which he would fix the car," and "he explained how he would fix the car." The assimilation of the handshapes and movements in this form gave rise to the sign in ASL. Today, it is almost exclusively reserved for formal registers.

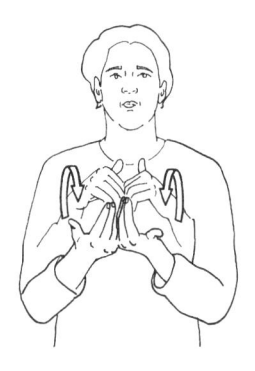

ASL HOW 1

❷ HOW 2 is a contemporary variant of HOW 1. The left hand remains still while the right hand exhibits a short back and forth rotation of the wrist. Additionally, signers are known to extend the little finger and the thumb of both hands, a shift that almost fully obscures the original symbolism of the sign. When the movement repeats, HOW 2 most commonly refers to the manner in

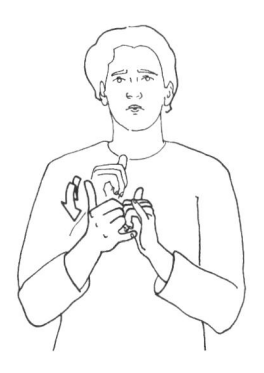

ASL HOW 2

which something is done. However, with a single rotation of the wrist, it can refer to how one is doing or feeling.

HOW MANY

Stemming from a counting gesture consisting of extending the fingers one after the other, this sign's origin is found in old descriptions of the LSF sign COMBIEN (how many). Ferrand (circa 1785) instructed signers to "count with the fingers one, two, three," and Lambert (1865) wrote "open the fingers of the right hand successively." Clark (1885) cites the same form in his entry for HOW MANY, only he indicates that the index finger (for the American sign ONE) is the first to be deployed: "Hold closed right hand in front of body, opening fingers, one after the other, commencing with the index." In the contemporary sign, the fingers open at the same time. HOW MANY and MANY (see entry) are distinguished from each other by their movements—a long emphatic movement and lowered eyebrows for HOW MANY and a short, repeated movement for MANY.

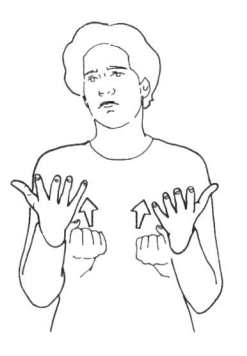

ASL HOW MANY

LSF COMBIEN
(IVT 1986)

HUMBLE

❶ HUMBLE and GOD (see entry) both come from the LSF sign SAINT (holy), in which "the right hand descends from the forehead down the length of the body by a curved line; at the same time the head bows down" (de Gérando 1827). This is a representation of the Holy Spirit that flows "from the forehead to the heart" (Lambert 1865). One of the characteristics of sainthood is humility, and the movement of the left hand under the right hand in the ASL sign reinforces the symbolism of submission. In an earlier variation documented by Michaels (1923), the sign began with the index finger posed on the mouth, probably a reference to the silence of one who is humble. The same symbolism is implicated in the sign described by Brown (1856), where the thumb glides the length of the lips symbolizing deprivation and resignation during the Catholic season of Lent (see PATIENCE).

❷ In a second variant first documented by Long (1910), the sign begins with the flat hand. This may have been inherited from the LSF SAINT or it could be the result of assimilation with the handshape in HUMBLE 1. Higgins (1923) notes both flat hands are drawn down with the "head bowing down" to indicate submission.

ASL HUMBLE 1

LSF SAINT
(YD, fieldwork)

ASL HUMBLE 2

(ONE) HUNDRED

Directly inherited from LSF, the handshape is the letter *C* for the French word *cent* (hundred). Abbé de l'Épée (1784) described the sign as follows: "CENT is produced like the Roman number by the letter *C*." The LSF sign can be produced without a number preceding it, and while this may have been true historically—Higgins (1923) cites the same variation—the contemporary ASL HUNDRED must always be preceded by a number.

ASL (ONE) HUNDRED

HURRY

Higgins (1942) described the sign as the right hand configured with the letter *H* "beckoning with quick jerks" as it moved forward on the axis of time. The jerking movement is seen in other signs that invoke speed, like the sign QUICK (see entry). Today, both hands are typically used instead of one. In addition, the hands can move forward (especially in the sense of *rush*) but do not have to.

ASL HURRY

HURT

Clark (1885) was the first to document this sign. He included it under his entry ACHE: "hold the extended index finger, others and thumb closed, over and parallel to surface, and then make thrusting motion to indicate the darting pain, sometimes first making the sign for SICK." In the early twentieth century, Higgins (1923) noted that the sign could be positioned in different locations to show where the pain occurred, a feature that remains in contemporary productions. Roth (1941) reiterated that the sign ACHE/PAIN is an indication of "a throbbing at the injured spot. (Similar to SIN from which it may have originated.)" This link between physical pain and moral deprivation is reflected in the related sign SIN (see entry).

ASL HURT

HYPOCRITE

The production of this sign combines several metaphors concerning deceit, underhandedness, and the association of the horned handshape with the evil eye (see "The Veiled Devil," p. 176). Long (1910) translates the sign as "humbug, impostor." In the early twentieth century, *humbug* commonly referred to a deceptive person; it is possible, then, that the movement of the right hand pressing down over the left represented a mask placed over the face to trick or deceive someone. Higgins (1923) has two entries relevant to HYPOCRITE, both of which contribute evidence that the sign likely merged two metaphors—"masks are a sign of deception" and "horns guard against the evil eye." He, too, documents the sign under his entry HUMBUG; however, he also lists the translation "hypocrite" under DECEIVE, where the horned handshapes "on both hands, palms down, extended to the left tandem wise, and right hand glides slowly outward along back of left hand as the left hand is withdrawn toward body." This entry provides evidence that an old French sign HYPOCRITE (hypocrite) is a likely ancestor. Lambert (1865) cites HYPOCRITE as a compound sign consisting of gliding the middle finger across the left palm for FACILE (easy) followed by the directional form of the old LSF TROMPER (deceive; see DECEIVE). Though there is no definitive proof of the sign's etymon, it is likely that a combination of these metaphorical forces influenced the form and its meaning.

ASL HYPOCRITE

LSF TROMPER
(Pélissier 1856)

I

ICE, FREEZE

Long (1910) notes that the fingers of the open hands bend into claws with a short movement toward the ground. The contemporary sign is the same, except that the hands move toward the body. The stiffening of the fingers symbolizes water solidifying under cold temperatures.

ASL ICE, FREEZE

IGNORE

In LSF, the nose is the location of intuition, a result of the polysemy of the French word *sentir*, meaning "sense" or "smell." The nose also has negative connotations in LSF and ASL (see DOUBT and LOUSY), and the twisting open hand away from the nose connotes negation (as in DON'T CARE and DON'T WANT, for example). The etymology of IGNORE is, in effect, "sense not."

ASL IGNORE

IMPORTANT

❶ Long (1910) and Higgins (1923) both included this sign, which is no longer used among mainstream Deaf Americans. Higgins (1942) wrote that the right hand was configured in the letter *I* for *important* and rested on the left fist while the two hands lifted in concert to "bring what is important to the top."

ASL IMPORTANT 1
(YD from Higgins 1923)

❷ IMPORTANT 2 is the conventional sign used today. It belongs to a family of signs with the ring handshape that pertain to worth or lack of worth (see WORTHLESS, WORTH, PRICE, and NOTHING). The first documented form in this family is the old LSF sign SANS, RIEN (without, nothing), which was transmitted to the U.S. as NOTHING and WORTHLESS. Over time, Deaf Americans derived WORTH from WORTHLESS via back formation, where the last part of the sign was interpreted as meaning "less" or "without." Stokoe, et al. (1965) cite WORTHLESS as a compound meaning "worth nothing." Higgins (1923) lists IMPORTANT 2 under his entry MERITS, and he provides the alternate translations "reward," "deserve," "worthy," and "desserts." IMPORTANT 2 is nearly identical to WORTH except for the movement, and it can be translated as "worth" in some contexts, such as "It was worth going to the event."

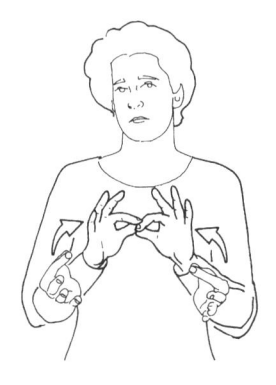

ASL IMPORTANT 2

IMPOSSIBLE

❶ The history of this sign is revealed in an older variant in which the right modified horn handshape marks an X, the sign of negation, on the left palm. This movement is seen in the old LSF sign JAMAIS (never), where the LSF letter *J* traces a cross in the air (Pélissier 1856). After transmission to the U.S., American signers added the extended thumb, thus obscuring the connection with the initialized French sign.

❷ In the most widely used form, the traced X has been replaced by a short, reduplicated knocking on

ASL IMPOSSIBLE 1

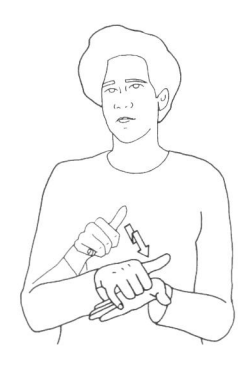

ASL IMPOSSIBLE 2

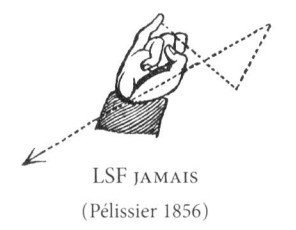

LSF JAMAIS
(Pélissier 1856)

the palm. This evolution completely obscures the etymological connection with the cross of negation.

IMPRESS, EMPHASIZE

This form is a gestural equivalent of the English words *impress*, *print*, and more specifically *fingerprint*. IMPRESS is identical to the French sign IDENTITÉ (identity), whose etymon is the sign EMPREINTE (fingerprint). The figurative uses of the sign in ASL are similar to those in English, all of which focus on extended meanings of *impress*—*emphasize* ("press a point"), *stress* ("pressure").

ASL IMPRESS, EMPHASIZE

IMPROVE

The movement of the right hand from the wrist to the top of the left arm is a visual metaphor for progress. The arm represents a measuring tool, which Long (1910) affirms in his description of the movement as "measuring off spaces of advancement." When the movement is inverted, the sign means DETERIORATE (see entry).

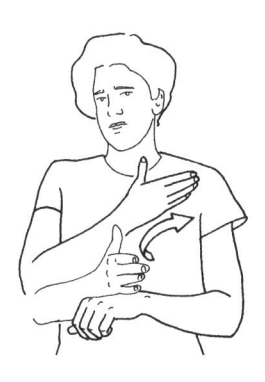

ASL IMPROVE

INFORM

The right, bundled hand on the forehead represents the grasping of ideas and the opening of the hands symbolizes releasing those ideas (see

"The Bundled Handshape," p. 217). The ASL sign is nearly identical to the old LSF ENSEIGNER (teach; Pélissier 1856). Long (1910) described an older version of the sign as a compound of KNOW and GIVE AWAY.

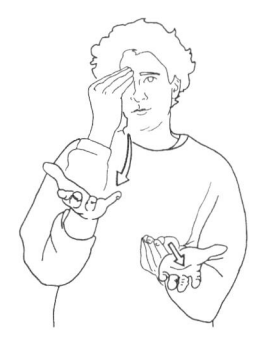

ASL INFORM

LSF ENSEIGNER
(Pélissier 1856)

INSECT

Historical documents describe the older version of this sign, which was produced in front of the body rather than on the nose, as "the crawling of the insect" (Higgins 1942; Long 1910). The change in location to the nose reinforces the association of the nose with negative or pejorative things (see DON'T CARE, IGNORE, and LOUSY).

ASL INSECT

INSULT

This sign comes directly from the old French sign INSULTE (insult), which Blanchet (1850) described as "tap the chest with the index extremity several times, if one wants to indicate that one has received the injury; make the sign in the opposite direction to indicate a person when the injury has been made to another." The index finger almost certainly represents a sword, an iconic form widely documented in LSF that was transmitted to ASL (see ARGUE, CANNOT, and STRUGGLE). Today, the wrist rotates up in an arc.

ASL INSULT

INTERESTING

❶ This sign is identical to the old ASL sign FASCINATED (see entry). The original ring handshape is still used by some older Deaf people (E. Shaw, field observation), and it suggests a delicate tugging on the heart and the head towards something outside the body. Higgins (1923) glossed it as YIELD, signifying yielding to pleasure or giving one's self over to something or someone else. Long (1910) also saw this meaning at work in the sign, which he said gave "the idea of drawing the attention out."

❷ In the subsequent evolution of the form, the handshape changed to small crescents that then contract into key handshapes. This variant is also frequently produced with only one hand.

❸ INTERESTING 3 maintains the drawn out movement of the earlier versions, but the dominant hand drops from the face to the center of the chest. The change from the ring handshape to the modified ring is a common phonological shift that has occurred in numerous ASL signs (see "Handshape Change," p. 148).

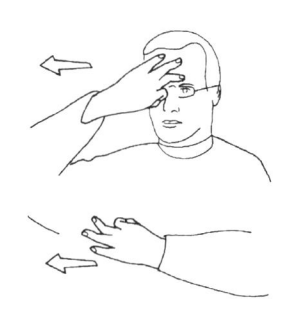

ASL INTERESTING 1
(YD from Higgins 1923)

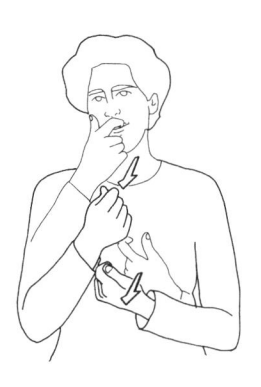

ASL INTERESTING 2

ASL INTERESTING 3

INTERPRET

This sign combines elements of two semantically related signs—the first part of LANGUAGE 1 (see entry) and the twisting movement of CHANGE. The twisting of the palm orientation signifies the conversion of one language to another. The same movement is seen in the ASL sign TRANSLATE.

ASL INTERPRET

INVENT

The handshape for this sign has been documented as the index finger (Long 1910), the flat hand (Costello 1994), and the open hand (Riekehof 1987). However, the movement has always represented the metaphor "ideas emerge from the head." The synonymous English expression *make up* reflects the same metaphor.

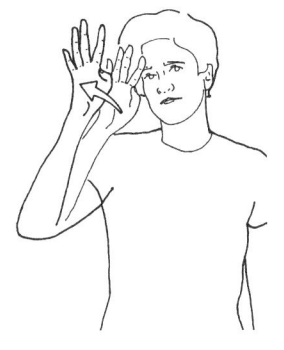

ASL INVENT

IRONIC

This sign derives from a mocking or injurious gesture commonly used among hearing people throughout the Mediterranean basin. Gesturers point the pair of horn handshapes toward an adversary to ward off the evil eye. The Deaf in France incorporated this form in many signs that convey mockery, deceit, and overall underhandedness (see MOCK and DECEIVE). The original configuration of the hand in the European gesture has been maintained in this ASL sign. Initiation of the sign near the nose carries additional meaning in France and, more subtly, in the U.S., where the nose is symbolic of funny or pejorative things (see DON'T CARE, FUNNY, and LOUSY). The sign is equally used to mean "sarcastic," which retains the form's semantic association with deception or masked meanings.

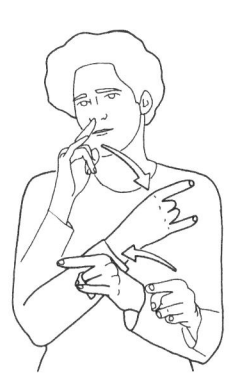

ASL IRONIC

Handshape Change

During the course of our historical analysis of ASL, we have uncovered some undocumented evolutionary tendencies. Nancy Frishberg's seminal work (1976) on historical change revealed that the vertical axis and the center of the signing space both exert a sort of gravitational pull on signs as they evolve over time. She posits that change will ultimately occur in signs whose locations are just outside these areas. We have found a class of signs where a similar "pull" operates on handshapes rather than locations on the body. We can categorize these into two groups: the flat handshape and the ring handshape.

The Flat Handshape

In the older forms of ASL and LSF, several signs with the flat handshape evolved into variations with a bent middle finger. Examples in ASL include EMPTY/BALD, FORGET, PITY, and SICK; and in LSF, NE PAS CONNAÎTRE (don't know)," S'ÉCHAPER (escape), and RETARD (late).

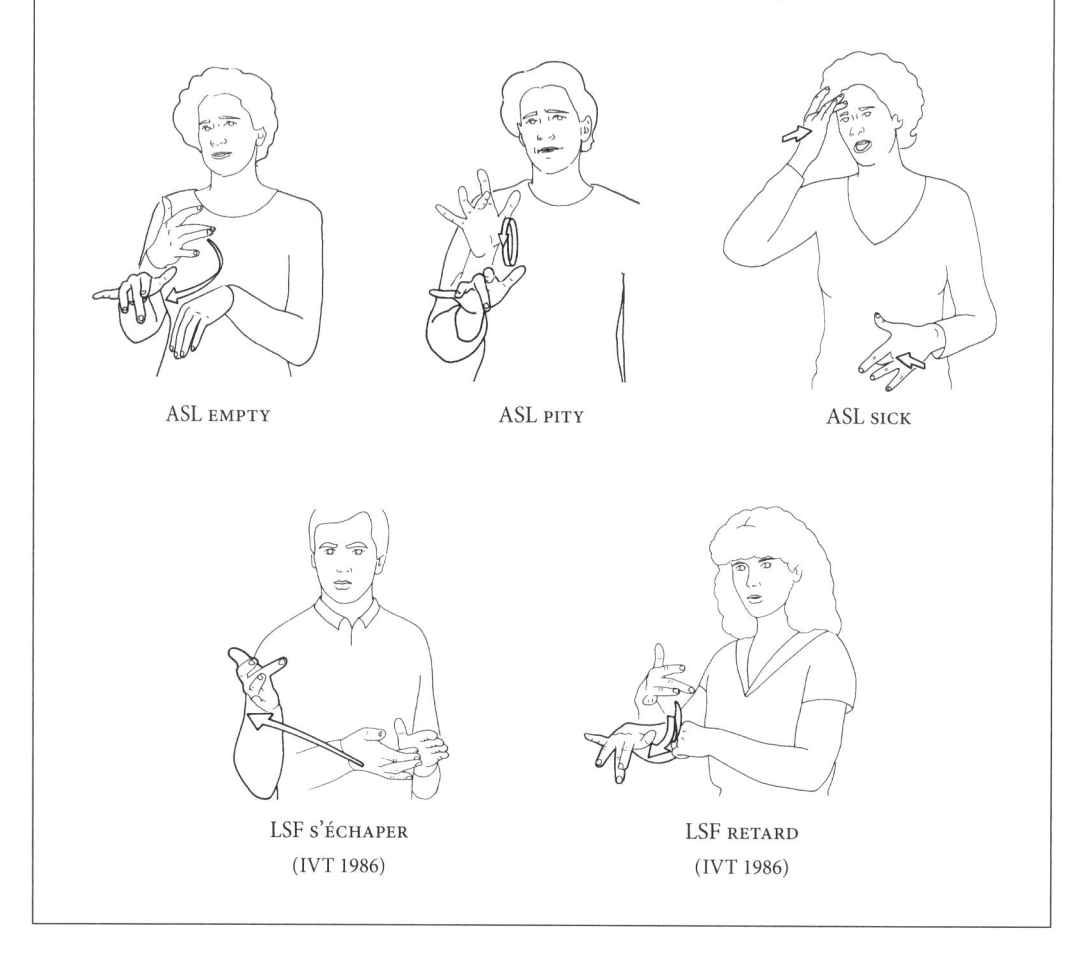

ASL EMPTY

ASL PITY

ASL SICK

LSF S'ÉCHAPER
(IVT 1986)

LSF RETARD
(IVT 1986)

This flat hand to bent middle finger evolution appears to be triggered by the hand's contact with the body.

The Ring Handshape

The ring handshape is typically implicated in signs that depict the grasping of thin objects such as COUNT and FIND. In several contemporary signs that use the modified ring handshape, where the thumb and middle finger make contact, their progenitors were produced with the ring handshape in at least part of the sign. These include CAT, CHOOSE, CONNECT, HATE, INTERESTING, LIKE, and TELL-A-STORY. All of these signs (some more than others) can still be produced with the ring handshape. This evolutionary tendency of the fingers drawn to the middle is not present in LSF but has proved widespread in ASL.

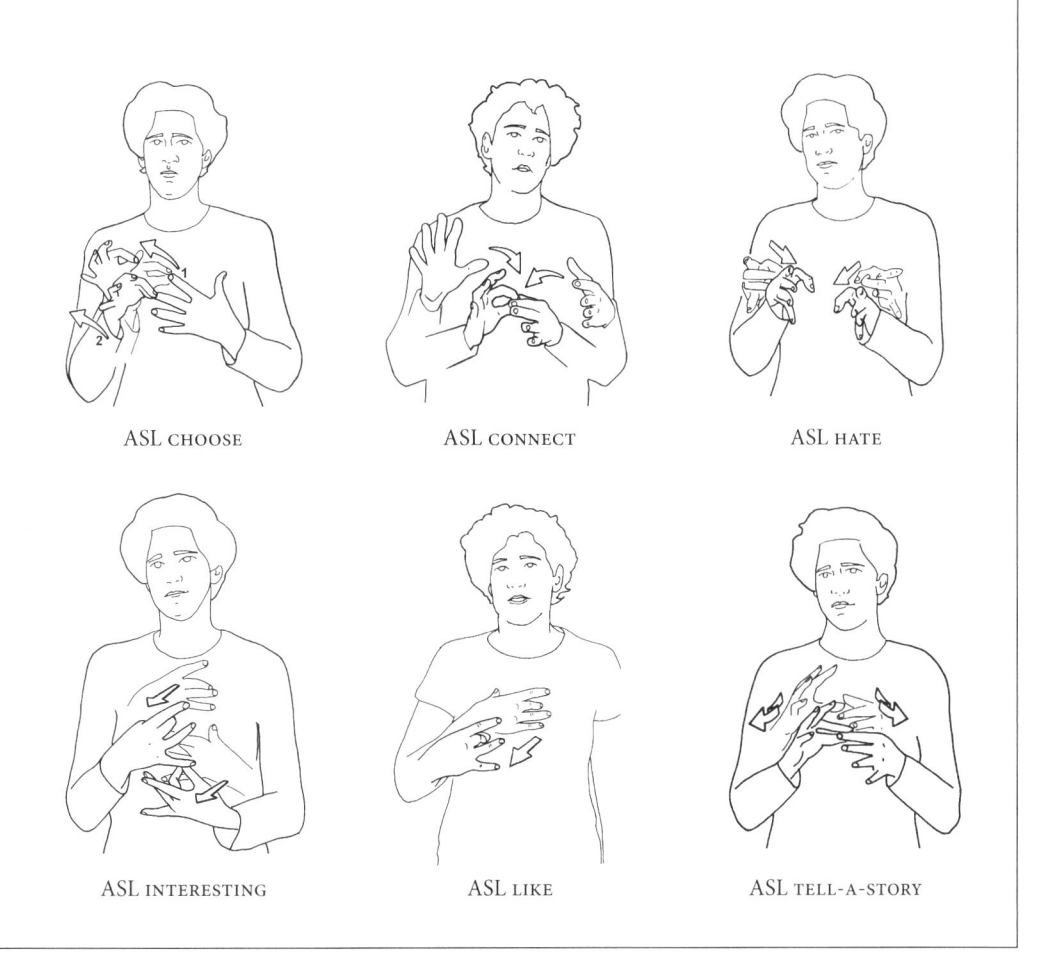

ASL CHOOSE

ASL CONNECT

ASL HATE

ASL INTERESTING

ASL LIKE

ASL TELL-A-STORY

HANDSHAPE CHANGE 149

J

JEALOUS

❶ This sign exists in other sign languages, including LSF, British Sign Language, and Lengua de Signos Española/Spanish Sign Language, suggesting it was borrowed from a gesture used in the larger hearing community. Littré (1863–1872) described the origin as "bite the fingers, actual act that is a sign of impatience, embarrassment, preoccupation." Costadau (1720) sees in this gesture "the sign of chagrin, sometimes a mark of menacing and vengeance." In transforming the gesture into a lexical unit for sign language, Deaf people restricted the meaning to "envious, jealous." In the old LSF variant of JALOUX (jealous), the sign remained the same as the gesture, and it is still seen in Saint-Laurent-en-Royans. However, in standard LSF, the index finger does not contact the teeth and the hand swings straight out in front of the mouth, as it does in the ASL sign. The added rotation of the wrist and bending of the index finger in the ASL sign further obscures its iconicity.

❷ A newer form is simply an initialized version of JEALOUS 1 that can originate close to the mouth or in more neutral space, thereby securing its distance from the iconic root.

ASL JEALOUS 1

LSF JALOUX
(YD from St-Laurent 1979)

ASL JEALOUS 2

JUSTICE

Ferrand (circa 1785) first documented the French sign JUGER (judge) as "hold the balance." Lambert (1865) later gave the following description of the LSF sign BALANCE (scales): "with the thumb and index of each hand, take the chains of the trays on a scale and with a light movement alternately raise and lower them." Thus, the ASL sign represents the trays of an old-fashioned scale, which is the symbol of justice prominently displayed in all courthouses. The iconicity is also seen in the ASL sign DECIDE (see entry).

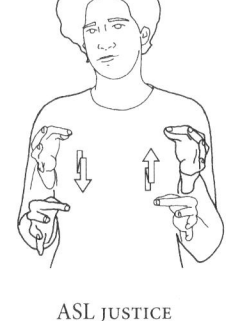

ASL JUSTICE

LSF BALANCE
(Lambert 1865)

Symbol of justice
(Pinloche 1922)

K

KID

Though this sign is not documented in any of the historical texts, it is often described as a depiction of wiping a runny nose. Some older Deaf people in Alabama point the index finger down and make a motion that depicts a runny nose (E. Shaw, field observation). Costello (1994) says it "suggests a child's runny nose"; Riekehof (1987) calls it "wiping the nose as children often do"; Sternberg (1994) says it is "the running nose"; and Stokoe et al. (1965) record that the index finger, rather than the horn handshape, is placed under the nose, noting that it is not used "in polite usage as the sign is imitative of runny noses."

ASL KID

KILL

This is one of many ASL signs in which the index finger symbolizes a sharp weapon such as a knife or sword (see ARGUE, CANNOT, and ENEMY, OPPOSITE). Documented in the U.S. since the nineteenth century (Clark 1885), the right index finger denotes a weapon that penetrates the body, represented by the left hand. Long (1910) confirms the iconicity in his description of the movement as: "the motion . . . of stabbing. Some follow with the sign for 'die.'"

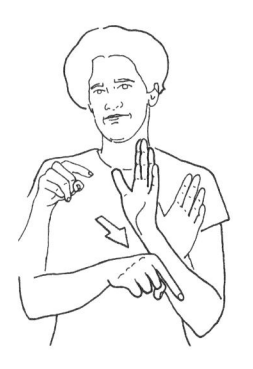

ASL KILL

KIND

This sign draws from a metaphor pervasive in ASL and LSF that means "the heart is the location of warmth and affection." It comes from the old French sign AMI (friend), in which "the two hands, one placed in front of the other near the heart in a horizontal position with the palms up, move over each other alternatively from the heart to paint the outpouring of the heart and its reciprocity" (de Gérando 1827). Paulmier (1844) speaks of a "current of affection that circulates from one heart to the other," and Lambert (1865) describes an "exchange of the heart." In contemporary ASL, KIND is typically used in more formal settings and can also mean "generous."

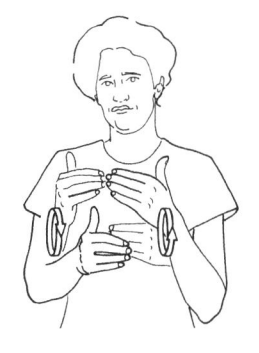

ASL KIND

LSF AMI
(YD from Oléron 1974)

KISS

❶ This variation of KISS was inherited directly from the French sign EMBRASSER (kiss), which mimics the customary French greeting of people kissing each other on both cheeks. In LSF, the fist symbolizes a person's head, and it touches each cheek. Because the custom does not exist in the U.S., the sign's form evolved in a way that obscures its literal origin. The hand assumes a bent mitten handshape and touches the area below and then above the mouth on the signer's cheek.

ASL KISS 1

LSF EMBRASSER
(Pélissier 1856)

❷ The bundled handshape in this sign represents the heads and, more specifically, the lips of two people engaging in a kiss. KISS 2 is almost identical to LSF AMOUREUX (in love), with the addition of a nonmanual marker of puckered lips.

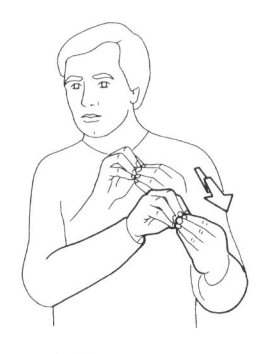

ASL KISS 2

LSF AMOUREUX
(IVT 1986)

KNOW

The bent mitten hand taps the forehead, the location of intellectual faculties. This sign comes from the French CONNAÎTRE (know), illustrated by Pélissier (1856) and described in Lambert (1865) as "gently tap the forehead two times with the tips of the fingers."

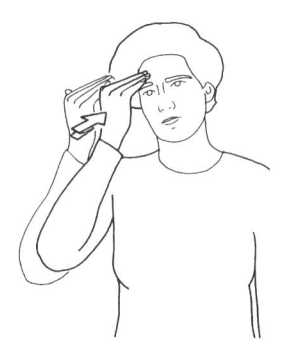

ASL KNOW

LSF CONNAÎTRE
(Pélissier 1856)

L

LANGUAGE

❶ In the early twentieth century, CHAIN, SENTENCE, and LANGUAGE all were produced with the "thumb and index of both hands, joined as if links, separating and joining repeatedly, as hands move rightward" (Higgins 1923). This version is nearly identical to the contemporary form SENTENCE 2 (see entry), where the hands assume ring handshapes that come together and stretch away from each other,—a representation of the "chain of speech," inherited from the French sign PHRASE (sentence). Over time, the rightward movement of the linked hands changed so that now the ringed hands touch in the first part of the sign and then draw outwards.

ASL LANGUAGE 1, SENTENCE 2

❷ Eventually, LANGUAGE 1 became initialized with the L handshape, resulting in a more targeted meaning. This change in form distinguished LANGUAGE 2 from the related signs CHAIN and SENTENCE, but also ruptured the sign's visual association with a chain.

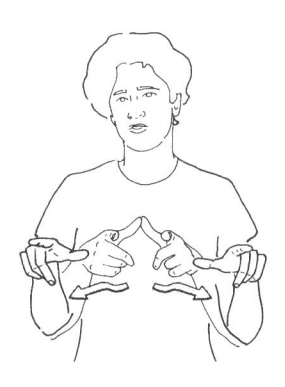

ASL LANGUAGE 2

LAST

❶ The right index finger taps the left little finger (Higgins 1923), just as the right index finger points to the left thumb in the counterpart sign FIRST (see entry).

ASL LAST 1
(YD from Higgins 1923)

❷ This contemporary form is the result of assimilation, where the right hand has borrowed the configuration of the left hand so that the right little finger, not the index finger, now strikes the left little finger.

ASL LAST 2

LATE, NOT YET

The old French sign APRÈS (after), first documented by Sicard (1808), is the etymon of this sign. The movement of the hand toward the rear is perplexing because in both ASL and LSF this motion typically indicates the past (see "Axis of Time," p. 286). This is a direct contradiction of the meaning, of LATE. The movement is explained by the polysemy of the French word *après,* which can mean "after something is finished" (e.g., *après dîner* [after dinner]) or "later" (e.g., *je viendrai après* [I will come after]). In ASL, if the sign is reduplicated and accompanied by a protruding tongue, it conveys the very specific meaning "not yet."

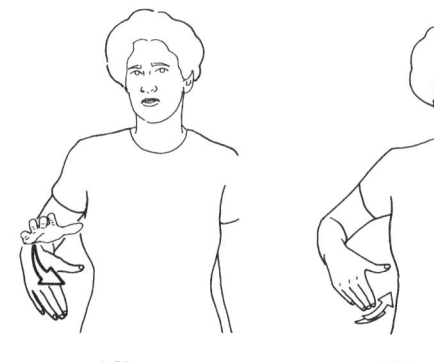

ASL LATE

ASL NOT YET

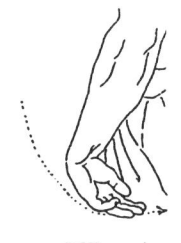

LSF APRÈS
(Lambert 1865)

LATER

❶ In LATER 1, the right thumb contacts the left palm while the index finger rotates down, iconically representing the movement of the minute hand on a clock. This sign closely resembles the ASL sign HALF HOUR (see entry), differing only by a shorter movement and initialized handshape.

ASL LATER 1

❷ Configured in the L handshape for *later*, this variant form projects away from the signer, symbolizing the passing of time toward the future (see "Axis of Time," p. 286). The sign is likely an initialized form of the semantically similar sign FUTURE, WILL (see entry).

ASL LATER 2

LAW

❶ In this early version of the sign in the U.S., the outer edge of the right index finger knocked against the palm of the left hand several times (Long 1910). LAW 1 is identical in both form and meaning to the old French sign LOI (law; Brouland 1855), where the flat left hand represents a tablet of laws (Lambert 1865) and the index finger symbolizes the articles written upon it.

❷ Under his entry BROTHER-IN-LAW, Clark (1885) shows an intermediary form wherein the L handshape replaces the original index finger (an initialization of *law*), and the palm faces away from the signer. In the contemporary form, the right hand retains the L handshape but the palms face each other, an evolution that likely occurred to ease production. The basic form of this sign has proved incredibly prolific in ASL where initialized extensions abound, including the signs AGENDA, a variant of BIBLE, CODE, ETHICS, FORMULA, POLICY, RULE, STATE, and TESTAMENT.

ASL LAW 1
(YD from Long 1910)

LSF LOI
(Brouland 1855)

ASL LAW 2

LAW 157

LAZY

The sign originates from the old French sign PARESSEUX (lazy), where the crossed arms rested on the shoulders to represent inactivity. In some areas (e.g., Indiana; E. Shaw, field observation; Shroyer and Shroyer 1984), an initialized version of the two-handed LSF sign with the letter *L* is still used. Today, LAZY is most often produced with only the right hand tapping the area of the chest near the heart. Fortuitously, this location on the chest is frequently indexed in signs that denote personal characteristics. As a result, the etymon of LAZY is largely unrecognized as a gesture of rest.

ASL LAZY

LSF PARESSEUX
(Pélissier 1856)

LEARN

This sign hails directly from the old French sign APPRENDRE (learn; Lambert 1865). Unchanged for centuries, it represents the transmission of knowledge from a book (signified by the left hand) to the head, the symbolic location of intellectual faculties. Sicard (1808) describes the form as "the action of taking, with the right hand, from the left palm, everything that one supposes is there and putting in the head that which one takes." The contemporary ASL sign STUDENT (see entry) originated as a compound of LEARN and PERSON.

ASL LEARN

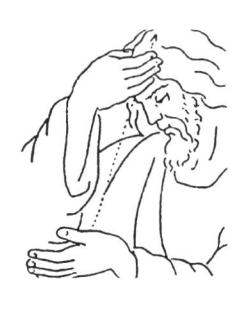

LSF APPRENDRE
(Lambert 1865)

LEAVE

The transition from the open to the bundled handshape visually represents the image of something going away and disappearing in the distance. A similar motivation can be seen in the LSF sign DISPARAÎTRE (disappear) and the ASL sign ABSENT (see entry), both of which involve the disappearance of someone or something.

ASL LEAVE

LECTURE

Higgins (1923) notes that the right hand is held "horizontal, pointing outward, palm leftward, moved up and down as if repeating gesture of emphasis." Similarly, Roth (1941) explains that the sign LECTURE is "the motion a speaker makes when delivering a lecture." Today, the hand is held higher, in front of the right shoulder, and the fingertips point upward in the initial position, rather than outward.

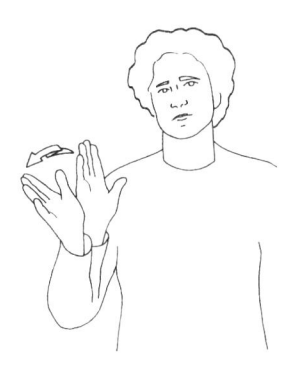

ASL LECTURE (YD)

LEND, BORROW

This sign derives from a compound of the signs GIVE and KEEP (Higgins 1923), where LEND requires movement away from the signer toward the one receiving the loan and BORROW requires movement in toward the signer, who is the receiver. GIVE is no longer realized in the contemporary form but for the slight bending of the wrists as the forked handshapes extend away from (or toward) the signer. The fork handshapes

ASL LEND, BORROW

maintain the sign's link to KEEP, which is also glossed as CAREFUL (see entry).

LESSON

This sign comes directly from the old French sign CAHIER (exercise book; Pélissier 1856). The left hand symbolizes a page in a student's lesson book, and the right hand marks the edges of the page. Higgins (1923) wrote a similar description: "divide the page represented by left palm."

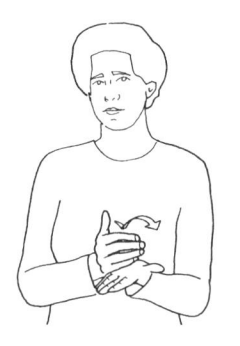

ASL LESSON

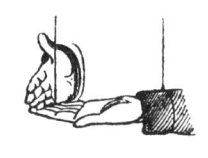

LSF CAHIER
(Pélissier 1856)

LETTER

LETTER comes from the LSF sign LETTRE (letter), which Blanchet (1850) described as "take the right thumb to the lips as if wetting a sealing wafer; imitate the act of applying it to a letter placed in the palm of the left hand." The symbolism of wetting a sealing wafer was later replaced by the image of the postal stamp. In both cases, the thumb represents bringing the wafer or stamp to the lips. The sign's form and meaning remain unchanged to this day.

ASL LETTER

LSF LETTRE
(Pélissier 1856)

LETTUCE, CABBAGE

❶ Both Long (1910) and Higgins (1923) give us the etymology of this sign: the fist handshapes tap the sides of the head just as "the wide leaves close together to form the head of a cabbage" (Higgins 1942).

ASL LETTUCE, CABBAGE 1
(YD from Long 1910)

❷ The sign has since evolved in two important ways. First, the handshape has changed to a claw, and second, the left hand has been dropped, likely to ease production, given the location of the sign at the height of the temple. These changes obscure the iconicity behind the sign.

ASL LETTUCE, CABBAGE 2

LIE

During the eighteenth century, the LSF sign MENSONGE 1 (lie) was produced by crossing the index fingers and shaking them over the mouth (Ferrand circa 1785). The crossed fingers symbolize an obstacle, in this case to the truth. The crossed fingers are also found in the LSF sign DIFFICILE (difficult), and a remnant can be seen in the ASL sign COMPLEX (see entry). By 1808, MENSONGE 2 had developed as a one-hand sign that Sicard described as "the act of tracing the index of the right hand the length of the mouth from right to left in an oblique line to express that the person of subject does not have the right, and that the expressions or the gestures announce falsity." In 1816, Clerc brought this form to North America. Today, the most frequently used variation of LIE is produced on the chin with a bent mitten handshape. However, in certain dialects (e.g., among some African American signers; E. Shaw, field observation), the form originally introduced by Clerc continues to be used today. The transverse movement of the index finger directly opposes that of its complement TRUE, which moves in a straight line away from the mouth.

ASL LIE

LSF MENSONGE 1
(Illustration by Pat Mallet)

LSF MENSONGE 2
(Pélissier 1856)

LIKE

Both Long (1910) and Higgins (1923) describe LIKE as produced with the thumb and index finger coming together "as if the heart was being drawn out toward the object" (Long). The same movement is present in the signs CONFIDENT, FASCINATED, and INTERESTING (see entries). In the contemporary sign, the middle finger and thumb draw away from the center of the chest (as opposed to the heart). The evolution in contact from the index to middle finger is common in ASL (see "Handshape Change," p. 148).

ASL LIKE

LIVE

❶ This very old sign was inherited from the LSF sign VIVRE (live), in which "the fingers unite by their extremity . . . raised from the bottom of the chest to the top" (Laveau 1868). Clark (1885), the first American author to record the imagery behind the form, wrote that the movement "denotes the flow of blood through the system." Long (1910) includes two forms in his dictionary—a sign having open hands that corresponds with the symbolism of LIVE 1, and a photograph showing the hands configured in fists, which corresponds to LIVE 2. In the mid-twentieth century, LIVE 1 was still interpreted as symbolizing "the blood . . . ascending the aortas" (Higgins 1942).

ASL LIVE 1, LSF VIVRE
(Laveau 1868)

❷ The subsequent evolution of the sign on American soil manifests a change in handshape so that the thumb extends from a closed fist. This variation is

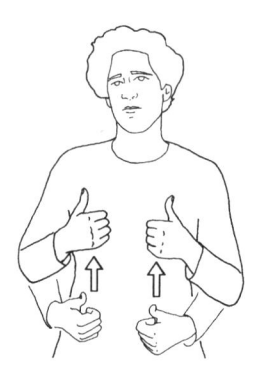

ASL LIVE 2

also used to mean "address" (as in one's residence or mailing address). LIVE 2 is frequently initialized with the L handshape, which further obscures the original imagery behind the sign.

LONELY

The form of this sign is similar to that of PATIENCE 2 (see entry), and it shares the meaning of enduring some kind of difficulty—in this case, solitude. Both signs belong to a family of signs whose origin is related to the practice of abstinence during the season of Lent (see HUMBLE, SECRET, and SUFFER). At the beginning of the twentieth century, LONELY was followed by the sign ALONE (Long 1910, Higgins 1923), which suggests that a compound sign, PATIENCE 2 + ALONE, might have preceded the contemporary form. If this were the case, the handshape of PATIENCE 2 assimilated with the handshape of ALONE (see entry) to create LONELY.

ASL LONELY

LONG

This sign was inherited from the French sign LONGUE (long). Sicard (1808) explained that "for the word *long*, I extend my left arm and with the right arm I run the length of the extension." The arm, then, serves as a measuring tool—a metonym also seen in the signs IMPROVE and DETERIORATE (see entries).

ASL LONG

LOOK FOR

Though some linguists consider the handshape for the ASL sign to be the letter C for the LSF CHERCHER (look for; see, for example, Baker-Shenk and Cokely 1980, 460; Cagle 2010), historical texts confirm that LOOK FOR derived from the LSF CURIEUX (curious). Blanchet (1850) explains that to produce CURIEUX, the signer must "form the manual letter C; bring it in front of the eye, like an eye glass; . . . shake it circularly several times." Higgins (1923) documents the ASL sign with additional translations ("look for," "seek," and "investigate") under his entry CURIOUS, which he describes as "vertical 'C' of right hand as if holding a magnifying glass before the eyes as the head turns from right to left as if searching." While CHERCHER has a close semantic link to LOOK FOR, its handshape has always been the double hook, *not* the letter C. CURIEUX is also the etymon of the contemporary ASL sign STRANGE (see entry), making LOOK FOR and STRANGE historically linked in spite of their semantic disparity.

ASL LOOK FOR

LSF CURIEUX
(Lambert 1865)

LOSE

LOSE is an iconic sign that originated in the French sign PERDRE (lose). Ferrrand (circa 1785) describes the production of PERDRE as "look in one pocket to search for a handkerchief or tobacco, then with the two hands joined at the fingertips, back-to-back, separate them with force while looking around saying 'it's lost!'" The meaning has since expanded to

ASL LOSE

LSF PERDRE
(Lambert 1865)

include "losing an object," "getting lost in a crowd," and even "losing one's place in a book."

LOSE A GAME

Long (1910), in his entry FAIL, characterizes LOSE A GAME as the act of standing and then falling down, literally conveying what it means to fail at a task. The first part of the sign has since dropped, so that now, only the palm of the right forked hand strikes the heel of the left palm. This change in form eased production and masked the iconicity behind the sign, but it also allowed for the emergence of the distinct sign FAIL (see entry).

ASL LOSE A GAME

LOUD

LOUD begins with the right open hand touching the ear and then both fists shaking at either side of the head. This action references the association of sound with the ear and visually represents the vibration of loud noises (see also NOISE). The fist handshapes add metaphorical meaning of strength or power (see BRAVE/COURAGE, DEFEAT, and STEEL).

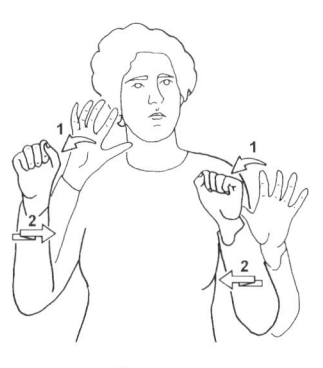

ASL LOUD

LOUSY

Although there are no historical records of this particular form, the rendition is consistent with the image of projecting mucus at something one deems "lousy." This metaphor is found in both LSF and ASL (see CURSE 1 and DON'T CARE). It is also possible that the "thumbing the nose" gesture influenced the form of this sign. In highly emphatic forms, the head can tilt to the side as the thumb presses into the nose.

ASL LOUSY

M

MACHINE

To produce this sign, the two claw hands fit together like the cogs of a wheel. This corresponds to Lambert's (1865) documentation of the French sign ENGRENAGE (gear), which he describes as "close both of the fists and then interlock the backs of the phalanges of the fingers one inside the other with the movement of the gears of two wheels." This sign is quite prolific in ASL; its meaning has extended to objects with actual cogs and wheels, (e.g., ENGINE) and to places where cogs and wheels might be located (e.g., FACTORY). In addition, if the movement is repeated with an added vibration of the lips, the sign means the machine or engine is running.

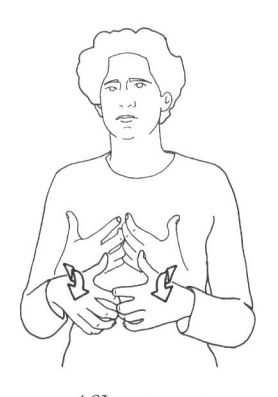

ASL MACHINE

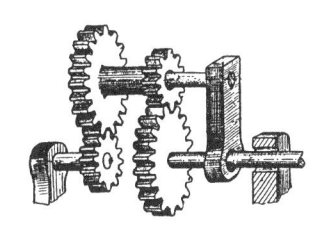

Gears
(Basquin, 1947)

MAD

The first description of MAD is found in Clark (1885) as a "clawing motion in front of face" with a "scowling expression." Long (1910) wrote that this handshape resembled "the talons of an eagle." In general, the claw handshape is associated with harsh or mean things (see ANGRY and COMPLAIN).

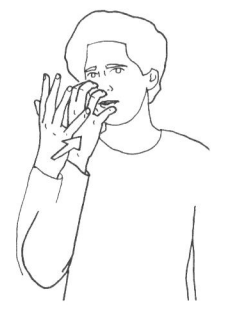

ASL MAD

MAKE

We uncovered the origin of MAKE in a gesture that depicts the act of manually creating something. Both Long (1910) and Higgins (1942) characterized the sign as the "action of twisting and pounding" (Higgins). Roth (1941) cites two movements in the sign's production—"strike the right fist on top of the left fist and then turn the striking fist this way and that way as if forming something." This sign is closely related to the French sign TRAVAILLER (work), which is produced by pounding the right fist over the left fist, as a laborer would employ an implement. TRAVAILLER is also the etymon of the ASL sign WORK 1 (see entry). In the eighteenth and nineteenth centuries, most Deaf people worked in manual trades, which creates an even stronger association between WORK 1 and MAKE. MAKE maintains the original orientation and point of contact of its French etymon, while the form of WORK 1 has since evolved.

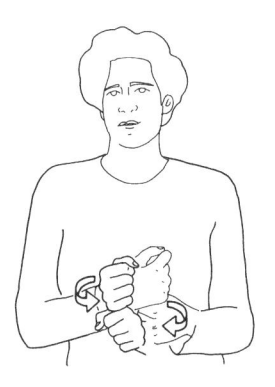

ASL MAKE

ASL WORK 1, LSF TRAVAILLER
(IVT 1986)

MAN

❶ This sign originates from a very old sign used in the French countryside (Chambéry, Angers, and Clermont-Ferrand), but never in Paris (Y. Delaporte, field observation). The thumb of the open hand touches the forehead then the chest, symbolizing two elements of the spectacular clothing worn by French noblemen and women before the French Revolution. Gentlemen wore tall hats that were often adorned with ostrich feathers, and

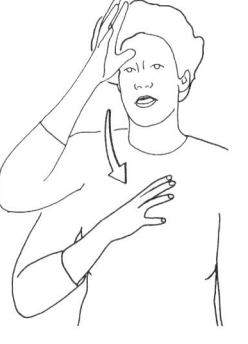

ASL MAN 1

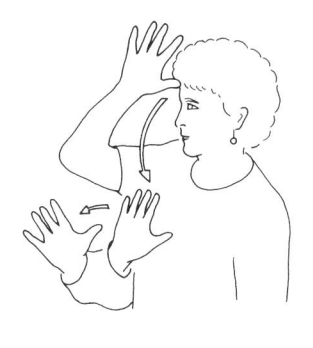

LSF MONSIEUR
(Chambéry; YD, fieldwork)

their shirts were decorated with ruffled lace. Until the 1950s, this same sign was used for MONSIEUR (gentleman) at the girls' campus of the school for the deaf in Chambéry. Coincidentally, the open hand with the thumb on the forehead was the sign ROOSTER at the same school. The first component of the compound MAN, therefore, most likely came from a depiction that mocked handsome gentlemen from the city—men adorned with feathered hats who dressed like proud roosters. The second part of the compound has the same origin as the sign FINE (see entry), which symbolizes the ruffles on a shirt.

❷ This variation begins with the thumb touching the forehead, which could be a remnant of BOY where the extended thumb handshape was a modification in anticipation of the open handshape of the sign FINE.

Ruffles of lace and three-cornered hat adorned with ostrich feathers circa 1700
(Agron 1970)

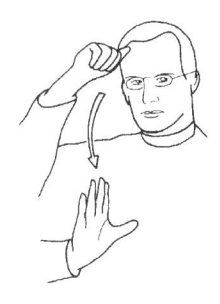

ASL MAN 2
(YD from Higgins 1923)

MANAGE, CONTROL

Ferrand (circa 1785) documented the metaphor behind the sign in his entry for ADMINISTRER (administer) as "take the reins." The French sign DIRIGER (manage), which is very similar to ADMINISTRER, is the etymon of MANAGE, and it represents the reins used to control horse-driven carriages.

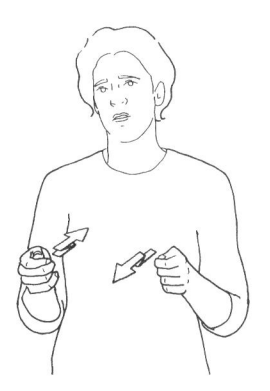

ASL MANAGE, CONTROL

LSF DIRIGER
(Lambert 1865)

A stagecoach in 1825
(Hallynck and Brunet 1948)

MANY

MANY hails from the French sign BEAUCOUP (many), which itself derives from the act of counting with the fingers. Ferrand's (circa 1785) description says to "close then open the right hand several times." The ASL sign has evolved to a simultaneous opening of both hands, which ultimately obscured its etymological link.

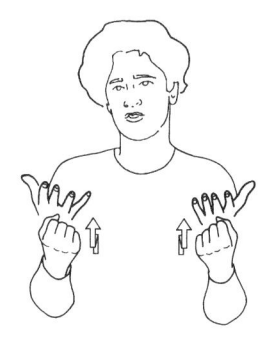

ASL MANY

MEAN

❶ Both Long (1910) and Higgins (1923) gloss this form as BACKBITE and show it configured with extended thumbs. The extended thumbs undoubtedly represent the French sign UN (one), which can also stand for an individual (see "UN (One): The Hidden Number," p. 239). Higgins' (1942) interpretation is that the "right hand is trying to beat the left thumb (a person) down and out of place." Long further specifies that MEAN can be preceded by the sign SHAME to produce the expression "shameful meanness." This compound might have influenced the contemporary sign MEAN 1, which has since been reduced to the claw handshape near the nose followed by the form described by Higgins.

ASL MEAN 1

ASL BACKBITE
(YD from Higgins 1923)

❷ To produce this variant the key handshape taps the nose several times. The nose is the site of several signs with negative connotations in LSF and in ASL (see entries DON'T CARE, INSECT, and LOUSY). This form is still used in some dialects (e.g., Chicago; E. Shaw, field observation).

ASL MEAN 2

❸ MEAN 3 is a regional variant found in Indiana (E. Shaw, field observation). It hails directly from the old LSF sign MÉCHANT, BLESSER (mean, injure), which is still used today in France. Using the mitten handshape, the signer cuts across the torso to symbolize an injurious act. In ASL, the movement has reversed from its French etymon.

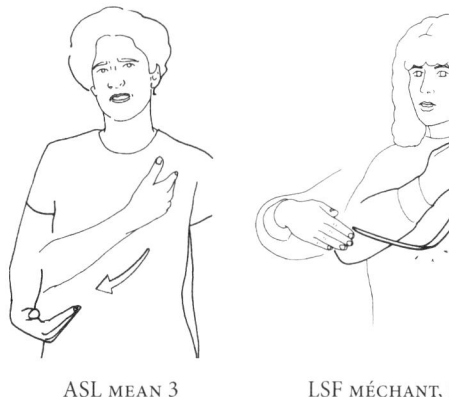

ASL MEAN 3

LSF MÉCHANT, BLESSER
(IVT 1986)

MEAN(ING)

This sign can be translated as "mean/meaning," "intend," and "purpose." The latter two translations provide evidence of the sign's link with its French etymon COMPAS (compass [used for measuring]), which also has an array of meanings, including "technique," "budget" (as in managing one's money), "follow a diet," "mark one's words," and "be prudent." The common denominator between the ASL and LSF signs is the idea *mesure* (measure), which has a double meaning in both English and French: "measure the dimensions of something" and "do something in a measured way, with wisdom and attentiveness." Clark (1885) was the first American author to document this sign in his entry PLAN, described as "touch forehead, and then hold tips of extended and separated first and second fingers on left palm, back of left hand down; the right hand is turned so as to give different position to the vertical fingers. (These latter probably are intended to indicate measurement with a pair of dividers.)" Creating a plan is another way of expressing intention or purpose. The image of a compass as an instrument of precision is uniquely

ASL MEAN(ING)

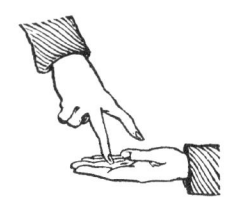

LSF COMPAS
(Pélissier 1856)

suited to convey concepts that involve measuring—intention and purpose both require some degree of thinking in a measured way. The use of the sign expanded to include "mean(ing)" via the polysemy of the word *mean* to indicate *intend*, as in "what do you mean to do?" When preceded by THINK, then, the ASL sign visually represents thought applied in a precise and measured way. Long (1910), like Clark, documents the sign as a compound consisting of THINK followed by the old LSF sign COMPAS, where the left palm faces up and the middle finger of the forked handshape rotates on it as a compass would on paper. Today, the wrist of the left hand of MEAN(ING) can also rotate towards the dominant hand, thereby obscuring the original imagery.

LSF TECHNIQUE
(IVT 1997)

MEASURE

Derived from the sign FOOT (unit of length), the tips of the thumbs touch while the hands twist (Higgins 1923) or tap each other (Sternberg 1994). Originally, the little fingers were flexed in a closed position (Long 1910); however, the evolution to the contemporary modified horn handshape is a shift also seen in a number of ASL signs (see STAY). The movement of MEASURE is likely an iconic representation of calculating a measurement with a ruler or tape measure.

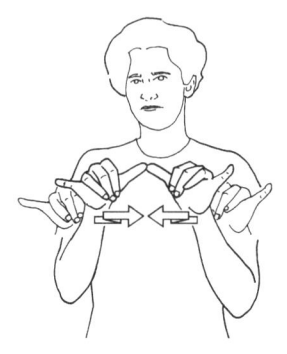

ASL MEASURE

MEAT

In this sign, we see the same form and meaning as the old French sign VIANDE (meat), which the Brothers of St. Gabriel (1853–1854) described as "one grasps the muscle between the thumb and the index finger of the right hand with the thumb and index finger of the left hand." The sign remains unchanged to this day.

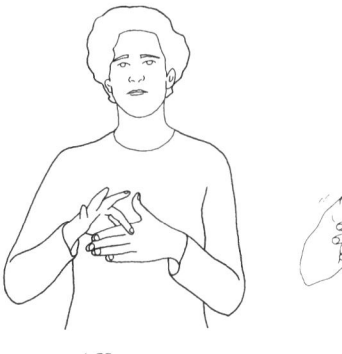

ASL MEAT

LSF VIANDE
(IVT 1986)

MEETING

This is identical to the old French sign SOCIÉTÉ (society; i.e., an organization; Oléron 1974). Higgins (1923) also glossed MEETING as ASSEMBLY. The metaphorical meaning behind the bundled handshape is an ensemble of things (see "The Bundled Handshape," p. 217), and, in this case, refers to people.

ASL MEETING

MENSTRUATION

Historically, in both ASL and LSF, signs on the cheek often denote the color red. Michaels' (1923) entry for APPLE, for example, includes the instruction to "rub the fist of either hand on your cheek (for color)." Lambert (1865) describes the sign VIN (wine) as "roll the manual letter V on the cheek" (1865); whereas Pélissier (1856) simply states that the sign "indicates the color of wine." This same symbolism is invoked in the sign SHAME, SHY (see entry), which Sicard (1808) explains as "showing the redness that divulges

ASL MENSTRUATION

MENSTRUATION 173

this emotion." Not surprisingly, MENSTRUATION is not recorded in historical texts. However, it is possible that the sign is placed on the cheek because of its association with the color red. In LSF, signers use ROUGE (red) for MENSTRUATION.

METAL

❶ METAL 1 consists of the fist striking the underside of the chin. The sign originated from the LSF sign FER, MÉTAL (iron, metal), which Lambert (1865) describes as "with the back of the right hand, strike beneath the chin." In both ASL and LSF, the chin is one location that is used to express hardness, in addition to the top of the hand, the head, sternum, and teeth (see DUMB, GLASS, HARD, AND TOUGH).

❷ This variant emerged in the nineteenth century with a slightly different handshape—a hooked index finger. The hooked index finger is used in a group of signs representing the metaphorical notion of harshness (see TEASE and WITCH). The same evolution from fist to hooked index finger has occurred in the contemporary LSF sign.

ASL METAL 1

LSF FER, MÉTAL
(Lambert 1865)

ASL METAL 2

LSF FER
(IVT 1986)

MISUNDERSTAND

The sign REVERSE (see entry) is produced at the forehead, the location of the sign UNDERSTAND (see entry). Its literal meaning is "understanding in reverse." Higgins (1942) describes the meaning as "I thought one way instead of the other." A similar sign, CHANGE ONE'S MIND, is produced with only the right hand where the tips of the index then middle finger touch the forehead.

ASL MISUNDERSTAND

MOCK

MOCK derives from the centuries-old gesture *mano cornuta* (horned hand), which is directed against one's adversaries and is widely used by hearing people throughout the Mediterranean basin. The extended index and little fingers are thrust toward a perceived threat and function as protection from the evil eye (see "The Veiled Devil," p. 176). In France, this gesture is the etymon of a number of LSF signs, including TROMPER (deceive), SE TROMPER (wrong), FAUX (false), and ARTIFICIEL (fake). The original handshape of the hearing gesture is preserved in MOCK, as well as in DECEIVE 1 and IRONIC (see entries).

ASL MOCK

Hearing children in France
(Illustration by Pat Mallet)

The Veiled Devil

Two codified gestures, strongly anchored in Western culture, share the configuration of the hands in the form of horns. One uses the extended index and little finger, and the other uses the extended index and middle finger. These two forms are rampant in the lexicon of several European sign languages and have become so entrenched in ASL that they are often unrecognized as being linked historically to European gestures.

The first gesture is called *faire les cornes* (make the horns) in French or *mano cornuta* in Italian. With only the index and little finger raised, the gesturer thrusts the hands toward a dangerous person, threatening to pierce the evil eye. This gesture from pre-Christian antiquity was used widely throughout the Mediterranean basin. It later became secularized and was commonly used as late as the twentieth century in French schoolyards by children to mock or deride an adversary. It has since dropped out of favor.

The horned fingers.
(Mural of Pompeii, First Century AD)

The second gesture consists of the extended index and middle fingers and is also directed away from the body. The configuration in the form of a fork evokes several symbols tied to the Devil: his horns, tail, claws, and hoofs, all of which are forked; in addition to the tools with which he torments the damned.

French Deaf people borrowed both gestures to create a number of signs with negative connotations, including MAUVAIS (bad), DANGER (danger), FAUX (false), and TROMPER (deceive). These gestures came to ASL through LSF and continue to be used, even though their original association with the Devil has been lost. The following examples illustrate how the gestures have been incorporated into ASL.

1. The gesture of protection against the evil eye (index and little finger extended) and later the gesture of mockery and derision is the root of the signs DECEIVE 1, IRONIC, and MOCK. Some signers in Colorado sign CHEAT in a way that resembles the sign for TEMPTATION, only with the handshape in horns referring without ambiguity to the Devil or the "demon tempter" (Shroyer and Shroyer 1984).

2. This same gesture (index and little fingers extended) was borrowed by French Deaf people and then underwent a transformation, so that now it is most often produced with the extended thumb and little finger. In LSF, the extended index and little finger configuration is rarely used. The transformation to the extended thumb and little finger handshape also occurred in many ASL signs. It appears in the sign WRONG, for example, which issues directly from LSF SE TROMPER (wrong) and whose etymology was clearly described as "make the horns to oneself" (Lambert 1865, 379) as a self-imposed deprecation. The sign was also passed on in a regional variant of FAKE (Shroyer and Shroyer 1984) that comes from the directional form of the LSF VOUS VOUS TROMPEZ (you are wrong), which, incidentally, also produced the French derivation FAUX (false) and the ASL (DECEIVE).

The ASL signs MOCK and DECEIVE are typically made with the index and little fingers extended, but they have also been documented with the thumb and little finger extended by Michaels (1923) in his entry MOCK and Higgins (1923) in his entry DECEIVE.

3. The fork of the Devil has a pejorative connotation in many signs, and it comes directly from LSF. The ASL sign WORSE is identical to the old LSF sign MAUVAIS (bad); CAREFUL is identical to the second part (DANGER) of the LSF compound FAIRE ATTENTION (be careful), which is composed of APERCEVOIR + DANGER (notice + danger).

ASL WORSE

Old LSF MAUVAIS (bad)
(Pélissier 1856)

MONEY

❶ This form is borrowed from a gesture where the thumb and index finger rub against each other "as if counting money into the palm" (Higgins 1923). This is the same form and meaning as the French sign ARGENT (money; Lambert 1865).

ASL MONEY 1, LSF ARGENT
(Lambert 1865)

❷ MONEY 2 was first documented by Clark (1885), who cited the right hand as flat (not bundled). Just a few decades later, Long (1910) described the contemporary form made with the bundled handshape. This newer form represents the grasping of money that is then placed on the left palm.

ASL MONEY 2

MONTH

This sign descends from the French sign MOIS (month), which Ferrand (circa 1785) described as "trac[ing] lines in the left hand up and down to represent the months as they are on the calendars." The difference in handshapes between the French and American signs is a result of the distinct numbering systems of each cultural group: Americans use the index finger to represent the number 1 while the French use the thumb (see "UN (One): The Hidden Number," p. 239). Thus, the respective signs reflect the cultural context in which they are used. A similar change occurred in the handshape of the American sign WEEK (see entry). Additionally, in the ASL sign MONTH, the left hand is configured with the index finger as a result of assimilating with the right hand (Long 1910; Higgins 1923).

ASL MONTH

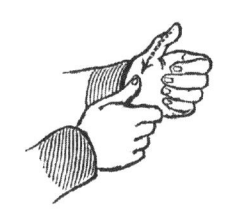

LSF MOIS
(Pélissier 1856)

MOON

The small crescent handshape for this sign is iconically motivated by the shape of a crescent-shaped moon. The initial location on the face conforms with stories and myths from many cultures that describe the Man in the Moon. Long (1910) described the movement of the sign as "upward toward an imaginary moon," placing this image at least referentially close to where the moon is found.

ASL MOON

The moon in popular iconography
(Blanchet 1864)

MORE

MORE derives from the French sign ENCORE (again), where the signer would "unite in a bundle the fingers of the right hand and hit it at the center of the palm of the left hand" (Lambert 1865). Long (1910) documents this same form in his entry. He also describes a variation that is strikingly similar to LSF AJOUTER (add), with both hands in the bundled handshape. The contemporary ASL sign exhibits a reduced movement due to the assimilation of the right hand to the left. Traces of the older arced movement can still be seen in emphatic instances of MORE.

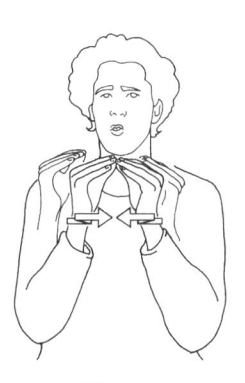

ASL MORE

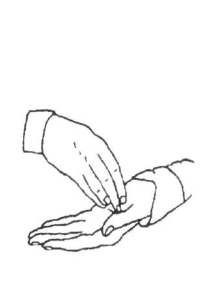

LSF ENCORE
(Brouland 1855)

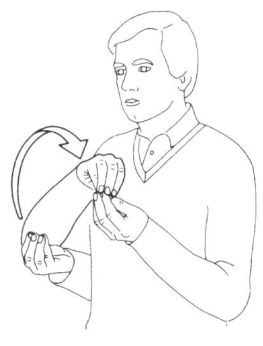

LSF AJOUTER
(IVT 1986)

MORNING

This sign originates from the French sign MATIN (morning), which represents the "rising sun" (Pélissier 1856). Sicard (1808) described the movement as "imitate with the right hand, the sun rising from our horizon." The iconicity of the sign is similar to that found in NIGHT (see entry), but with the opposite movement.

ASL MORNING

LSF MATIN
(Pélissier 1856)

MOST

This sign's form derives from the LSF sign PLUS QUE (more than), in which the extended thumb holds the value of "one" or "first" (see "UN (One): The Hidden Number," p. 239). The movement in producing MOST shows that one thing is above another. The concept of the superlative is relayed through the metaphorical representation that superior things are higher than the norm.

ASL MOST

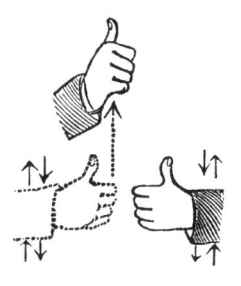

LSF PLUS QUE
(Pélissier 1856)

MOTHER

The origin of this sign is closely intertwined with the etymons of WOMAN 1, FATHER, and MAN (see entries) and likely resulted from an assimilation of the location of GIRL with the handshape of the sign FINE, the two parts of the compound WOMAN 1. Like FATHER, there are two variations of MOTHER: the thumb can tap the chin, or the thumb can rest on the chin while the fingers oscillate.

ASL MOTHER   ASL WOMAN 1

MOVIE

Each historical author in the U.S. reports a different variation of this sign based on representing either the projector that casts images or the actual fluttering of the images on a screen. The origin of MOVIE seems to be linked to the old French sign THÉÂTRE (theater), where the signer "run[s] the right hand over the back of the left hand as the curtains in a theater are raised" (Lambert 1865). This form was used in Chambéry for CINÉMA (movie, movie theater). Old movie theaters traditionally had curtains over the screen that would either rise or draw open at the beginning of the movie. This imagery is perhaps at work in a variant form used in Pennsylvania (Shroyer and Shroyer 1984, 150), where the two open hands face out and slide in small lateral movements. In ASL, as in LSF, the symbolism of the contemporary sign was reinterpreted as the fluttering of images on the screen.

ASL MOVIE

LSF CINÉMA
(YD from Chambéry 1982)

MUSIC

MUSIC comes from the old French sign POÈME (poem). The iconic motivation behind it, according to Blanchet (1850), is to "simulate the length of a verse." The sign, then, initially referred to written poems that were studied by deaf students at the school in Paris. The sign used today is documented in Long (1910) and Higgins (1923), who gloss it as POEM, SONG. In Roth's dictionary (1941), he imagined that the left arm represents "a song book or a piece of music," and the right hand moves over it "in rhythmic cadence." Once the initialized sign POEM emerged, the original form took on the more specific meaning of "music" and "song."

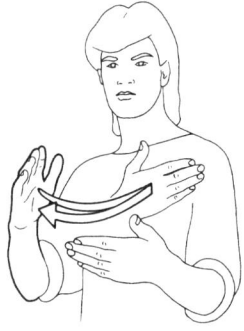

ASL MUSIC

LSF POÈME
(IVT 1986)

MUST

This sign comes from the French sign FALLOIR (must), which Blanchet (1850) described as "the index of one hand, bent and turned toward the ground, is brought downward in this position several times from high to low." Lambert illustrated the same sign in 1865. In European hearing culture, the gesture is used to convey a command or an order. In ASL, MUST has a single downward movement, but when it is repeated with a different facial expression, it is glossed as NEED (see entry) and SHOULD.

ASL MUST

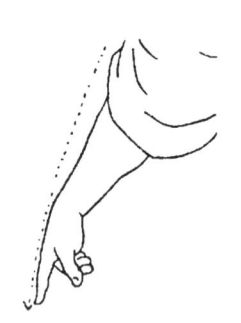

LSF FALLOIR
(Lambert 1865)

N

NAME

ASL NAME originated as the old LSF sign NOM (name), in which "the index finger of the right hand hits the index of the left hand two times in the shape of a cross" (de Gérando 1827). This sign is an iconic representation of the X illiterate people used as their signature. Before the advent of schools for the deaf, many deaf people signed documents this way. Clark (1885) reported the sign was formed with both index fingers, but eventually in both France and the U.S., the N handshape replaced the cross to indicate the first letter in the words *nom* and *name*.

ASL NAME

LSF NOM
(Pélissier 1856)

NATURE, NATION, NORMAL

The symbolism behind this sign derives from the old LSF sign NORMAL, NATUREL (normal, natural), where the index finger moved in a circle over the signing space, essentially circumscribing the natural world as a symbol of the normalcy of things. For Abbé Jamet (circa 1830), this was also the verb ÊTRE (be). Long (1910) documents a similar form in his entry RULE, in which the right hand circumscribes the left hand (representing the land), indicating dominion over it. Long also cites the initialized form under his entry NATION, where the N hand makes a smaller circle over the left hand before

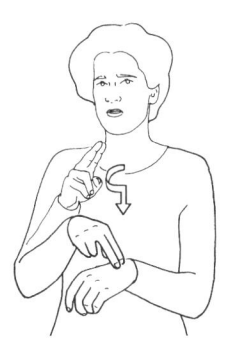

ASL NATURE, NATION, NORMAL

contacting it. In contemporary ASL and LSF, the sign's circular movement is the only remnant of the etymon. The polysemy of the sign already existed in the early twentieth century; Higgins (1923) notes that NATION can be used to mean "nature (natural)," "nation(al)," "of course," and "normal."

ASL RULE
(YD from Higgins 1923)

NEED

NEED is a derived form of MUST (see entry), which itself originated in the LSF FALLOIR (must). Whereas in MUST, there is one emphatic movement, the movement in NEED is short and repeated from the wrist. In addition, the mouth is open and the lips spread as if saying "ee" for *need*.

ASL NEED

NERVY

Nearly identical to the French sign S'ÉNERVER (become annoyed, agitated by) NERVY can be used to describe a pushy person who has annoyed or agitated others, as in the expression *he has a lot of nerve!* In both languages, there is a link with the word "nerve." The French word *énerver* (annoy) has several meanings, but in this case it refers to touching a sensitive area (as in the expression *hit a nerve*). A bold or pushy person touches the nerve of one who is agitated. Both signs employ the double hooked handshape, which is metaphorically linked to harsh things (see HARD and PROBLEM) and is also used in signs related to extraction (for

ASL NERVY

LSF S'ÉNERVER
(IVT 1997)

184   NEED

example, TONSILLECTOMY, STEAL [see entry], and QUOTE FROM). Given the placement of the sign on the cheek, it is possible that the form was originally motivated by the extraction of a tooth.

NEVER

This sign comes from the old French sign JAMAIS (never), where the signer "trace[s] a cross in the air in a rapid motion" (Blanchet 1850). The same movement is documented by Long (1910) and Higgins (1923), and it was inherited from a more general gesture of refusal or negation where the two hands, palms down, crossed over each other and then moved outward (see DON'T WANT). The complete movement of the cross has become so abbreviated that the origin is no longer perceptible. Stokoe et al. (1965, p. 20) characterize the shape of the movement as a "7 or ?."

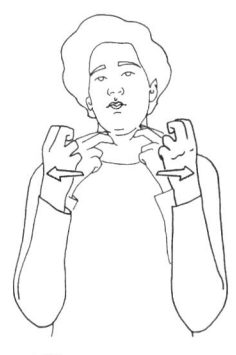

ASL TONSILLECTOMY

ASL QUOTE FROM

ASL NEVER

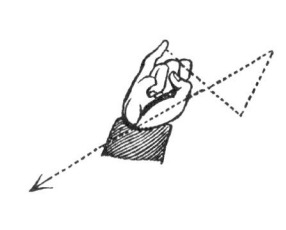

LSF JAMAIS
(Pélissier 1856)

NEW

The back of the right hand slides across the left palm as it moves upward, evoking the appearance of something new. Clark (1885) describes this same form under his entry MARVELLOUS (*sic*). The link between *marvelous* and *new* hinges on the characterization of novelty as wondrous or marvelous. This symbolism was not documented in the twentieth century; instead, Higgins (1942) interpreted the etymology as "bright new metal pushed out of the mold."

ASL NEW

NIGHT

Directly inherited from the LSF sign SOIR (evening), this sign shows "the sun that lowers and sets" (Sicard 1808). The iconicity of the sign is similar to that found in MORNING (see entry), but with the opposite movement.

ASL NIGHT

LSF SOIR
(Pélissier 1856)

NOISE

The direction of movement in the sign NOISE is identical to that of the French sign BRUIT (noise). The movement is explained by Jamet (circa 1830) and Lambert (1865) as take the index or the hand to the ear and "quickly separate them with a startled expression." The sign, then, does not represent the perception of sound, as is the case for HEAR and LISTEN where the movement is directed toward the ear. Rather, the sign represents the reaction to sound, that is, the negative reaction hearing people have to a loud noise. This interpretation of the sign is confirmed by Higgins (1923) and Sternberg (1994), who both relate the sign to *thunder*.

ASL NOISE

(*Journal de Bébé* 1938)

NOSY

The movement of the index finger from the nose to the left fist is a gestural representation of the expression "put one's nose in someone else's business." The hooked handshape in the second part of the sign adds a negative connotation that is also present in signs like TEASE and WITCH (see entries).

ASL NOSY

NOT

Inherited from the French sign RIEN (nothing), NOT descends from a hearing gesture used in Europe that consists of flicking the thumbnail from under the teeth as an act of defiance and contempt. The gesture originally signified "I will not surrender to anything," but later took the more neutral meaning "nothing." Abbé de l'Épée (1784) explained that "the sign RIEN is known by everybody. We take our fingers between the extremity of two teeth and then draw out the hand with haste: the deaf and mute all know this sign even before coming to our classes." Abbé Lambert (1865) mentioned other uses for the sign beyond *nothing* that included *nobody* and *none*. In ASL, the location of the sign lowered to the chin and is used exclusively to mean "not."

ASL NOT

LSF RIEN
(Lambert 1865)

NOT RESPONSIBLE

In both French and English, responsibility is metaphorically associated with a weight on the shoulders (e.g., in the expression *shoulder a burden*). In the ASL sign RESPONSIBLE, Higgins (1923) notes the hands are placed on the shoulder and bear down on it. To produce NOT RESPONSIBLE, the bent middle fingers flick away from either shoulder, indicating that one is brushing off or shirking responsibility. Though no historical documentation verifies the link, a similar sign C'EST PAS MOI (it's not me) exists in LSF and may share the etymon of this ASL sign.

ASL NOT RESPONSIBLE

LSF C'EST PAS MOI
(IVT 1986)

NOTHING

❶ NOTHING 1 is derived from a nineteenth-century French sign glossed as AUCUN (no one), RIEN (nothing), and SANS (without), where the signer "blow[s] on the palm of the left hand held horizontally" (Blanchet 1850). Today, the sign has evolved such that the hand moves from left to right in front of the mouth while the mouth releases a small puff of air.

❷ The second sign also invokes the act of blowing away an object. NOTHING 2 is inherited from the LSF sign SANS, RIEN (without, nothing) where the ringed hands are brought to the mouth then figuratively blown away to signify that nothing is left. George Veditz signs this same form in his film *Preservation of the Sign Language* (1913), in the phrase "KNOW NOTHING." Today, the initial position is typically under the chin, while the initial handshape has changed to the fists. These slight changes have blurred the connection with the sign's etymon. The same etymon gave rise to the ASL signs WORTH, WORTHLESS, and SIMPLE (see entries).

ASL NOTHING 1

LSF AUCUN, RIEN, SANS
(Lambert 1865)

ASL NOTHING 2

LSF SANS, RIEN
(IVT 1986)

NUMBER

NUMBER most likely evolved from the French sign PROBLÈME (difficulty; see PROBLEM). The bundled handshape metaphorically invokes an ensemble or grasping of things (see "The Bundled Handshape," p. 217), while the movement represents the act of folding and refolding things into a complex whole. The pivoting movement is found in several French and American signs—PROBLÈME (problem), COMPLIQUÉ (complicated), and STRUCTURE (structure) in LSF, and NUMBER, PROBLEM, and PUZZLE in ASL.

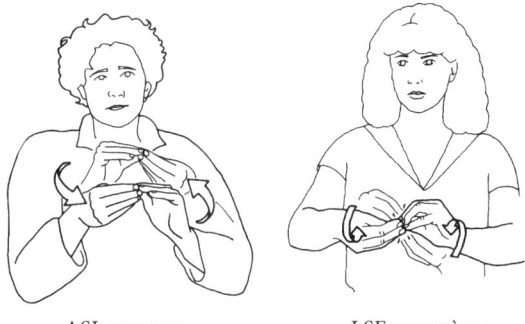

ASL NUMBER

LSF PROBLÈME
(IVT 1986)

NUT

Long (1910) describes the sign NUT as a compound, slightly different than the contemporary form, consisting of NUT followed by the old form of STONE—"Bite the end of the right thumb of 'A' hand, nail down, and strike the top of the left 'S' hand with the right 'S'." Higgins (1923) interprets the symbolism as "cracking a nut with the teeth." We propose a different etymology of the sign, one rooted in the old LSF sign RIEN (nothing; see NOT), which has the same form as the sign NUT. The French word *rien* has the same figurative meaning as "peanuts," as in "something of little importance." The phrase *de petits riens* (little nothings) equates to the English expression "to work for peanuts." The etymological connection between RIEN and NUT has long since ruptured, but the form remains intact.

ASL NUT

O

OBEY

This is the old French sign OBÉIR (obey), which was produced with a bowed head symbolizing the spirit and the hands put at the disposal of God (Ferrand circa 1785; de Gérando 1827). Long (1910) said that the sign represented "submission to authority." In the contemporary sign, the head does not lower in reverence. Coincidentally, OBEY is a homonym of the ASL sign INFORM (see entry).

ASL OBEY

OBSESS

Likely a compound of the signs THINK and TOUCH, OBSESS has evolved so that only the handshape of the second part of the compound is produced. The sign is a visual representation of what it means to be obsessed with something—to think about one thing for an extended period of time.

ASL OBSESS

OFTEN

OFTEN is derived from the sign AGAIN (see entry), which itself is from the LSF ENCORE (again). The repeated movement relays the meaning of doing something again and again.

ASL OFTEN

OH I SEE

From the intermediary IMPOSSIBLE (see entry), the sign OH I SEE derives from the mocking gesture typically used throughout the Mediterranean basin to ward off the evil eye (see "The Veiled Devil," p. 176). The meanings "impossible" and "oh I see" both refer to something that is not yet seen or is difficult to believe. The same relationship exists between the French signs AH BON? (really?) and FAUX (false), whose forms and meanings are also close to the American sign IMPOSSIBLE.

ASL OH I SEE

LSF AH BON?
(IVT 1986)

OLD

Although all of the older American texts propose that the imagery behind OLD is the long beard of an elderly man, French historical documents reveal an entirely different etymology. OLD comes from the French sign VIEUX (old) whose origin is firmly established in eighteenth- and nineteenth-century documents as follows: "sign CANE, GLASSES, curve over, sign FEW TEETH" (Ferrand circa 1785); "figure the action of pressing both hands on a cane" (Blanchet 1850); and "as if holding a staff with both hands underneath the chin" (Lambert 1865). It is common throughout regions of France for elderly people to sit outside and rest their chins on their canes as they watch passersby. However, this practice is not typically associated with seniors in the U.S. The oldest record of the sign in ASL conforms with Lambert's description of VIEUX: "denote extreme age by placing side of curved right index,

ASL OLD

LSF VIEUX
(Lambert 1865)

Two elderly men in the South of France
(Illustration by Yves Lapalu)

other fingers and thumb closed, against the chin and lowering the head with a tremulous motion" (Clark 1885). By the twentieth century, however, the sign had evolved and the etymological link was broken. The hand no longer rested on the chin but was drawn away from it; Long (1910) wrote that the S hand pulled down, "as if pulling an imaginary beard." The initial closed fist soon evolved into a slightly open claw handshape that closes into a fist at the end of the sign's movement, thus marrying the form with the reinterpreted etymology of a long beard. Michaels (1923) explained it as "hold both hands with the fingers closed under your chin; move them downward in a shaky manner," and this exact form appears in John Hotchkiss's *Memories of Old Hartford* (1913). Higgins (1942) made a tentative guess to reconcile the competing forms with the explanation "the hand of the aged shakes when stroking whiskers."

ONCE, TWICE

These signs come directly from the French signs UNE FOIS (once) and DEUX FOIS (twice). In the French numbering system, the thumb means "one" and the extended thumb and index finger means "two" (see "UN (One): The Hidden Number," p. 239). In ASL, the handshapes for the numbers 1 and 2 replaced the original UN (one) and DEUX (two).

ASL ONCE

ASL TWICE

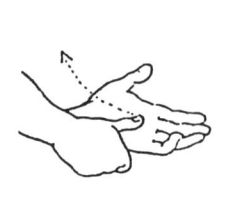

LSF UNE FOIS
(Lambert 1865)

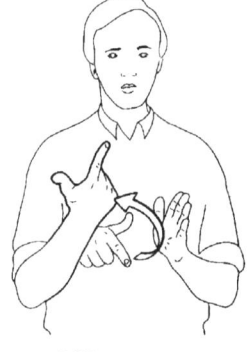

LSF DEUX FOIS
(IVT 1990)

OPERATE, RUN

The proximity in form between OPERATE, RUN and GET GOING, LEAVE (see entry), as well as a wide range of meanings, makes the origin of this sign difficult to determine. The form of OPERATE, RUN seems to be a reduplicated instantiation of GET GOING, LEAVE, which can be translated by a slew of English expressions, including "get going," "leave quickly," and "gotta run." The two signs are also semantically linked through the polysemy of the English word *run*, which has many meanings, including "run away," "leave," and "operate a machine." There is additional evidence that the meaning of this ASL sign expanded from *run* to *run a machine* via the symbolism of the sign SHARP, which Long (1910) and Higgins (1923) describe as "using the right open hand as a whetstone make motion of whetting against the edge of the open left hand" (Long). The very literal act of whetting a sharp implement over a whetstone was extended to a range of machines. The meaning "operate a machine" is a recent development in the history of the sign. Higgins glosses the contemporary form as RUN, and Long glosses it as RUN AWAY.

ASL OPERATE, RUN

ASL SHARP
(YD from Higgins 1923)

OR, THEN

This is the old French sign OU (or) that Lambert translates as "this or that" (1865). OR, THEN retains a trace of the French numbering system where the thumb represents 1 and the extended thumb and index finger represent 2 (see "UN (One): The Hidden Number," p. 239). The adaptation to the American numbering system produced a second variation where the right index finger touches the left index and then middle finger. In contemporary ASL, the older sign is widely used to mean "then"; an initialized version with the letter O for *or* has emerged as a product of Signed English.

ASL OR, THEN

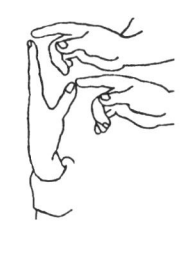

LSF OU
(Lambert 1865)

OTHER

This sign is borrowed from a gesture used by hearing people to indicate a person or thing situated a distance away. Long (1910) writes that the extended thumb "describes a semicircle in the air." Given the form's proximity to the sign ANY (see entry), it is possible the two are linked historically.

ASL OTHER

OWE

❶ This variant is from the French sign DEVOIR, DETTE (owe, debt), where the index finger, pointing toward the ceiling, drops suddenly downward. This is a gesture of commandment borrowed from hearing people in France. Its use for this sign is explained by the

ASL OWE 1, LSF DEVOIR, DETTE
(Lambert 1865)

polysemy of the French word *devoir*, which can mean "falloir" (have to, must) and "avoir une dette" (owe). The oldest mention of the sign is in Abbé Ferrand's text (circa 1785): "hit the table with the end of the index finger several times," referring to the table Abbé de l'Épée used during instruction of his students. The palm of the left hand eventually replaced the table as the point of contact, which Lambert (1865) recorded: "DEVOIR, with the meaning DETTE: bring the right index on the left hand." The earliest documentation of OWE in ASL shows the same form imbued with directionality, and Long (1910) explains it as "move both hands forward toward imaginary person. To indicate the debt is due to oneself, with hands in similar position draw them toward you." Higgins (1923) describes its production as "both hands moved toward creditor or away from debtor."

❷ Today, the directionality has largely disappeared, and the long, single movement of the right index finger has been replaced with short, reduplicated movements.

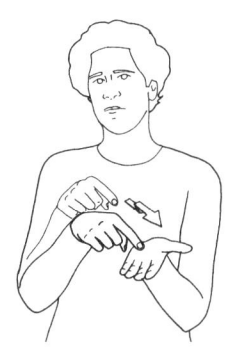

Abbé de l'Épée hits the table with his index finger during instruction
(Illustration by Pat Mallet)

ASL OWE 2

OWN

The open hands draw toward the body as the fingers contract into bundled handshapes. The transformation of the hands indicates taking possession of something (see "The Bundled Handshape," p. 217).

ASL OWN

P

PAPER

This sign is identical in form to the French sign IMPRIMER (print), which Lambert (1865) describes as "press the palm of the right hand on the palm of the left as if to print an imprint." Long (1910) glosses this same sign as PUBLISH, which he explains is used "to indicate something is published [that is, printed] and announced in a newspaper." The act of imprinting text onto a page with a press motivated the form, and explains its original association with *news* and *newspaper*. Over time, however, the use of this old sign shifted in the U.S. to mean "paper." Michaels (1923) describes the production of PAPER as "strike the balls of your hands together." Today, an entirely different ASL sign, PRINT (see entry), is used for *newspaper* and the verb *to print*.

ASL PAPER

LSF IMPRIMER
(Clamaron 1875)

Printing press
(Blanchet 1864)

PATIENCE

❶ Higgins (1923) translates this sign as "abstain" or "fast from food." He states that the signer must first produce "EAT and make a cross on the lips with the thumb." In a later edition of his book (1942), he explains that in producing PATIENCE "the lips are sealed (with a cross because of the Catholic law of fasting)." PATIENCE 1 comes from the same root as FAST (see entry). The same form in contemporary LSF means

ASL PATIENCE 1, LSF SACRIFICE
(IVT 1990)

196 PAPER

"sacrifice"; however, the form used in the Belgian dialect of LSF retains the older meaning "day of fasting."

❷ Today, PATIENCE 2 is a reduced form with a vertical movement only. The sign no longer refers to fasting, but instead denotes any act of self-restraint. This variant form is used with the newer meaning in several countries, including France, Spain, Italy, Greece, Great Britain, and Quebec, Canada. The World Federation of the Deaf recognized the universality of the sign and has adopted it into International Sign.

ASL PATIENCE 2

PEACE

❶ PEACE 1 hails from the old French sign PAIX (peace), which Lambert (1865) explains as "take one's hands, one in the other, in the guise of peace." In what amounts to two partners shaking hands in agreement, the movement later became reduplicated in France and in the U.S. Higgins (1923) describes the sign as "right hand grasps the left as if to shake it and the left hand grasps the right."

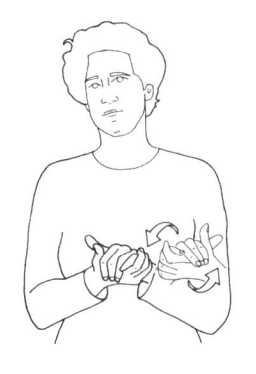

❷ Today, the contemporary form is the result of a compound in which the first part is produced with flat hands like the contemporary LSF sign PAIX and the second part is the ASL sign CALM. Both Long (1910) and Michaels (1923) described PEACE 2 as a compound, but Higgins (1942) treated the second part as optional. The iconicity of the sign eventually diminished as the handshake transformed into a smooth rotation of both flat hands. This change resulted in the first part of PEACE 2 becoming a

ASL PEACE 1

LSF PAIX
(Lambert 1865)

ASL PEACE 2

LSF PAIX
(YD, fieldwork)

homonym of the sign BECOME, which allowed for a reinterpreted etymology as BECOME + SETTLE to emerge (Costello 1999).

PENIS

The nose is the site of several ASL signs with negative connotations (see DON'T CARE, LOUSY, and FOOL, JOKE). Although Americans do not ordinarily associate the nose with sexual innuendo, the connection is widespread in LSF as a result of European folklore from the Middle Ages to the Renaissance (Bakhtin 2008). For example, in the LSF signs FAIRE L'AMOUR (make love) and JOUIR (orgasm), the nose serves as a substitute for the penis. In the American sign PENIS, the handshape is initialized for the English words *penis* and also *pee* in some contexts. The ASL sign ORGASM is also produced on the nose. The identical location of production in both ASL and LSF is compelling, especially given the fact that the nose does not carry the metaphorical association with the male sexual organ in America.

ASL PENIS
(YD)

LSF FAIRE L'AMOUR
(IVT 1986)

ASL ORGASM

LSF JOUIR
(IVT 1990)

PENNY, CENT

DOLLAR is the only monetary sign recorded in the American historical texts. PENNY is colloquially linked with two signs associated with the head: Abraham Lincoln (Sternberg 1994), whose head is printed on all pennies and the sign SENSE because of the phonemic homophony of the English words *cents* (another word for *penny*) and *sense* (one's intellectual faculty). In essence, the sign PENNY could be glossed SENSE ONE. Additional signs for the value of different coins (NICKEL, DIME, and QUARTER) simply incorporate the numerical value with the sign PENNY, CENT (for example NICKEL = PENNY, FIVE).

ASL PENNY, CENT

PEOPLE

This sign is a derivation of the singular sign PERSON (see entry), initialized with the letter *P*. In *Preservation of the Sign Language* (1913), George Veditz used the repeated circular movement in this sign to signify a vast ensemble of people. Higgins (1942) describes this sign as "show[ing] many individuals."

ASL PEOPLE

PERFORM, PLAY

Higgins (1923, 1942) documents the origin of the sign in his entry ENTERTAINMENT, where the flat hands with palms facing away from the signer move alternately up and down "to indicate the raising and the lowering of the curtain" (1942). Lambert (1865) describes similar imagery for the old French sign THÉÂTRE (theater; see MOVIE). Long (1910), however, cites the use of the extended thumb handshape in his description of the sign for "a play at the theatre or acting." Like in Higgins and Lambert, Long documents the hands as moving alternately up and down. At some point in the ASL sign's

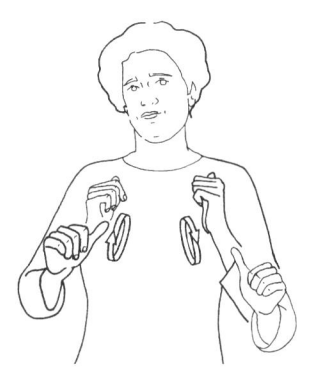

ASL PERFORM, PLAY

evolution, the hands gravitated closer to the chest and rotated alternately toward the chest. Consequently, the contemporary form no longer exhibits the original iconic motivation of stage curtains.

PERSON

The contemporary form of PERSON is similar to the old French signs formerly glossed HOMME (man) and INDIVIDU (person). Puybonnieux (1846) describes HOMME as "run the length of the body from the head to the feet with two hands," and Lambert (1865) explains INDIVIDU's form as "the two hands run the length of the body from the chest to the thighs, indicating the human body." In both signs, the fingertips touch the body. The old ASL sign also made contact with the body, as can be seen in the film *Preservation of the Sign Language* (Veditz 1913), and in Higgins' (1923) entry for ER (meaning an occupation). Today, the hands no longer touch the torso; instead, the fingertips point out and the hands are drawn down in neutral sign space. The sign continues to function as an agentive marker when produced after a verb (e.g., TEACH + PERSON = TEACHER). This practice was common in old LSF, but because it was introduced by hearing instructors as part of Signed French, it was widely discarded by French Deaf people. American Deaf people do not have the same association with the sign and still use it as part of their discourse, both as a stand-alone sign and as an agentive marker. The initialized version with a P handshape is widely used in the U.S. today for *person*.

ASL PERSON
(YD)

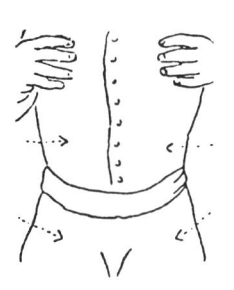

LSF INDIVIDU
(Lambert 1865)

PHYSICS

This sign derives from ELECTRICITY, which represents the connection of two electrical wires (see entry). Here the double hooked handshapes are used instead of single hooks.

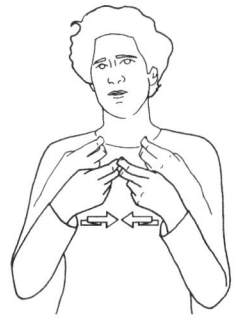

ASL PHYSICS

PICK ON

This sign hails from the old French sign AGACER QUELQU'UN (irritate someone), which Ferrand (circa 1785) calls a natural sign (that is, a gesture) and describes as "irritate someone by fooling him." Long (1910) cites the sign in his entry "find fault." His depiction of the sign is consistent with the contemporary form, where the dominant hand assumes the key handshape. In this form, the extended left index finger represents a person—a productive iconicity that is also employed in signs like FLATTER and SITUATION (see entries).

ASL PICK ON

PICTURE

❶ Long (1910) writes that PICTURE can be signed by drawing a "C or crooked forefinger downward against the face." Clark (1885) describes the same sign made with the hooked index finger, and Hotchkiss signs it this way in his filmed narrative *Memories of Old Hartford* (1913). That form is also the first component of the old LSF compound sign IMAGE (picture), which was followed by PETIT CARRÉ (little square) and symbolized a face in profile (Pélissier 1856).

ASL PICTURE 1,
LSF PORTUGAL
(IVT 1990)

LSF IMAGE
(Pélissier 1856)

An identical sign in contemporary LSF now means PORTUGAL, whose shape resembles the profile of a face. IMAGE is also the origin of the ASL sign DOLL (see entry).

❷ Long (1910) and Higgins (1923) describe PHOTOGRAPH as a compound consisting of Long's PICTURE 1 with the crescent handshape followed by placing the edge of the right crescent hand on the left palm. In English, *picture* and *photograph* are used synonymously, and in ASL, PICTURE 2 can also mean "photograph."

ASL PICTURE 2

PIG

The American sign PIG originates from the old French sign COCHON (pig), where the fingers of the right hand represented a pig's snout, and the movement mimicked "rustling the ground" (Lambert 1865). Clark (1885) was the first American author to describe PIG, stating that its form "indicate[s] the rooting with extended right hand under chin." Higgins (1923) characterizes the form as "the wallowing of the animal in the mire." Although semantically related, this sign is distinguished from the sign DIRTY (see entry) in two ways: its handshape is a bent mitten instead of an open hand, and all of the fingers bend instead of oscillate.

ASL PIG

LSF COCHON
(Pélissier 1856)

PITY

❶ Early American authors (Long 1910; Higgins 1923; and Michaels 1923) describe a compound sign where the signer first produces FEEL and then "bring[s] the open hand out extended toward the imaginary object of pity, making a kind of stroking or circular motion with the hand, as if giving comfort" (Long). The first part of this compound is closely linked to the ASL sign TOUCHED (see entry), which itself is identical in form to the LSF sign PITIÉ (pity).

❷ PITY 2 is a reduced form of PITY 1. The bent middle finger handshape of the first part of PITY 1 became integrated with the movement and orientation of the second part. The bent middle finger is used in LSF and ASL to represent emotional contact (see "Handshape Change," p. 148).

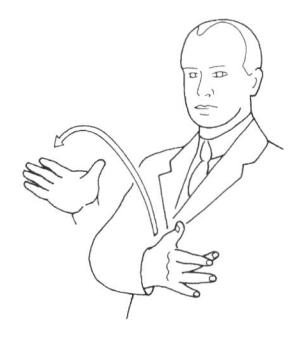

ASL PITY 1
(YD from Long 1910)

LSF PITIÉ, TOUCHÉ
(Lambert 1865)

ASL PITY 2

PLAY

The ASL sign PLAY comes from the LSF sign S'AMUSER, JOUER (have fun, play), which is produced by "mak[ing] two Js . . . with small rotations of the hands" (Blanchet 1850). The handshape is not Y for the last letter in the English word *play*, but the LSF letter J for the French word *jouer*. The handshape in PLAY is definitive proof of the link between the two signs.

ASL PLAY

LSF S'AMUSER, JOUER
(IVT 1986)

POOR

This sign, which is an iconic representation of the clothes of a poor person, comes from the French sign PAUVRE (poor). Pélissier characterizes PAUVRE as a "hole in the sleeve" (1856). Clark (1885) describes a slightly different hand configuration, stating that one would "clasp the sleeve on under side with thumb and index, dropping hand as though indicating that same was torn into strips or rags." Today, all of the fingers of the right hand grasp the elbow of the left arm before pulling down and closing into the bundled handshape.

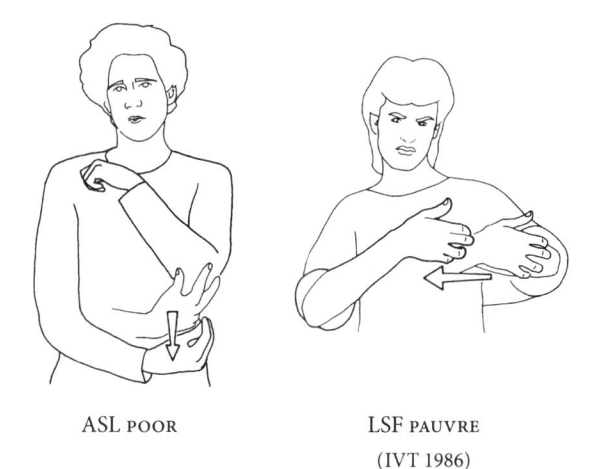

ASL POOR

LSF PAUVRE
(IVT 1986)

POPULAR

In this iconic sign, the palm of the right claw hand presses against the left index finger to represent a large number of people converging on an individual. The extended index finger is often employed in ASL to signify an individual, such as in the signs CHAMPION, FLATTER, PICK ON, and SITUATION (see entries).

ASL POPULAR

POSTPONE

Long (1910) notes that this sign can be produced with either one or two hands. Today, POSTPONE is always two-handed, and the left hand can either remain in place or move in concert with the right along the axis of time (see "Axis of Time," p. 286). This sign comes from the LSF sign REPORTER (postpone), which differs mainly in handshape. The use of the ring handshapes in POSTPONE may be a remnant of de l'Épée's methodical sign TEMPS (time), a sign Sicard (1808) described as "trace a straight line to depict length and time" with the hands configured in the LSF letter T, which is almost identical to the ring handshape in ASL.

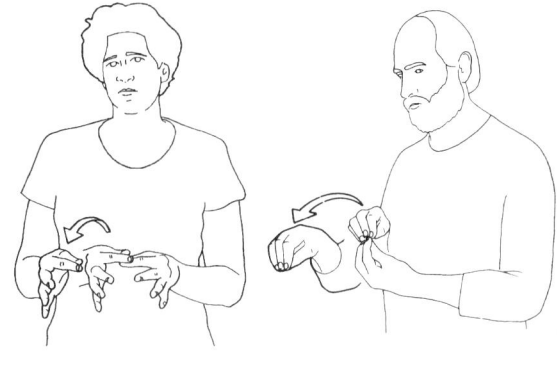

ASL POSTPONE   LSF REPORTER
(IVT 1986)

POWER

The right flat hand traces the contour of flexed biceps to show strength. Except for the handshape, this ASL sign is almost identical in form to the semantically related French sign ÉNERGIE (energy). The ASL signs AUTHORITY and ENERGY derive from POWER as a result of initialization.

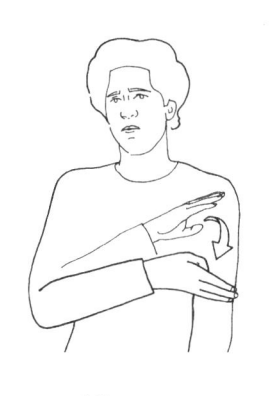

ASL POWER   LSF ÉNERGIE
(IVT 1990)

(Illustration by Pat Mallet)

PREACH

Historically, PREACH was produced higher and further away from the signer, much like LECTURE (see entry). Higgins (1942) is the only author to explain that the handshape was the letter "*F* for 'friar preachers' and gesture for emphasis." It is possible that the symbolism behind PREACH is in fact more metaphorical than that. Long (1910) defines the sign REVIVE as "bring up something from the past," and the form lends some clues as to PREACH's possible etymon: "reach the hands back over the right shoulder and grasp imaginary object and drag it forward." Long does not describe the hand configuration, but in many other entries (see CHOOSE, LIKE, and Clark's description of POOR), the ring handshape represents grasping. It is possible, since pastors preach through stories revived from the past, that the contemporary sign PREACH is simply a truncated and reduplicated instantiation of the now extinct sign REVIVE. The delivery of sermons in religious revivals is additional evidence of the sign's roots.

ASL PREACH

PRECIOUS

This sign has been described as a variant of the sign JEWISH, invoking negative stereotypes that Jewish people are greedy (cf., Stokoe et al. 1965, 153). PRECIOUS is more likely inherited from the French sign AVOIR ENVIE (want to, feel like—literally "have envy"), where the fingers of the claw handshape tap the chin, an area of the body associated

ASL PRECIOUS

with good and sweet things (for example, CUTE, DELICIOUS, and SWEET). AVOIR ENVIE likely derived from the gesture of biting the fingers in envy (see also JEALOUS). Once incorporated into LSF, the form lowered to the chin to facilitate lipreading. In ASL, the hand contracts into a fist. The addition of the fist enhances the symbolism behind the sign's meaning, literally grabbing onto that which is precious or dear.

LSF AVOIR ENVIE
(YD, fieldwork)

PREDICT

PREDICT has remained unchanged since the nineteenth century. Clark (1885) described the form as "carry right fixed as in SEE or LOOK under left. (Seeing under left hand, seeing things partially hidden.)" The movement of the right hand under the left expresses the notion that prediction involves uncovering hidden information. In writing "looking through the veil of the future," Higgins (1942) clearly reflects this motivation behind the sign. The handshape and movement of the right hand also symbolize a long-term view along the axis of time (see "Axis of Time," p. 286).

ASL PREDICT

PREFER

This old ASL sign is still used in some regions of the U.S., including in Illinois (E. Shaw, field observation) and among older signers. The fingers of the flat hand touch the side of the chest, then flex into a thumb handshape as the hand draws out to the right. PREFER descends directly from the LSF signs AIMER (like) and PREMIER (first), illustrated by Lambert in 1865, which later compounded into one sign.

ASL PREFER

LSF AIMER
(IVT 1986)

LSF PREMIER
(Lambert 1865)

PREPARE, PLAN

Besides the more obvious symbolism of "putting things in order" (Higgins 1923), PREPARE, PLAN may have derived from the old French sign PRÉPARER (prepare) in which the edge of the right hand hits the left palm in several places, indicating a progression of things. The sign also meant PEU À PEU (little by little; Lambert 1865). Clark (1885) describes the same sign in his entry ARRANGE. Higgins (1923) glosses it with several English equivalents, including "arrangement," "classed," "complete," "degree," "order," "plan," "prepare," "put in order," and "ready." He also notes that the rightward movement with repeated stops shows "division or arrangement." The concept of "preparation," which is equally at work in the ASL sign, is actually closer to that of "progression" than "putting things in order." In both LSF and ASL, the production of PREPARE, PLAN, and READY 1 (see entry) are closely linked, demonstrating that one must prepare in order to be ready.

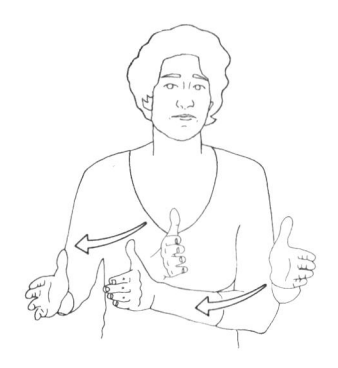

ASL PREPARE, PLAN

PRESERVE, SAVE

Ferrand (circa 1785) was the first to describe this sign under his entry CONSERVER (conserve)—"Take the left hand and press it against the chest, something that one is glad to have and take the right hand over it to show that one does not want to let it go." Higgins (1923) described the same sign in his entry SAVE. In the early twentieth century, PRESERVE, SAVE also meant "salvation" in religious contexts (Long 1910; Higgins 1923). However, now, the sign is almost exclusively used as it was in France during the late eighteenth century in the sense of conserving something. Today, the hands no longer contact the chest, and the forked handshape of the right hand is possibly a trace of initialization with the letter *P* for PRESERVE.

ASL PRESERVE

PRESIDENT

Both Long (1910) and Higgins (1942) agree that this sign symbolizes the "horns of authority." Higgins (1942) goes further to say that "chieftains affected the horns as part of headdress." Roth (1948) instead correctly interprets its origin as "George Washington's three-cornered hat," an image that was certainly in the history books that Deaf children would have seen in school. Confirmation of Roth's proposed etymology is found in LSF, where the same sign means GENDARME (constable; Pélissier 1856; Clamaron 1875), and is documented as symbolizing the three-cornered hats worn by French police officers during the nineteenth century.

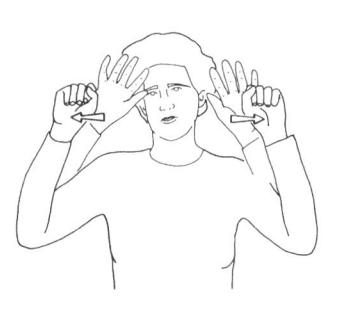

ASL PRESIDENT

George Washington

LSF GENDARME
(Clamaron 1875)

Illustration of a constable
(Clamaron 1875)

PRESIDENT   209

PRIDE

PRIDE comes from the old French sign ORGUEIL (pride), the form of which Lambert (1865) describes as "raise the right hand the length of the chest: swollen heart." In ASL, this sign has been documented since the nineteenth century with the fingers flexed and the thumb extended (Clark 1885). This change in handshape partially obscures the etymological link; however Higgins (1923) noted the symbolism of "a swelled chest."

ASL PRIDE

LSF ORGUEIL
(Brouland 1855)

PRINCIPAL

❶ We first find this sign in Clark (1885), and later in Higgins (1923), who translated it as *authority*, *control*, and *rule*. Higgins describes PRINCIPAL 1 as "the right open prone palm, circled horizontally over the left prone closed hand." Roth (1948) provides a clear description of the symbolism behind this form: "The left hand represents the physical aspects of a place, and the right hand the controlling factor over it." The same form is implicated in the sign NATURE, NATION, NORMAL (see entry).

ASL PRINCIPAL 1 (RULE)
(YD from Higgins 1923)

❷ It is possible that this initialized form emerged during the 1970s, when Signed English gained favor in American schools for the deaf. The long, circular movement of the dominant hand in PRINCIPAL 1 was replaced by a short one. This change also occurred in the semantically related sign NATURE (see entry). Today, the metaphorical motivation behind this contemporary form is no longer apparent.

ASL PRINCIPAL 2

PRINT

❶ Long (1910) cites the motivation behind this sign as "make motion of printer putting type into a stick." Similarly, Higgins (1923) describes the movement of PRINT 1 as "picking the type from the font and placing them in the left palm as into the composing stick." This is the first part of IMPRIMER (print), an old compound sign in LSF, which Ferrand (circa 1785) describes as "take characters from the different cases, arrange them in order between the thumb and index of the left hand, then turn them over on the hand with force to give the impression of printing." Today, the meaning of the old IMPRIMER has changed to "typesetter."

❷ The form and movement of the contemporary variant has changed slightly, such that only the right index finger moves, while the thumb maintains contact with the palm of the left hand. The meaning of the sign has broadened to include the English equivalents "newspaper," "printer," and "publish." Now typesetting is largely obsolete; however, it was a popular profession among Deaf Americans in the nineteenth and twentieth centuries. Although technology has changed rapidly in the last century, PRINT 2 continues to refer to text that is printed on a page.

ASL PRINT 1, LSF TYPOGRAPHE
(IVT 1990)

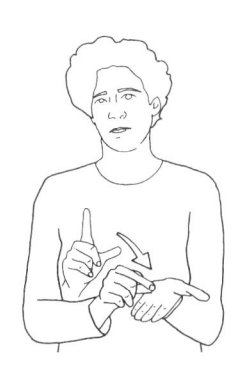

ASL PRINT 2

Typesetter
(Illustration by Pat Mallet)

PROBLEM

Higgins (1923) documents one variant of this sign where the "bent knuckles of 'V' hands, palms inward, struck together from the sides," which denotes a collision, hindrance, or difficulty encountered. It is possible the twisting movement in PROBLEM was inherited from the LSF sign PROBLÈME (difficulty, problem), which Ferrand (circa 1785) discusses in his entry COMPLICATION (complication) as "fold and refold together" meaning "the two open hands, supine, turn over from the right over the left and back again" (Jamet, circa 1830). The LSF sign PLIER (fold) demonstrates Jamet's citation. The metaphor of "folding something to complicate it" motivates the French word *compliqué* (complicated), which comes from the Latin *complicare* (fold).

ASL PROBLEM

LSF PROBLÈME
(IVT 1986)

LSF PLIER, ASL FOLD
(YD, fieldwork)

PROMISE

In this sign we see traces of the gesture one makes when taking an oath—raising the flat hand—a gesture that has been used in Christianity since the Middle Ages (Schmitt 1995). The sign was first documented in France by Blanchet (1850) and in the U.S. by Long (1910) with the right hand open and flat. Another variant, where the flat hand raises "in nature of an oath" (Long 1910) in the second part of the sign, was also present in the early twentieth century. In contemporary ASL, the index finger is first placed on the lips, a semantic association with the speech coming from the person who is making a promise. The last part of the sign,

ASL PROMISE

LSF PROMETTRE
(YD from St-Laurent 1979)

where the palm of the open hand makes contact with the left fist, continues to exist in one regional dialect of LSF (Saint-Laurent-en-Royans).

PROOF

This sign is similar in form to its French counterpart PREUVE (proof), which Lambert (1865) describes as "hit the back of the right hand on the palm of the left hand." He adds that this form is a gestural representation of the metaphor "all cards on the table." Higgins (1942) saw in this sign the gesture that "goes with 'Prove it,' put the evidence there so we can see it." That same form can be initialized to mean "evidence," "fact," and "witness."

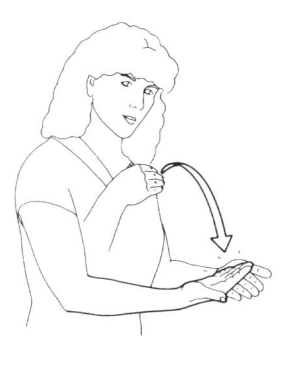

ASL PROOF

LSF PREUVE
(IVT 1986)

PROSTITUTE

PROSTITUTE was first recorded by Clark (1885) as a compound consisting of FEMALE followed by SHAME (see entry). The contemporary ASL sign is distinguished from SHAME based on a reduplicated movement, which may, in fact, be the sole trace of FEMALE, the first part of the original compound sign.

ASL PROSTITUTE

PROTEST

This sign comes directly from the semantically related LSF sign DÉSOBÉIR (disobey). Lambert's (1865) form of the sign came from an image clearly described by de l'Épée (1786), in his entry PÉCHER (sin). De l'Épée states that "we make the same sign of the elbow that the children do when they do not want to do what they have been told. God commands, one disobeys, one makes a transgression." As in the signs RESIST and WON'T (see entries), the fist handshape in PROTEST conveys the meaning of force and opposition. Long (1910) shows an intermediary form in which both the wrist and the elbow twist. Today, only the wrist twists, and the sign has taken on the more specific meanings of "protest" or "revolt."

ASL PROTEST

LSF DÉSOBÉIR
(Lambert 1865)

ASL DISOBEY
(YD from Long 1910)

PSYCHOLOGY

There are two possible etymologies for this sign. The first is the old French sign PSYCHOLOGIE (psychology), which relates to the idea of transparency; the fingers of the right hand penetrate the hollows of the left as if to see a cross section of the patient's spirit. The contemporary LSF sign is now identical to the ASL sign. The second possibility for the sign's origin, one which Deaf people in France favor, is the manual representation of the Greek letter *psi*, the first syllable of the word *psychology* and the symbol for psychology around the world. However, these two possible etymologies are not mutually exclusive, the second could have easily stemmed from a reinterpretation of the older LSF sign.

ASL PSYCHOLOGY

LSF PSYCHOLOGIE
(YD from Poitiers 1982)

The Greek letter *psi*

PUBLICIZE

This sign issues from the second part of an old French compound sign PUBLIER (publish, publicize), which represents the town crier blowing his trumpet before announcing "the decrees of Parliament" (Ferrand circa 1785). The LSF etymon gave rise to two variations based on the symbol of the trumpet—one long single movement to show the trumpet's shape, and the short repeated movement of the right hand away from the body depicting the trumpet's sound. Though news is no longer announced with trumpets, the sign remains in ASL's lexicon to refer to all sorts of media communication, particularly advertisements.

ASL PUBLICIZE

A trumpeter announcing the decrees of Parliament
(Illustration by Pat Mallet)

PUNISH

❶ Higgins (1923) describes the iconicity of this sign as follows: "grasp the culprit by the collar, and right hand strikes the culprit with the right index used as a rod." Long (1910) noted this same form of the sign.

❷ Later, the left arm lowered to ease production, as did the index finger, which now makes brushing contact with the elbow. Abbé Laveau (1868) drew this same form in his entry PUNIR (punish). This combination of changes ruptures the variant's link to its etymon. Parenthetically, this particular evolution of components is also evident in the sign COUNTRY (see entry).

ASL PUNISH 1
(YD from Higgins 1923)

ASL PUNISH 2

LSF PUNIR
(Laveau 1868)

PUT

The bundled handshape typically symbolizes an assembly of things (see "The Bundled Handshape," p. 217). In this sign, the hand configuration also conveys the grasping of some object to be moved or placed somewhere else. The exact same sign exists in LSF.

ASL PUT

PUZZLED

Originally, the index finger would trace the shape of a question mark at the height of the forehead (Clark 1885). However, the contemporary form of PUZZLED is produced by flexing the index finger as it is drawn toward the forehead. Interestingly, Clark documented this sign under his entry MEDICINE, which in the late nineteenth century was still a perplexing, if not mysterious, profession.

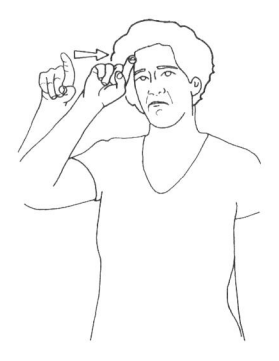

ASL PUZZLED

The Bundled Handshape

The bundled handshape is a common configuration in the gestures of hearing people. Kendon (2004) analyzed hundreds of hours of conversations between hearing people and found that the handshape is used extensively to mark a discourse topic, ask questions, demand explanations, or emphasize a topic as pertinent to a discussion. An oscillating bundled handshape tends to accompany utterances that implore an interlocutor to pay attention to what is being said. When the bundled handshape moves toward an interlocutor and then opens, the speaker is typically commenting on, proposing, or completing a topic of discussion (see Kendon 2004, chapters 11 and 12, for a full discussion). In ASL, the bundled handshape conveys several meanings, depending on what immediately precedes or follows it.

1. When no other handshape precedes the bundled handshape, it represents one of two things:

    a. The union or grasping of things (concrete or metaphorical), as in ABOUT, BUY, EAT, FLOWER, GIVE, MAKEUP, MONEY, MORE, PUT, and SELL. The metaphorical meaning of this union of abstract things is also seen in the gestures hearing people produce when "appear[ing] to mark the topic" (Kendon 2004, 228).

    ABOUT   EAT   GIVE   PUT

    b. The head, as in DINOSAUR, KISS, any classifier predicate for the head of an animal (like a dog), and HEAD NOD.

    DINOSAUR   KISS   HEAD NOD

2. When an open hand or a slightly bent open hand precedes the bundled handshape, it has two possible meanings.

   a. A grip. Examples include AND, ACCEPT, ADD, COPY, LEARN, OWN, VACUUM, and WHITE (pinching the shirt). Out of all possible symbols, Long (1910) selected the ampersand (&) to represent this handshape in his dictionary.

   AND　　　　LEARN　　　　OWN　　　　VACUUM

   b. A disappearance, as in ABSENT and LEAVE, OUT.

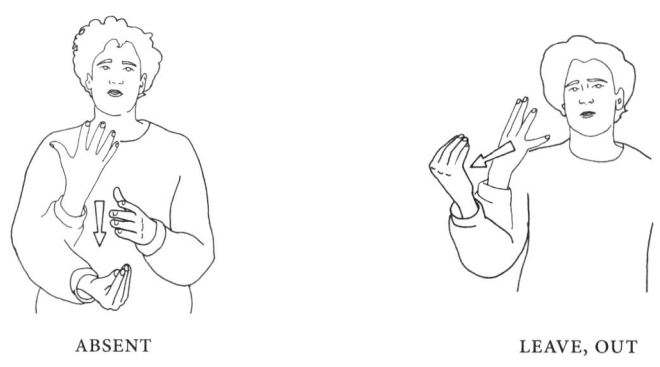

   ABSENT　　　　LEAVE, OUT

3. When an open or slightly bent open hand follows the bundled handshape, it has the following symbolism:

   a. An opening, as in the signs CLEAR and GROW.

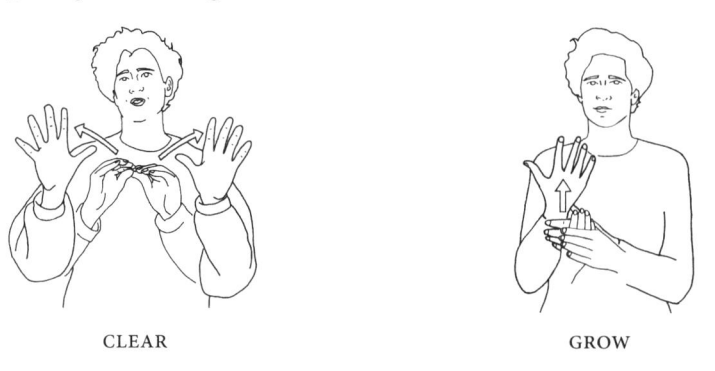

   CLEAR　　　　GROW

b. A diffusion, such as an escape or a projection of something. Examples include the signs ADVISE, DON'T CARE, GIVE OUT, INFORM, LOSE, and SPREAD.

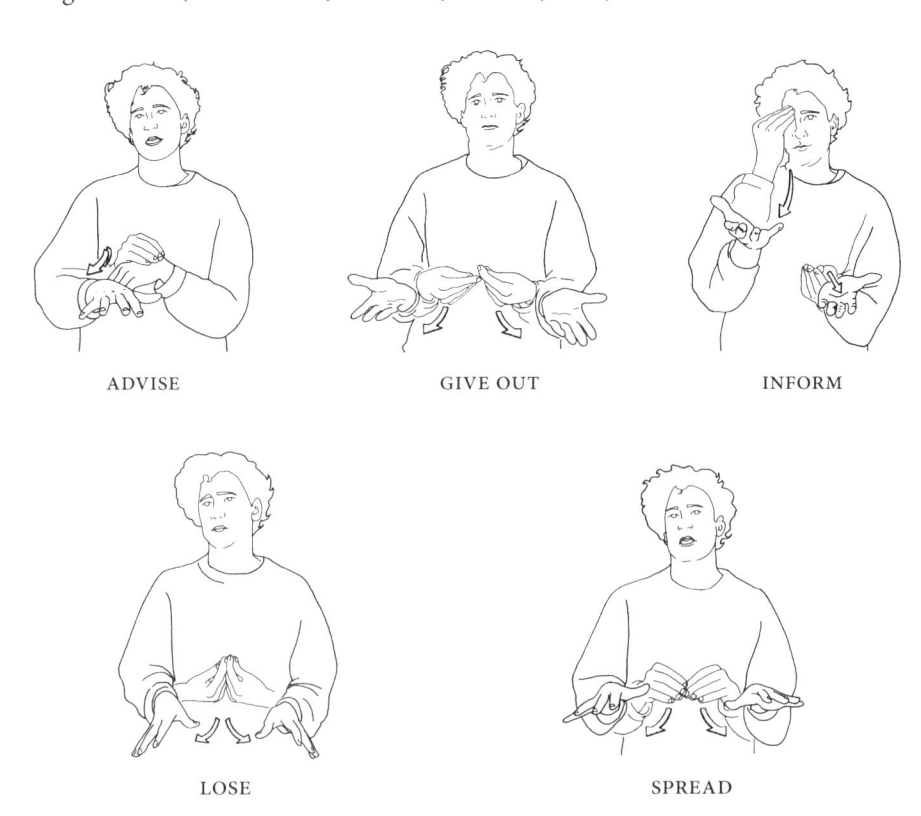

ADVISE

GIVE OUT

INFORM

LOSE

SPREAD

    The deconstruction of the symbolism behind the bundled handshape allows us to recognize symbolic, meaningful, and systematic patterns that exist in this particular sign language. The analysis might also inform how scholars interpret the meaning of handshapes in gestures that hearing people use.

Q

QUAKER

The sign for QUAKER is borrowed from the gesture known as "twiddling the thumbs" that hearing people ordinarily use to mean "I have nothing to do" or "I'm bored." The sign's meaning narrowed in ASL to refer to the Quakers, as well as the Amish, perhaps because during Quaker services parishioners sit in silence, waiting for inspiration from the Holy Spirit. In LSF, the same gesture motivated the sign LOISIRS (leisure time).

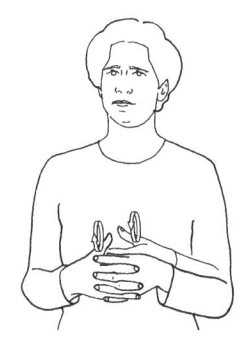

ASL QUAKER

QUICK

ASL QUICK was inherited from a French gesture used by hearing people to indicate "just a little bit." In LSF, the gesture became the sign PEU (few), which was the second part of BIENTÔT (soon; FUTUR [future] + PEU), a compound used in nineteenth-century France. In contemporary ASL, authors no longer perceive the sign's link with the gesture, instead describing it as "a quick movement" (Sternberg 1994) or "as fast as shooting a marble" (Riekehof 1987).

ASL QUICK
(YD)

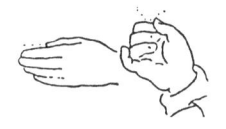

LSF BIENTÔT
(Lambert 1865)

QUIET

❶ The index finger is brought to the mouth to symbolize closing the lips when commanding silence. This form is borrowed from a hearing gesture used to tell others to be quiet. In contemporary ASL, the sign means "hold my tongue" or "I'm not saying a word."

❷ Issued from the French sign CALME (quiet), the lowering of the hands is a gestural metaphor for reducing noise or agitation. Long (1910) describes a compound sign consisting of QUIET 1 followed by QUIET 2; this same compound is described by Michaels (1923) in his entry BEHAVE.

ASL QUIET 1

ASL QUIET 2

LSF CALME
(Lambert 1865)

R

RABBIT

❶ In this iconic sign, the extended index and middle fingers of both hands placed on each side of the head represent the ears of a rabbit.

❷ In a more perplexing variant, the paintbrush handshapes of the crossed hands are generally interpreted as representing rabbit ears. The hands moved from the head to the chest to ease sign production. It is more likely, though, that the evolution occurred as a result of assimilation of the old LSF sign LAPIN (rabbit), in which the right forked hand pointed up to represent the ears, and the left forked hand pointed toward the ground to represent the rabbit's body. In LAPIN, the two hands moved forward with an oscillating movement depicting a rabbit jumping. Over time, the forked fingers closed, the orientation of the hands rotated 45 degrees, and the oscillating movement of the hands transferred to the fingers, thus fully rupturing the etymological root.

ASL RABBIT 1

ASL RABBIT 2, LSF LAPIN

(From a leaflet of a deaf peddler, c. 1800s)

RAT

The contemporary ASL sign maintains the same form as its French counterpart RAT (rat), where the signer "place[s] the manual letter *R* on the nose, with a light movement imitate[s] the snout of the rat" (Lambert 1865). Higgins (1942) saw a slightly different symbolism, noting that the movement represented nibbling. The semantically related ASL sign MOUSE is exactly the same except for its handshape (the index finger instead of R).

ASL RAT

READY

❶ The connection between the signs PREPARE (see entry) and READY 1 was present in LSF in the nineteenth century (Lambert 1865) and in ASL in the twentieth century. Both Long (1910) and Higgins (1923) described the sign similarly; Long cites the compound ARRANGE + FINISH and Higgins cites CLASSED. The contemporary variant, initialized with the R handshape, maintains the original left to right movement of the sign PREPARE.

ASL READY 1

ASL READY 2

❷ Because the hands in READY 2 move away from each other, the etymological link with the symbolic ordering movement in PREPARE becomes weaker.

❸ In this regional variant, (Alabama, E. Shaw field observation), the hands configured in the fist handshape drop and open as they cross over each other. READY 3 is directly inherited from the LSF sign PRÊT (ready), which itself emerged from the LSF PRÉPARER (prepare).

ASL READY 3
(IVT 1986)

LSF PRÊT

REASON

The R handshape rotates in small circles in front of the temple, visually indicating the movement of thoughts. The etymology of REASON is linked to only one of the definitions of the English word *reason*—the capacity for rational thought, rather than cause or motive. Given the productivity of initialized signs in ASL, REASON has become a catch-all sign for semantically similar English words beginning with the letter *R* that refer to thoughts, including *rational*, *realize*, and *reasonable*.

ASL REASON

RECENT

Today, two variants of RECENT exist in the U.S., neither of which is documented by the early twentieth-century authors of ASL signs.

❶ RECENT 1 derives from the old LSF sign IL Y A UN INSTANT (just a second ago) first described by Laveau (1868) as "the right hand over the right shoulder slightly agitates the index finger and the thumb." The finger points behind the signer, which metaphorically indicates the past. In RECENT 1 the thumb contacts the cheek while the index finger oscillates. This is an intermediary form between the old LSF sign and RECENT 2.

❷ The second variant consists of the outer edge of the hooked index finger touching the cheek, palm facing in, while the index finger oscillates. The prominence of the index finger in this variation completely obscures the thumb.

ASL RECENT 1

LSF IL Y A UN INSTANT
(Laveau 1868)

ASL RECENT 2

RECRUIT

In line with several signs (see CHAMPION, FLATTER, POPULAR, and SITUATION) where the extended index finger iconically depicts an individual, here the double hooked handshape draws the index finger toward the signer as one might enlist another for duty.

ASL RECRUIT

RED

Often in evolving sign languages, there are no particular signs for colors; people point to objects situated in the vicinity to indicate a specific color. In ASL, LSF, BSL (Brien 1992), Plains Indian sign languages (Clark 1885), and among Cistercian monks (Barakat 1975), the lips are the location for the color *red*. Long (1910) described RED as "draw the end of the forefinger . . . downward across the lower lip, two or three times." In contemporary ASL, the index finger has lowered from the lips to the chin, and the thumb has extended. The ASL sign PINK is an initialized derivative of RED.

ASL RED

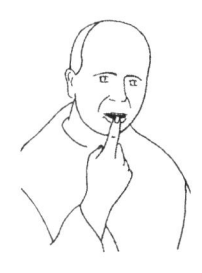

RED used among Cistercian monks
(YD from Barakat 1975)

RELIEVED

With the palms of both flat hands facing down and thumbs under the palms, the hands trace the length of the chest. This is a gestural equivalent of the onomatopoetic expression *whew!* that imitates the expiration of breath when one unloads a great weight. De Gérando (1827) recognized the same metaphor in the old LSF sign MODÉRATION (restraint), stating that "the two open hands lower from the top of the chest toward the heart, as if calming the agitation."

ASL RELIEVED

RELIGION

❶ In this earlier sign symbolizing religious faith, the letter *R* for *religion* touches the heart and then swings out and up toward God in heaven (Long 1910; Higgins 1923).

❷ For ease of movement, the sign has evolved so that the hand is directed away from the body but not toward the sky.

ASL RELIGION 1
(YD from Higgins 1923)

ASL RELIGION 2

REMEMBER

The earlier form of REMEMBER consisted of the index finger (Long 1910) or the flat hand (Higgins 1923) touching the forehead, followed by the French sign RESTER (stay), which Higgins (1942) interprets as "the thoughts stay." Over time, these handshapes assimilated so that both hands assume the extended thumb handshape. The same evolution occurred in LSF, and REMEMBER and SE SOUVENIR (remember) are now identical.

ASL REMEMBER

LSF SE SOUVENIR
(IVT 1986)

RESERVE

❶ Long (1910) and Higgins (1923) gloss this sign as ENGAGEMENT. It consists of three components: PROMISE (see entry), followed by a circular movement of the two hands that Higgins translates as "arrangement," and then BOUND, based on the image of shackled hands (see HABIT). Though this sign is no longer used in ASL, it is similar in form to the contemporary LSF ARRANGEMENT (arrangement). It is probable that the second part of the sign came from LSF but had already disappeared in ASL by the early twentieth century.

ASL RESERVE 1
(ENGAGEMENT)
(YD from Higgins 1923)

LSF ARRANGEMENT
(IVT 1997)

❷ Over time, the sign has evolved, probably for ease of production. Similar changes have also occurred with NATURE and PRINCIPAL (see entries). In RESERVE 2, the first part of RESERVE 1 has been dropped, but it retains a trace of the circular movement and it ends with BOUND.

ASL RESERVE 2

RESIST

Higgins (1923) shows RESIST produced with both hands, and it resembles the gesture of defending oneself (see DEFEND). The fist handshape conveys the meaning of force and opposition (see DEFEAT, PROTEST, and WON'T).

ASL RESIST

RESPONSIBLE

The sign RESPONSIBLE derives from the French sign CHARGE (burden), which Ferrand (circa 1785) interpreted as "the action of a man who would put a stack of wheat on his shoulders with an air of weight." Blanchet (1850) writes that CHARGE is "express[ed] by tossing the hand on the shoulder that one buckles under the weight of an object that is carried." Trappist monks use a one-hand version of Blanchet's sign to designate the person who is tasked with a specific chore in the monastery; for example, "a Brother charged with sweeping." When signed with one hand in ASL, RESPONSIBLE can also mean "fault," as in "you are responsible (at fault) for what occurred."

ASL RESPONSIBLE

Trappist Monk sign, Old LSF CHARGE
(YD, fieldwork)

REST

Long (1910) says signers "fold the arms across the breast." This sign hails from the canonical gesture of crossed arms as a symbol of repose. Its most prominent use is in the image of one who rests eternally, as in the expression "rest in peace" inscribed on tombstones.

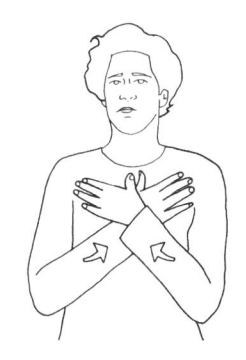

ASL REST

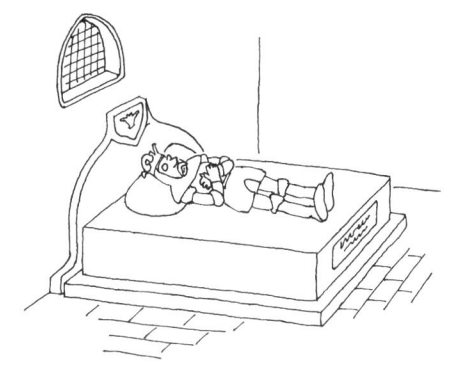

(Illustration by Pat Mallet)

REVENGE

Bent index fingers convey hardness or harshness (see MEAN 2, METAL 2, and WITCH) and are frequently used in signs where there is a conflict in social relations (see TEASE). Here, the hands are configured in the key handshape. Higgins (1942) saw the symbolism as "the beaks of two fighting roosters in action." We see a different symbolism in the location of the hands: the right hand is placed below the left when the hands draw together. The implicit underhandedness of the sign's meaning is conveyed through the inferior position of the dominant hand. The same symbolism is at work in DECEIVE 1 and STEAL 2 (see entries).

ASL REVENGE

REVERSE

Rotating the hand designates the act of inversion in both the concrete and abstract sense. Among hearing people, this image is often used to signal a logical opposition (Calbris and Montredon 1986). The sign REVERSE originates from the French sign ENVERS (reverse), which is made with a fork handshape. The handshape comes from Signed French, a manual code used by hearing educators of the eighteenth and nineteenth centuries. The word *envers* was broken into two morphemes EN (in) followed by VERS (toward), and the handshape was the letter *V* (Ferrand circa 1785). Americans have no awareness of REVERSE's link to the invented code in France.

ASL REVERSE

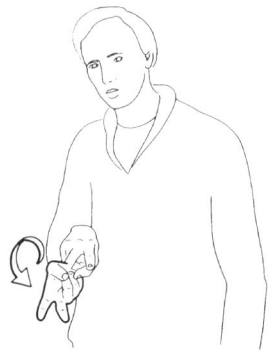

LSF ENVERS
(IVT 1990)

REVIEW

The sign is an initialized version of a more iconic variant where the outer edge of the left hand, configured in either the index finger or the fork handshape, traces an arc from the little finger to thumb of the left hand to indicate looking over things (E. Shaw, field observation). Deaf people often use the open left hand to represent a list of things that they reference by pointing to each finger with the right index.

ASL REVIEW

REVOLVE, MIX

This is the French sign RÉVOLUTION (revolution), which has multiple meanings, but in this case refers to the orbit of a planet, from its origin and back" (Sicard 1808). The configuration of the hands represents spherical objects, in particular, the celestial bodies that turn around each other.

ASL REVOLVE, MIX

LSF RÉVOLUTION
(IVT 1990)

RIGHT, CORRECT

In the first part of the twentieth century, RIGHT, CORRECT was produced by holding the two hands far from each other, then precisely striking them together in parallel; Higgins (1923) glosses this form as PERFECT and states the signer shows "an effort to make the indices exactly parallel." The parallel movement of the hands was a metaphor representing the alignment of two things. The sign has since evolved such that only the right hand moves now and, to ease production, the fingers are no longer precisely aligned.

ASL RIGHT, CORRECT

RUBBER, GUM

Documented in Long (1910) under his entry GUM, the hooked index finger strokes down the bottom of the cheek twice, symbolizing the movement of chewing. While some signers (e.g., in Maryland; E. Shaw, field observation) still use the sign with a slight movement backward along the cheek to refer to chewing gum, in contemporary contexts the sign most frequently refers to rubber. Long and Higgins (1923) list a different sign under their entries for RUBBER. However, the two terms were linked in English at that time; for example, *gums* and *rubbers* were used interchangeably to refer to rain boots (Roget's Thesaurus 1911). At some point, then, the meaning of the sign GUM expanded to include "rubber." Incidentally, the sign also refers to the city of Akron, Ohio, where a large population of Deaf people once worked at the Goodyear and Firestone tire factories.

ASL RUBBER, GUM

RUIN

RUIN is linked with the semantically similar signs TEASE and TORTURE, both of which use hooked index fingers to metaphorically convey hardness or harshness. In these signs, the hooked index finger represents an implement used to poke or prod someone. Today, the three signs are distinguished by movement alone.

ASL RUIN

S

SAD

While the signs expressing joy (see EXCITED and HAPPY) are animated by an upward movement, those expressing sadness are produced with a downward movement. These movements are based on the metaphors "good is up" and "bad is down," which are found in American and French cultures. In SAD, placing the hands near the face and then dropping them down conveys the visible drop in expression of a sad person's face. Clark (1885) was the first to document this sign, which he cited as made with one hand.

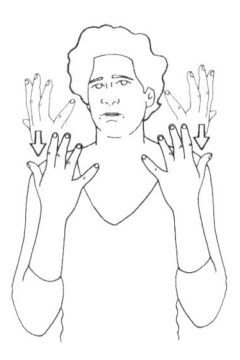

ASL SAD

SAME

The original French sign MÊME (same) was adapted from a gesture used by hearing people throughout the Mediterranean basin (for example, in Italy, North Africa, and Lebanon). This gesture has also been observed among hearing populations who use sign language, such as the Plains Indians and Cistercian monks (Clark 1885; Hadley 1893). In the LSF sign, the contact between the two index fingers symbolizes social proximity or complicity. The contemporary ASL sign has maintained the same form and meaning as its French counterpart.

ASL SAME

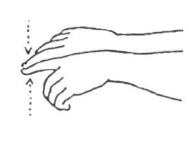

LSF MÊME
(Lambert 1865)

Gesture for *very good friends;* a Lebanese hearing gesture
(Srage 1991)

SAME AS

Long (1910) glosses this sign THE SAME; today, it is widely used to indicate similarity between two or more things. The history of this sign is complex. Stokoe et al. (1965) wrote extensively about its relation to the signs CONTINUE, STILL, STAY, and LATE, NOT YET (see entries), which all "express the concept of continuity, or duration, or lack of change." Etymologically, this sign was influenced by the old LSF RESTER (stay; Brouland 1855), a sign that is very different today in form and meaning from SAME AS (for a full discussion, see "Axis of Time," p. 286). The ASL sign is incredibly productive due to its flexibility in movement and, therefore, its ability to express a number of meanings. With short horizontal movements, the sign equates two things; with a circular, horizontal movement, it conveys universal similarity; with a downward, vertical movement, it means a lack of change; and with a vertical, circular movement, it conveys redundancy.

ASL SAME AS

ASL SATISFY

SATISFY

This ASL sign is the same as the old LSF sign AVOIR (have), which is produced when the signer "open[s] the two hands and bring[s] them towards the self in a half-circle" (Ferrand circa 1785). The ASL sign HAVE (see entry) also derives from AVOIR, but it has evolved into a different form. SATISFY, on the other hand, retains the same form as AVOIR, but it has a more specific meaning: "have enough"

LSF AVOIR (two hands)
(Pélissier 1856)

LSF AVOIR (one hand)
(Lambert 1865)

instead of simply "have." Like HAVE, SATISFY can be signed with one hand, a variant also found in old LSF.

SAVE

This comes from the French sign LIBRE (free), whose own origin is the iconic representation Lambert (1865) characterized as "break[ing] out of the shackles while lifting the arms." In the early twentieth century, this sign took on the religious connotation of salvation, which is supported by Higgins' (1923) gloss of the sign as DELIVER. Semantically related signs such as FREE and INDEPENDENT were subsequently derived from SAVE via initialization.

ASL SAVE

LSF LIBRE
(Lambert 1865)

A slave breaks his chains
(from *Nos loisirs* 1914)

SCHOOL

Clark (1885) first documented this sign in the late nineteenth century. It stems from the old practice of school teachers clapping their hands to attract their deaf students' attention. Higgins (1923) remarked that in the schools for the deaf this act would "call the children to class," later adding that teachers would use this attention-getting method "instead of ringing a bell" (1942). Though the orientation of this sign has since shifted from the hands held vertically to horizontally, some older Deaf people still hold their hands in the vertical position when they sign SCHOOL (e.g., Alabama; E. Shaw, field observation).

ASL SCHOOL

(Illustration by Pat Mallet)

SCIENCE

❶ In the early twentieth century, this sign was a compound of the ASL signs THINK and DEEP (Long 1910; Higgins 1923), which, incidentally, is also the etymon for the semantically related sign WISE (see entry).

❷ In an entirely different form, the extended thumbs were selected as iconic representations of the pipettes used to pour liquids together during science experiments. This form has proved prolific in ASL, generating subsequent derivatives through initialization, such as BIOLOGY, CHEMISTRY, and EXPERIMENT.

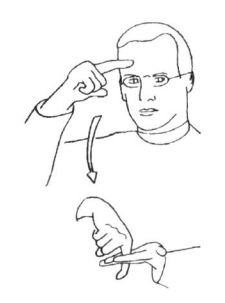

ASL SCIENCE 1
(YD from Higgins 1923)

ASL SCIENCE 2

SECOND

Today, this sign is used during formal meetings following parliamentary procedures where motions require a *second* to pass. A different sign is used as the ordinal number SECOND. The twisting movement of the wrist was inherited from LSF and is seen in the sign DEUXIÈME (second), which Lambert (1865) describes as the "sign DEUX (two) while imprinting a half-circle movement from front to back." The parliamentary SECOND also retains the handshape of DEUX, which is signed with the index finger and the thumb extended.

ASL SECOND

LSF DEUXIÈME
(Lambert 1865)

SECRET

The thumb placed on the mouth ties SECRET to a family of signs whose origin, both figurative and literal, is related to the season of Lent (see FAST and PATIENCE 1). Keeping a secret implies an effort equal to the abstinence undertaken during Lent. Higgins (1923) documents the sign as a compound (SECRET followed by HIDE), but in contemporary ASL, only the first component is used, reinforcing its relationship to PATIENCE 2 (see entry).

ASL SECRET

SECRETARY

Variations of the sign begin at different locations (either near the ear or the mouth), but they end with the sign WRITE. These forms reflect the old practice of taking dictation by writing on a notepad. Long (1910) states that the sign begins at the ear "as if you take an imaginary pen from behind the ear." Higgins (1923) notes in his entry PENCIL that the hand is "placed to the lips as if moistening the pencil and then writing." Even with the advent of computers, where typing has superseded writing by hand, SECRETARY maintains its original form without change.

ASL SECRETARY

SEEM

SEEM derives from the old LSF sign CONNAÎTRE (know), which Ferrand (circa 1785) described as "present oneself with vivacity to the hand, and signal through the eyes and the air of the face, oh yes I know you." Long's (1910) description of SEEM is very similar to CONNAÎTRE, explaining that the signer must "bring the open right hand up in front . . . turn the hand so as to present the palm toward self and fix the eyes upon it." Long also glossed the sign as APPEAR and LOOK LIKE. Over time, the meaning expanded to include "apparently." A semantically related form produced with both hands is glossed as COMPARE (see entry).

ASL SEEM

SELF

This is a cognate of the French sign MOI-MÊME (myself), documented by Lambert in 1865. Among hearing French people, as in LSF, the raised thumb carries the value 1 or *first* (see "UN (One): The Hidden Number," p. 239). In LSF, the sign UN produced a number of derivatives, including PREMIER (first), UNIQUE (unique), and MOI-MÊME. SELF has two acceptable forms, unlike its French counterpart. When the intended meaning is "myself," the point of contact of the hand can be either the closed fingers or the thumb of the thumb handshape. When the meaning is extended to include "yourself," "himself/herself," or "themselves," the sign is directed outward toward the position of the referent.

ASL SELF

LSF MOI-MÊME
(Lambert 1865)

UN (One): The Hidden Number

In LSF, UN (one) is produced with an extended thumb and DEUX (two) is produced with the extended thumb and index finger. These signs conform to the counting conventions used by all French people. According to their culture, counting begins with the extended thumb followed by the sequential unfolding of the index (DEUX), the middle finger (TROIS [three]), the ring finger (QUATRE [four]), and then the little finger (CINQ [five]).

LSF UN
(Lambert 1865)

A significant quantity of signs in LSF incorporate UN: L'AN PROCHAIN (one year in the future), L'AN DERNIER (one year in the past), PENDANT UNE HEURE (for one hour), MIEUX (better—BON + PREMIER [good + first]), OU (or; a sign from the nineteenth century that has disappeared today in France and is used to mean "which," "or," and "one or the other" in the U.S.), and COMPÉTITION (literally, "who will be first?"). In addition, LSF has a group of signs that refers to the uniqueness and singularity of the individual: SEUL (only); UNIQUE (unique); UNI (plain); a single sign that can be glossed as MOI-MÊME, CÉLIBATAIRE, PRIVÉ, ARTISAN (myself, single, private, artisan); ÉGOÏSTE (egotistical); AUTONOME (independent); and CHAQUE, CHACUN (each, each one). Counting in this manner also influenced the production of the signs TOUS LES JOURS (every day), PLUSIEURS (several), and COMBIEN (how much, how many).

Conversely, in ASL, ONE is made with an extended index finger and TWO is made with the extended index and middle finger, in accordance with the counting conventions practiced in American culture. Laurent Clerc introduced many signs of French origin that incorporate the LSF UN to his American students. These signs continue to be used today just as they are in France; however, Americans do not recognize the extended thumb as representing the number 1. The following list contains ASL signs that integrate the French UN:

FIRST: One of two variants consisting of the index finger touching the left thumb which, in this case, is the first finger of the French counting system.

ANY: From the LSF sign CHAQUE, characterized by the repeated movement (UN + UN + UN). Both Higgins and Long described this sign in the beginning of the twentieth century, but the form has since changed.

MYSELF: Directly from the LSF sign MOI-MÊME without modification.

BRAG: A derivative of MYSELF where the signer indexes oneself repeatedly, just as ÉGOÏSTE in LSF is a derivative of MOI-MÊME.

WHICH: From the old LSF sign OU without modification.

OR: From the LSF sign DE DEUX CHOSES L'UNE [UNE CHOSE OU UNE AUTRE] (of two things [one thing or another]) without modification.

BETTER, BEST: From the LSF sign MIEUX, BON EN PREMIER, meaning "good in first place."

MOST: This sign is interpreted as "one superior to another."

CHIEF, SUPERIOR: From the LSF sign PREMIER (first).

TOMORROW: Taken from the LSF sign DEMAIN without modification, meaning "one day into the future."

YESTERDAY: Taken from the LSF sign HIER without modification, meaning "one day in the past."

FEW, SEVERAL: Taken from the LSF sign PLUSIEURS (several).

SOON, IN A FEW DAYS: This sign incorporates the French numbers, UN, DEUX, TROIS . . . , extended away from the side of the chin, as in the LSF sign TOUS LES JOURS (every day) and BIENTÔT (soon).

Inevitably, the rupture of the etymological link behind the extended thumb and its original meaning has led to reinterpreted etymologies in the U.S. For example, ANY is often interpreted as being an initialized sign, and SOON is widely interpreted to be the lexicalized S-O-O-N (see SOON 1).

The French UN has also left numerous traces in ASL's numbering system. The ASL sign TEN comes from the original LSF sign DIX (ten—UN followed by ZÉRO [zero]). In today's form, the sign has been reduced to the first sign in the compound along with the movement originally added to link the signs UN and ZÉRO. In the cases of 20, 21, 23, and 24 through 29, the raised thumb and index finger show traces of the French sign DEUX; and in 30 through 39, the raised thumb, index, and middle finger are traces of the LSF sign TROIS (three).

The numbering system in ASL, then, is a true hybrid resulting from contact between two systems belonging to two different cultures.

SELFISH

Historically, SELFISH was configured with a different handshape and at least two different movements. Long (1910) cites the right claw scraping the left palm to indicate greed, which is identical in form and meaning to the French sign AVARE (greedy). Lambert (1865) describes AVARE as being produced "with the clawed fingers of the right hand, scrape the palm of the left hand as one would greedily take money toward the self." Higgins (1923) documents that in the ASL form, both claw hands are drawn toward the body. Today, the sign has changed slightly so that the hands, configured as double hooks, contract as they move toward the body. The handshape also reflects the symbolism of hardness (see DIFFICULT, HARD, and PROBLEM).

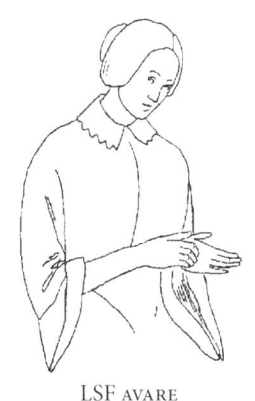

ASL SELFISH

LSF AVARE
(Brouland 1855)

SELL

This is a very old sign, first recorded in the U.S. in the late nineteenth century by Clark, who describes it as "raise hands in front of body, as though holding up a piece of cloth for exhibition" (1885). This is the cognate of the French sign VENDRE (sell; Pélissier 1856). De Gérando (1827) provides the clearest and most assured etymology of VENDRE, citing its source as the marketing custom of the era where "the two hands, lifted to the height of the head, shake back and forth like those of the merchants who shake handkerchiefs by their two corners to attract customers." Some regions in France retain a ring handshape (Y. Delaporte,

ASL SELL

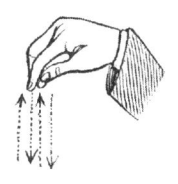

LSF VENDRE
(Pélissier 1856)

field observation)–a configuration that, in both LSF and ASL, represents the grasping of a thin or pliable object (see COUNT and EXPLAIN). This variation also exists in some regions in the U.S., such as Maryland (E. Shaw, field observation).

SENTENCE

❶ The variant form SENTENCE 1 comes from the image of a chain. This etymology is documented by Long (1910), who describes it as "lock the thumbs and forefingers of both hands together like the link of a chain," and by Higgins (1923), who describes it as the "thumb and index of both hands, joined as if links, separating and joining repeatedly, as hands move rightward." This form is similar to the French sign PHRASE (sentence), which is based on the same imagery that is also reflected in the French expression *chaîne parlée* (speech chain). This form has a shared etymology with the semantically related sign LANGUAGE (see entry).

❷ The interlocking of the two ring handshapes eventually disappeared, thereby obscuring the etymological link with the expression *chaîne parlée*. In addition, an initialized sign emerged for *language* that is different from SENTENCE 2 by only the handshape (see LANGUAGE 2), allowing for SENTENCE 2 to have its own distinct form and meaning. This form can also mean "phrase" and, when the movement is repeated, "closed captioning."

ASL SENTENCE 1
(YD from Higgins 1923)

LSF PHRASE
(YD from Le Puy 1984)

ASL SENTENCE 2

LSF PHRASE
(IVT 1997)

SEVERE, SERIOUS

SEVERE, SERIOUS shares many of the same features as DISAPPOINTED (see entry), even employing the same facial expression. The main difference between the two is that the index finger twists in SEVERE, SERIOUS. There is no other historical documentation of this sign to provide additional insight into its origin, but its proximity to DISAPPOINTED suggests that it likely derived from the same etymon.

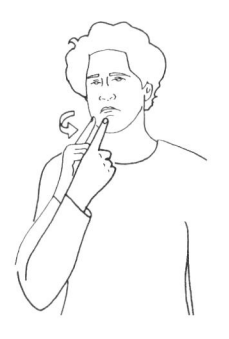

ASL SEVERE, SERIOUS

SEX, GENDER

This sign comes from two signs Abbé de l'Épée invented to translate into LSF the French gendered definite articles *le* and *la* (the). The masculine article *le* was represented by hooking the index finger on the forehead as if raising a hat. The feminine article *la* was also represented by the hooked index finger, which was placed near the ear "where the hairstyles of the person of the sex [i.e., females] terminate" (de l'Épée 1784). Further strengthening the link between the sign and written French, de l'Épée chose to use a hook handshape because it symbolized the grammatical function of the articles, which he explained was to "join words" as the articulations of the fingers "join our bones." Incidentally, during this era the French word *article* (article, item) also referred to the bending movement of the fingers. In contemporary French and English, *articulation* is used in lieu of the older *article*. The amalgamation of these linguistic symbols gave rise to the two invented signs that quickly fell

ASL SEX, GENDER

LSF HOMME
(Pélissier 1856)

LSF FEMME
(Pélissier 1856)

out of favor among French Deaf people but remained in LSF's lexicon meaning "man" and "woman." After transmission to the U.S., the forms persisted. The location of the index finger at the forehead and the ear subsequently lowered to the top and bottom of the cheek. The contemporary ASL sign can be translated as "gender," but it is widely associated with the English word *sex*, likely due to the resemblance between the hook handshape and the manual letter X. A reinterpretation of this sign's origin in the U.S. was possible because of the dual meaning of the English word *sex* as both "gender" and "the act of copulation."

SHAME, SHY

Issuing from the French sign HONTE (shame), this sign is described by Sicard (1808) as "passing the reverse of the two hands over the two cheeks, as if showing the redness that divulges this emotion." In the U.S., early records show that the sign could be produced with either one or two hands "to denote the blush or color" (Clark 1885). This sign shares a common etymon with EMBARRASS and PROSTITUTE (see entries).

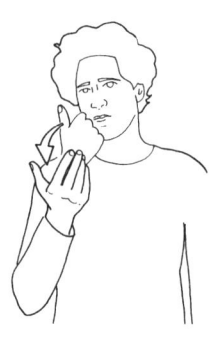

ASL SHAME, SHY

LSF HONTE
(IVT 1986)

SHOES

According to Clark (1885), SHOES was produced by thrusting "the right hand, as far as the knuckles, into the partially-closed left." Today, this describes the act of putting on or taking off shoes. In contemporary ASL, the sign for actual shoes is made by tapping the two fists together. This is likely an initialized form of the LSF sign CHAUSSURES (shoes), which is produced by clapping the two palms together, as if tapping shoes to remove dirt.

ASL SHOES

LSF CHAUSSURES
(IVT 1986)

(Illustration by Pat Mallet)

SHORT

Long (1910) cites this form under his entry "TIME (a short period of)," for which he explains the signer must "place the right 'H' hand, pointing outward, across the left 'B' hand held in front [...] with a scraping motion move it back and forth along the top of the forefinger of the left hand." The left hand represents a measuring device over which the right hand indicates the short length of the entity in question. Today, due to assimilation, both hands are configured with the paintbrush handshape. The metaphorically abstracted sign SOON 3 (see entry) uses the same handshape to express a short amount of time.

ASL SHORT

SHOW

SHOW comes directly from the French sign MONTRER (show), which was first documented by Ferrand (circa 1785). Lambert (1865) explains that to produce MONTRER the signer must "open the left hand and pass it in front of the body with the palm facing outwards and the right index posed in the center." Ferrand documented the semantically related sign EXAMPLE as "trace something in the left hand and present it." In ASL, EXAMPLE is almost identical except for its two short movements.

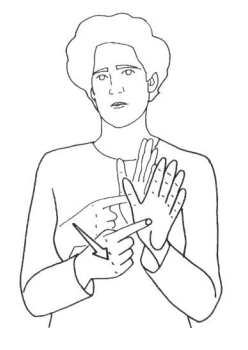

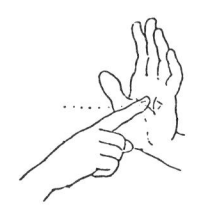

ASL SHOW

LSF MONTRER
(Lambert 1865)

SICK

Clark (1885) describes an earlier form of this sign in which the signer would "lean the head forward, place palm of left hand on forehead, and palm of right at upper part of chest or against the heart." Over time, the flat handshapes were replaced by the bent middle fingers, a common evolution in ASL (see "Handshape Change," p. 148). The location of the left hand also has lowered to the signer's stomach instead of the heart.

ASL SICK

SILLY

❶ This form derived from the French sign IDIOT (silly). The modified horn handshape symbolizes the horns of an animal. An identical metaphor motivates the sign STUPID (see entry). It is equally likely that the configuration represents the letter *I* for the French word *idiot*. At one point in ASL, the hand hovered in front of the forehead (Clark 1885; Long 1910), but now it is located near the nose. This change of location may be due to the negative and humorous connotations of the nose (see also DON'T CARE, FUNNY, and LOUSY). With the wrist rotating away from the nose, SILLY 1 means "silly" or, as Long (1910) characterized it, "absurd, trifling, and to indicate that something receives one's disapproval."

❷ A contemporary variant of this sign maintains the same handshape as SILLY 1 but changes to a circular movement around the nose. This sign generally denotes something that is outrageous or beyond the pale, and it is identical to the contemporary LSF sign IDIOT (silly).

❸ SILLY 3 is an emphatic variant used to indicate extreme outrageousness. In this sign the hands move in opposing circles in front of the signer's nose.

ASL SILLY 1

ASL SILLY 2

LSF IDIOT (IVT 1986)

ASL SILLY 3

A dispute between two French Deaf hunters: IDIOT (left) and BÊTE (stupid [right]) (from *Le Réveil des sourds-muets* 1901)

SIMPLE

This sign is inherited directly from the LSF sign SANS, RIEN (without, nothing), from which the sign WORTHLESS is also derived (see entry). Higgins (1923) describes an intermediate form of SIMPLE in his entry NOTHING, where the right ring handshape moves from the signer's mouth toward the lowered left ring hand. In his description of that form, Higgins offers "unjust" and "unfair" as translations. Even though SIMPLE shares the same handshape as the other two signs mentioned, its location and movement are different. While today SIMPLE can refer to something that is easy to do, it is more accurately characterized as meaning "unfit," "of a small amount," or "inconsequential." These meanings reveal the sign's connection with WORTHLESS and SANS, RIEN. The differences in composition between SIMPLE and WORTHLESS precipitated the distinct semantics of each sign.

ASL SIMPLE

LSF SANS, RIEN
(IVT 1997)

SIN

The origin of this religious sign is its secular counterpart HURT (see entry). Roth (1941) mentions that the sign for *ache-pain* is an indication of "a throbbing at the injured spot [that is] similar to SIN, from which it may have originated." While Roth connects the signs SIN and HURT conceptually, historical data suggest that HURT emerged before SIN. In the early twentieth century, two variations of SIN existed. Long (1910) describes

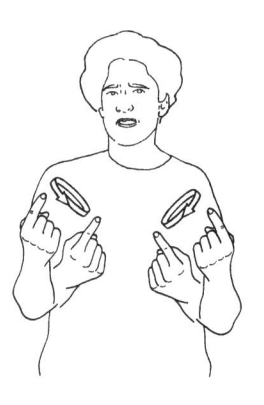

ASL SIN

it as a compound of the signs LAW and BROKEN, while Higgins (1923) cites hooked index fingers like the contemporary form.

SINGLE

❶ At the beginning of the twentieth century, different compound signs were used to describe the characteristics of an unmarried person. For example, the ASL signs MALE and FEMALE followed by OLD ONE meant "bachelor/old maid" (Long 1910). Higgins (1923) described *bachelor* as MALE followed by ALONE or NOT MARRIED.

❷ This contemporary sign comes directly from a variant of PATIENCE in which the thumb glides down the length of both sides of the mouth. The meaning behind all of the signs for *patience* originated in the act of fasting or abstinence during Lent. Today the meaning is closer to an act of self-restraint. In many cultures, including the U.S., single people were expected to practice sexual abstinence, which could be viewed by many as a test of patience. The sign BACHELOR is an initialized variant of SINGLE 2.

ASL SINGLE 1 (MAN + ALONE)

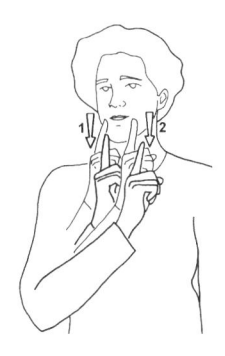

ASL SINGLE 2

SISTER

❶ This sign was originally a compound consisting of GIRL followed by SAME (see entries). It has the same form and meaning as the nineteenth-century French sign SŒUR (sister), which is still used today in the regional dialect of Saint-Laurent-en-Royans.

❷ Over time, the handshapes in SISTER 1 evolved into right angle handshapes—a melding of the thumb of GIRL and the index finger of SAME. The final position also changed so that the right hand comes down on top of the left hand. The use of the right angle handshape will likely obscure this form's etymology for future generations, especially as SISTER 1, while still recognizable today, becomes increasingly obsolete.

ASL SISTER 1

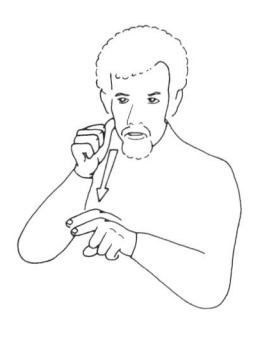

LSF SŒUR
(YD from St-Laurent 1979)

ASL SISTER 2

SITUATION

The extended left index finger in this sign is an iconic representation of an individual. This symbolism is found in many other ASL signs, including CHAMPION, FLATTER, PICK ON, and RECRUIT (see entries). The circular movement of the right hand is inherited from the LSF CIRCONSTANCE (circumstance), which both Ferrand (circa 1785) and Lambert (1865) link to the Latin word *circum*, meaning "around." The configuration of the right hand in a fist is likely the letter S, an initialization of the English word *situation*. Subsequent initialized derivations have developed in ASL, including ATMOSPHERE, CULTURE, and ENVIRONMENT.

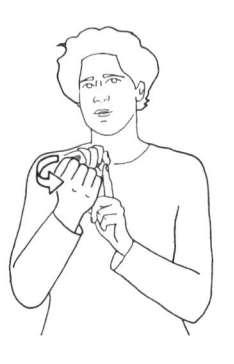

ASL SITUATION

SKILL

❶ Both Long (1910) and Higgins (1923, 1942) document the sign with the gloss SHARP, which Higgins describes as "using the whetstone to sharpen the lower edge of the left hand" (1942). Before the meaning expanded to denote all sorts of capabilities, SKILL 1 originally referred to manual competencies—an attribute long associated with Deaf people because they were historically limited to working as manual laborers. Long was the first to cite the expansion of that literal meaning to include the personal characteristic of sharpness as an intellectual trait. In his entry SHARP, SHREWD, he describes the right flat hand as symbolizing a whetstone and making a "motion of whetting" against the left hand. Today, the right hand grasps the edge of the left flat hand and then pulls away from it into an extended thumb handshape.

❷ The modified ring configuration of the dominant hand in this variant form links directly to Long's entry "SHARP (a sharp edge)." Both SKILL 1 and SKILL 2 metaphorically abstract the concrete reference to the sharp edge of a knife to the "sharp wit" of a person's intellect. They are used widely to mean "skillful," "competent," "qualified," and simply "good at." They can also be used to describe language fluency (e.g., "He is fluent in ASL"). The outer edge of the nondominant hand in TECHNICAL (see entry) also denotes precision.

ASL SHARP
(YD from Higgins 1923)

ASL SKILL 1

ASL SKILL 2

SKINNY

❶ This variant form descends from the French sign MINCE (slim), which itself comes from the gesture used by hearing people "to make another feel that one regards them as slack and cowardly, as if he had less strength in his body than is contained within the little finger that is shown him" (Costadau 1720). SKINNY 1 reflects that same symbolism.

❷ SKINNY 2 was first described by Sicard in 1808 as "imitate a person whose cheeks are hollowed: and this sign is made by taking in the skin of the face as much as possible." The thinness of the face is shown by moving the extended thumb and index finger down either side of the mouth. This sign's meaning can also apply to inanimate objects such as a thin broth.

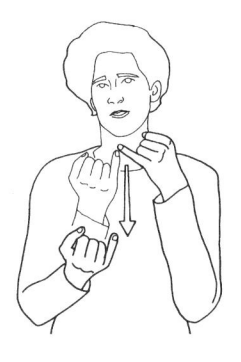

ASL SKINNY 1

LSF MINCE
(Lambert 1865)

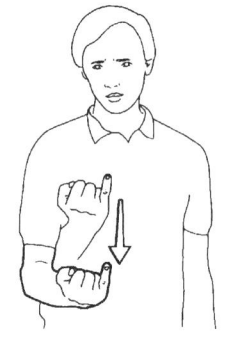

LSF MINCE
(IVT 1990)

Gesture for *skinny*; a hearing Algerian gesture
(Marie Virolle-Souibès 1985)

ASL SKINNY 2

SKIP

While no historical documentation of this sign exists, the configuration of the left hand follows a family of signs associated with touch (see OBSESS, SICK, and TOUCHED). It is likely that a metaphorical abstraction is at work here, invoking a failed attempt at contact. The sign can also mean "absent from."

ASL SKIP

SKUNK

This sign clearly symbolizes the trademark white stripe on the head of a skunk. The handshape is widely misattributed to be the letter K for the last letter in the English word *skunk*. Costello (1994) describes the sign's form as "bring the right K hand, palm facing left, from near the forehead back over the top of the head." The first documentation of this sign, however, shows a more iconic rendering where the index and middle fingers of the fork handshape made contact with the head. Clark (1885) explains that in this older configuration the signer would "indicate this [stripe] by drawing tips of index and second finger up over face and top of head."

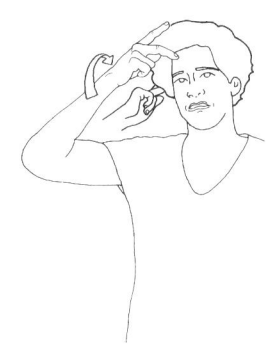

ASL SKUNK

SLOW

This sign has been the subject of much debate concerning the iconicity of ASL (e.g., Klima and Bellugi 1979, p. 30; Taub 2001, p. 228–29), where the movement of the hand is considered to belie its meaning. The placement of the right hand and the direction of movement, in fact, also played a role in the etymology of this sign. The left arm represents an object of measurement, as in the signs DETERIORATE, IMPROVE, and LONG (see entries), over which the right hand moves to demarcate temporal progression. The direction of movement toward the back gesturally translates one of the meanings of *slow*, which is "to be late."

ASL SLOW

SMART

❶ Michaels (1923) documented the oldest form of SMART as "push the index finger of the right hand from the bridge of the nose up across the forehead." This description aligns with the old LSF sign SIGNIFIER (signify), where the index finger moved from the forehead to the nose, indexing the symbolic locations of intelligence and intuition in French culture. The nose is associated with intuition in the LSF sign DEVINER (guess) and in the French expression *avoir le nez fin* (have a fine nose), which means "guess what it is." Indexing the forehead as the location of intelligence is also noted by the Brothers of St. Gabriel (1853–1854) in their entry for the LSF sign INTELLIGENT (intelligent), which they describe as "the sign of KNOW with the index of the right hand; the facial features indicate the difference between this word and KNOW."

❷ In SMART 2, the inner edge of the index finger contacts the forehead then moves away in a short, quick motion. This is likely an evolved form of SMART 1, where the connection with the nose (which carries no association with intuition in ASL) has disappeared.

❸ Also initiating at the forehead, SMART 3 is produced with the bent middle finger handshape and an added rotation of the wrist. Long (1910) cites this sign in his entry SHARP, BRIGHT, INTELLECTUALLY BRILLIANT, where he links the handshape to the sign SHARP (edge), indicating this sign employs the double meaning of *sharp* as a descriptor of physical objects and a descriptor of intellectual faculties (see SKILL).

ASL SMART 1
(Michaels 1923)

LSF SIGNIFIER
(YD from the description in Lambert 1865)

ASL SMART 2

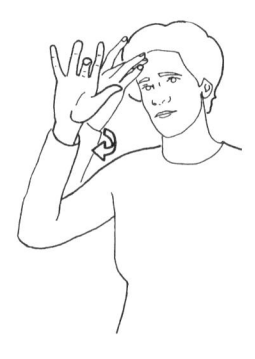

ASL SMART 3

SOCKS

Though this sign is not recorded in the older dictionaries, Roth (1941) describes a compound that is likely the etymon of SOCKS—"make the sign for KNIT as if your index fingers were the knitting needles, and then point to the foot." The movement of the first sign, KNIT, likely assimilated with pointing to the foot to create the contemporary sign.

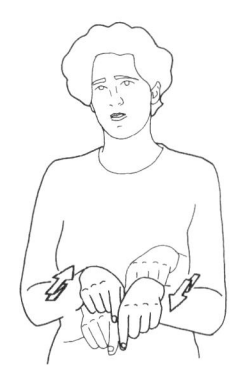

ASL SOCKS

SOME

This sign is polysemous; it is used to mean "some," "part," and related synonyms like "component" and "portion." The sign's form can be accounted for by the meaning of the English word *part*: the right hand traces the division of the left palm into two parts.

ASL SOME

SOMETIMES

❶ This sign is similar in form to the semantically related sign ONCE (see entry). ONCE derives from the French sign RECOMMENCER (start again), which was documented by Lambert (1865). The distinction between SOMETIMES 1 and ONCE, however, is that SOMETIMES 1 is repeated several times (Long 1910). This reduplication of ONCE reflects the root of the English word *sometimes*, which means "more than one time."

❷ To convey an extreme inflection of SOMETIMES meaning "very rarely" or

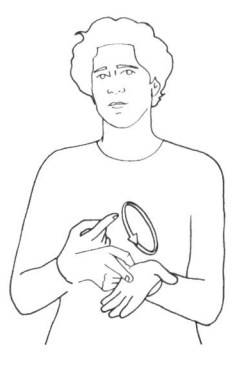

ASL SOMETIMES 1

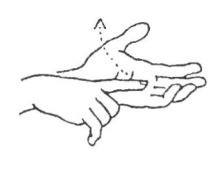

LSF RECOMMENCER
(Lambert 1865)

"occasionally," the extended index finger brushes the palm of the left hand, then moves up while the hand opens and the fingers oscillate, and then the entire sequence is repeated. Here, we see a trace of the etymon RECOMMENCER inflected with a depiction of the passing of time through the movement of the right hand. The oscillation of the fingers could be a trace of counting to five.

ASL SOMETIMES 2

SOON

❶ Though commonly believed to be an initialized sign, where the letters S then N are projected forward from the side of the chin, this regional variation of SOON (e.g., Maryland and Indiana; E. Shaw, field observation) is in fact rooted in the old LSF sign BIENTÔT (soon), which has the same handshape, location, and movement. The contemporary ASL form exhibits a shift in palm orientation from its French etymon, which likely triggered (or was triggered by) its reinterpreted etymology.

ASL SOON 1

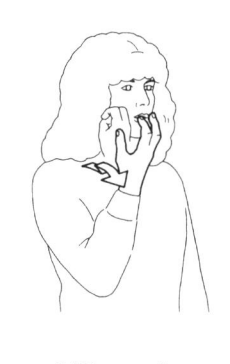

LSF BIENTÔT
(IVT 1986)

❷ SOON 2 does not have a clear history, since it is not documented in any of the historical texts. Some Deaf people in California, Oregon, and Washington produce the sign on the nose (E. Shaw, field observation), which suggests that it may be related to NEARBY, a semantically similar sign, in that something that is temporally close is figuratively near. The use of the ring handshape in this particular location evokes the notion of precision, which also is at work in the sign EXPERT.

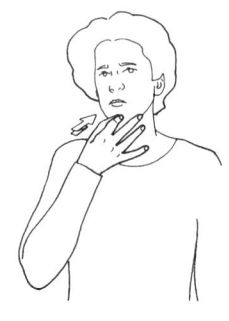

ASL SOON 2

❸ SOON 3 is simply a variation of the sign SHORT (see entry), where temporal distance and physical distance are conceptually linked. In SOON 3, the movement is repeated, but in SHORT, it is not. Long (1910) described SOON 3 as "a short period" of time, which accounts for it sometimes being glossed as TEMPORARY.

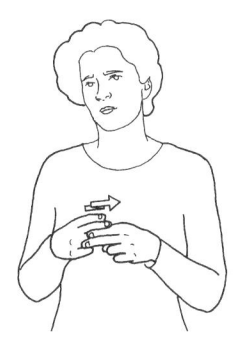

ASL SOON 3

SORRY

The contemporary ASL sign SORRY is from the old nineteenth-century French sign DÉSOLÉ (sorry), which also was glossed CHAGRIN (grief) and PEINE (sorrow). Brouland (1855) describes DÉSOLÉ as "press the fist against the chest." The sign is a gestural metaphor for squeezing the heart, the feeling expressed by "a broken heart."

ASL SORRY

LSF DÉSOLÉ
(Brouland 1855)

SOUR

This sign hails directly from the LSF AIGRE (sour), which Ferrand (circa 1785) describes as "pricks the tongue." In ASL, the sign is accompanied by a grimace to depict one's reaction to tasting something that is not sweet. Long (1910) describes that the index finger makes contact with the mouth, but the location of the contemporary form has lowered to the chin where the index finger twists.

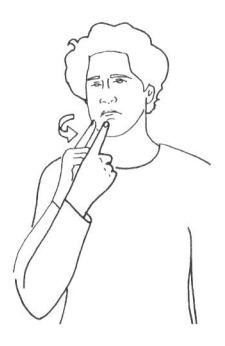

ASL SOUR

SPECIAL

SPECIAL is inherited from the old LSF sign EXCEPTÉ (except), which Sicard (1808) describes as "show all of the fingers of the right hand; action of separating one of these fingers from the others and distinguishing it from them." This older form, from which the contemporary sign developed, was produced with the open left hand held upright while the right ring hand pulled the left index finger upward. In the contemporary sign, only the left index finger is extended, and the right hand is configured in the ring handshape. This handshape is used to depict picking up something small, thin, or fine (see CHOOSE, COUNT and SELL), and also connotes the idea of something very specific (see also EXPERT and SOON 2).

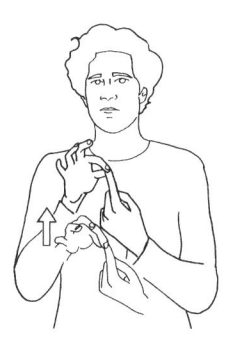

ASL SPECIAL

SPECIALTY

Close in form to the sign STRAIGHT, SPECIALTY is rooted in the same metaphor indicating a straight and narrow path one follows without deviation. When the right hand is configured in a flat handshape, the sign can mean "career," "field," and "major." When the hand is configured in a P handshape, the sign means "profession(al)."

ASL SPECIALTY

SPIRIT

Both of the ASL signs come from LSF, and they can be translated as *soul* or *ghost*.

❶ This older sign is motivated by the medieval concept that the soul of a dying person exits the body through the mouth. Brown (1856) describes the form as "hands put at the sides of mouth brought down with the breath." This etymology matches that documented by Jamet (circa 1830) for the LSF cognate ESPRIT, which is produced when "the right hand is brought to the mouth that is partially open, as if to take a breath."

❷ By the early twentieth century, the hands had lowered to the chest (Higgins 1923). The movement of the hands away from each other represents the soul leaving the heart to go to God. A variant that ends with the hands in the bundled handshape (Long 1910) is identical to one of several signs for *spirit* in contemporary LSF.

ASL SPIRIT 1, LSF ESPRIT
(Lambert 1865)

ASL SPIRIT 2

SPRING

SPRING originates from the old LSF sign PRINTEMPS (spring), which Lambert (1865) explains as "flowers spring up." In contemporary ASL, the semantically related sign GROW exhibits the same single upward movement as PRINTEMPS, whereas SPRING is a reduplicated form of GROW.

ASL SPRING

LSF PRINTEMPS
(Lambert 1865)

STAR

Higgins (1942) saw in this sign the impact of flint and steel struck together to produce sparks that resemble stars. The actual etymology is much simpler; it is the old French sign ÉTOILE (star), which Ferrand (circa 1785) described as "show different points in the firmament." Sicard (1808) wrote that the hands "indicate with the two indexes the celestial arch and point, as if we were seeing, as we see them during the night, the stars that are strewn across the sky"; and Lambert (1865) said the index fingers "indicate the place of the stars in space." The contemporary French sign ÉTOILE has an entirely different origin, and the older LSF form is now glossed as ASTROLOGIE (astrology). The English word *astrology* and the French *astrologie* derive from the Latin *astrum* meaning "star." In ASL, the two index fingers moved closer together so that they make contact, an evolution that has obscured the sign's simple etymology.

ASL STAR

(Illustration by Pat Mallet)

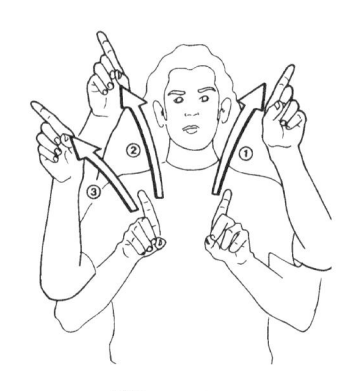

LSF ASTROLOGIE
(IVT 1997)

START

The ASL sign START comes from the French sign COMMENCER (start), which was documented by all of the French authors, from Ferrand (circa 1785) to Lambert (1865). The right index finger glides between the middle and index fingers of the left fork hand to announce the arrival of something new. One variant of the sign in ASL retains the fork handshape of the left hand, while the more common variation utilizes an open handshape. The Brothers

ASL START

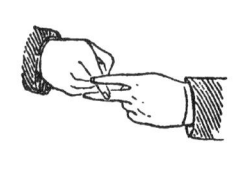

LSF COMMENCER
(Pélissier 1856)

of St. Gabriel (1853–1854) first documented the rotation of the right index finger, which ultimately obscured the sign's etymology when the form was transmitted to the U.S.

STAY

STAY 1 and STAY 2 stem from the French sign DEMEURER, RESTER (remain, stay), which was described as "the right thumb presses transversally on the left thumb" (de Gérando 1827), and "press the thumb of the right hand on the left with an expression of consistency" (Lambert 1865). Lambert provides a description of a similar form in his entry FIXER (affix, set). The symbolism derives from an object that can be affixed to something, such as a stamp on an envelope. Much later in LSF, DEMEURER, RESTER became symmetrical; the right thumb no longer pressed the left, but both thumbs lowered in unison. Two evolutions in form ultimately distanced the ASL sign from its French etymon. First, the little fingers extended—an evolution also at work in the sign WRONG (see entry). Second, two alterations in the downward movement of the hands emerged.

❶ In STAY 1, the right hand moves down after first making contact with the left hand.

❷ In STAY 2, both hands move down but never touch each other. These signs belong to a large family that includes CONTINUE, SAME AS, and STILL (see entries), which are all characterized by movement along the axis of time (see "Axis of Time," p. 286).

ASL STAY 1

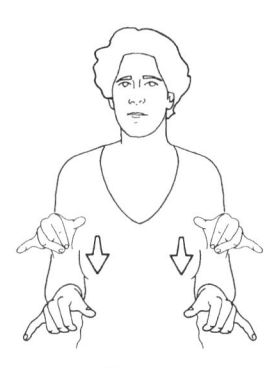

ASL STAY 2

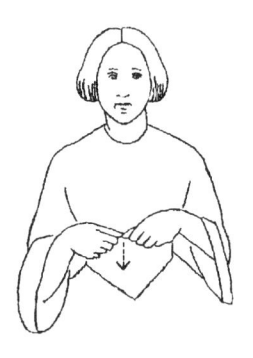

LSF DEMEURER, RESTER
(Brouland 1855)

STEAL

❶ The fingers of the open right hand close while the hand moves under the left elbow, as if grabbing something clandestinely (Clark 1885; Long 1910; Veditz 1913; Michaels 1923). The position of the right hand under the left elbow denotes concealment of an underhanded act, as we see in the signs TEMPT and REVENGE (see entries).

❷ In the contemporary form, STEAL 2, the right hand is first configured in a fork handshape, which then bends into a double hook as the hand moves along the length of the left forearm. This variation was already in use in the early twentieth century, being documented for the first time by Higgins (1923) who describes the handshape "as a hook to take something from under the left elbow." The double hook handshape is metaphorically associated with hard or harsh things in both ASL and LSF and with extraction in ASL (see NERVY).

ASL STEAL 1
(YD from Long 1910)

ASL STEAL 1
(Michaels 1923)

ASL STEAL 2

STEEL

An old sign, STEEL was first recorded in the U.S. by Clark in 1885. Later documented by Long (1910), Higgins (1923), and Michaels (1923), the sign's form was described as representing a hammer striking an anvil to forge a bar of iron. Michaels explains that to produce this sign, one must "strike in a gliding manner on the thumb and index finger of the left hand with the right fist." This sign has since dropped out of the lexicon of contemporary ASL because steel production methods have

ASL STEEL
(YD from Long 1910)

changed, but the form is still used as one of the name signs for the Pittsburgh Steelers NFL football team.

STILL

STILL shares the same ancestor as CONTINUE, SAME AS, and STAY (see entries)—the old LSF RESTER (stay) described by Brouland (1855). Long (1910) glosses the sign as YET, STILL and describes the form as "place the right Y hand at the side and carry it out straight forward from the side. This also conveys the idea of continuity." The metaphor behind the sign is "the future is ahead" (see "Axis of Time," p. 286). Today, STILL is produced with one or both hands, which twist out rather than move forward as Long documents.

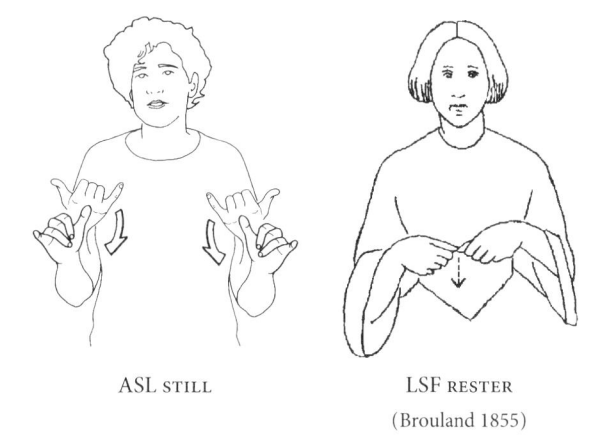

ASL STILL

LSF RESTER
(Brouland 1855)

STONE

❶ An older variant of STONE was produced on the chin, a location in both ASL and LSF frequently used to express hardness (see METAL 1).

❷ STONE 2 is very similar to HARD (see entry), differing only in the handshape. This contemporary form comes from a regional LSF variant PIERRE (stone), identical to the nineteenth-century sign DUR (hard; Brothers of St. Gabriel 1853–1854), which is still used in Poitiers, France.

ASL STONE 1

ASL STONE 2

STONE   263

STOP

Clark (1885) glosses this sign as HALT and describes the form exactly as it is produced today: "strike the left palm with the lower edge of the right hand sharply." In contemporary LSF, this form is the sign FINIR (finish).

ASL STOP

STRANGE

A sign with a long history, STRANGE is surprisingly rooted in the French sign CURIEUX (curious), as a result of the polysemy of the English word *curious*, which can mean "inquisitive" or "peculiar." The French sign is motivated by both the letter *C* from the French word *curieux* and by the act of looking for something through a magnifying glass. Blanchet (1850) describes it as "form the manual letter C; bring it in front of the eye, like an eye glass; . . . shake it circularly several times." After its transmission to the U.S., CURIEUX transformed into two ASL signs, each with a distinct meaning—LOOK FOR and STRANGE. Long's (1910) entry CURIOUS is identical to its French ancestor, which he described as "move the 'C' hand [. . .], in front of the face, describing a circle from right to left." Today, STRANGE has only a single arced movement, while the repeated circles from CURIEUX remain in LOOK FOR (see entry).

ASL STRANGE

LSF CURIEUX
(Lambert 1865)

STRICT

The double hooked handshape and the location of this sign represent two different metaphors. The handshape invokes harshness, as in the signs HARD and PROBLEM (see entries) and the location on the nose signifies negative concepts (see DON'T CARE and LOUSY). Though not documented by historical authors, it is possible that the sign is a gestural translation of the semantically equivalent English expression "hard-nosed." It is equally tempting to link this sign with the LSF MANIAQUE (finicky, fussy), where the hooked index finger strokes the length of the nose.

ASL STRICT

LSF MANIAQUE
(IVT 1997)

STRUGGLE

The two index fingers in opposition to each other iconically represent the conflict inherent in a struggle. The index fingers originally represented swords, thus linking STRUGGLE to a family of signs whose meanings reference some sort of discord (see ENEMY, HURT, OPPOSITE, and SIN). The etymon of all these signs is the LSF sign ENNEMI (enemy). The circular movement of STRUGGLE may represent the advance and retreat of one's opponent, similar to what one experiences in a conflict.

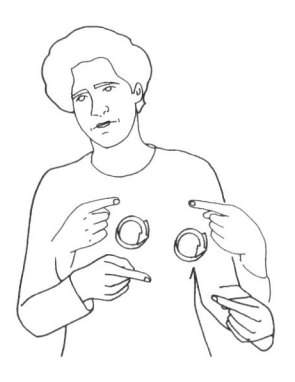

ASL STRUGGLE

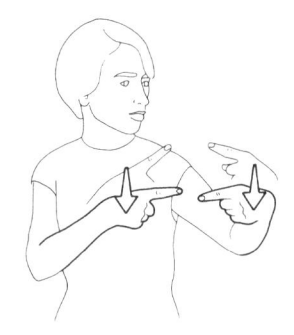

LSF ENNEMI
(IVT 1986)

STUBBORN

Drawing from the stereotypical quality of a donkey, the animal notorious for its obstinate personality, STUBBORN symbolizes one of the donkey's ears bent forcefully.

ASL STUBBORN

(Illustration by Pat Mallet)

STUCK

The neck or throat represents a passageway that, in this case, is impeded by a forked implement. STUCK likely comes from the LSF sign ÊTRE COINCÉ, SE FAIRE PIÉGER (stuck, trapped), which shares all the same features of the ASL sign except for handshape. ÊTRE COINCÉ, SE FAIRE PIÉGER is most frequently produced with a ring or small crescent handshape. The ring handshape also exists in older variations of STUCK in ASL (E. Shaw, field observation). The same imagery is present in the semantically related sign CLOGGED where the crescent handshape grasps the throat, which is even more similar to the form of ÊTRE COINCÉ, SE FAIRE PIÉGER.

ASL STUCK 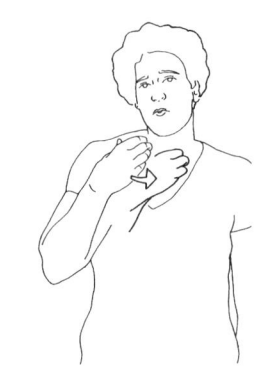   ASL CLOGGED

LSF ÊTRE COINCÉ, SE FAIRE PIÉGER
(IVT 1986)

STUDENT

❶ We see in this sign a compound of LEARN (see entry), where the sum of knowledge is symbolically gathered into a bundled handshape and placed at the forehead, and PERSON (see entry), indicated by both open hands running down the sides of the torso. This form appears to have originated in the old LSF sign ÉLÈVE (student), which Sicard (1808) also describes as having two components: "1. Bring all of the closed fingers to a point on the forehead several times to designate a student receiving lessons. 2. Represent a student." Lambert's (1865) entry APPRENDRE (learn) is practically identical to the first part of STUDENT 1.

❷ Over time, the sign underwent several changes as a result of compounding. The right bundled handshape still rises from the left palm, just as it does for LEARN, but it no longer makes contact with the head. The second component, PERSON, has reduced to the dropping and opening of the right hand. STUDENT 2, then, retains a trace of the PERSON marker inherited from one of de l'Épée's invented methodical signs. The French Deaf community discarded this agentive marker long ago.

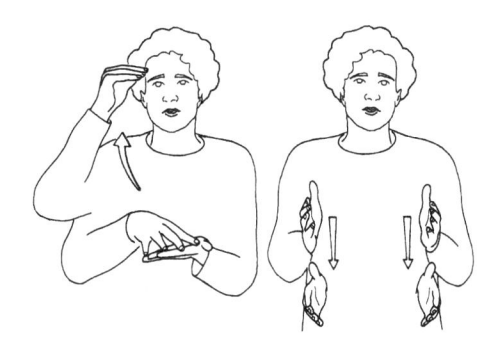

ASL STUDENT 1 (LEARN + PERSON)
(YD)

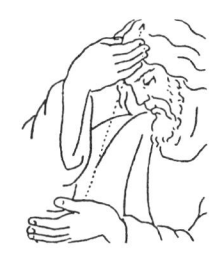

LSF APPRENDRE
(Lambert 1865)

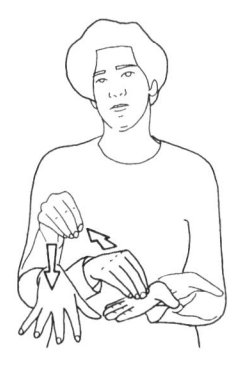

ASL STUDENT 2

STUPID

STUPID is one of a handful of ASL signs derived from LSF calques (or loan translations) of French words (see also REVOLVE, MIX). This sign, in particular, comes from the LSF sign BÊTE (stupid), whose form iconically represents the horns of an animal. BÊTE is founded on the polysemy of the French word *bête*, which can be used to literally mean "animal" or "beast," and figuratively to mean "stupid." The etymology of BÊTE is also documented by Sicard (1808), who describes it as being "made by placing the two index fingers on the head like the horns of an animal." In America, the standard translation of the sign as "stupid," breaks all connections with the association to a horned beast.

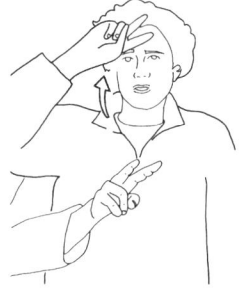

ASL STUPID

LSF BÊTE
(Pélissier 1856)

(Illustration by Pat Mallet)

SUFFER

❶ SUFFER 1 is identical to PATIENCE 2 (see entry), except for a short twisting of the wrist. The base form of the thumb placed over the mouth is linked to the season of Lent.

❷ SUFFER 2 has the same form and meaning as the French sign SOUFFRIR (suffer), which was documented in the eighteenth century by Ferrand (circa 1785), who characterized it as "pass the closed fists in front of the stomach over several turns." In the nineteenth century, Blanchet (1850) described it as "turn both fists one around the other like boxers," and Lambert (1865) described it as "roll the fists one around the other." Subsequent evolutions, where the movement of the fists

ASL SUFFER 1

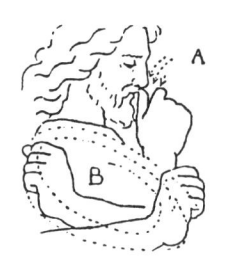

A. LSF PATIENCE
B. LSF SOUFFRIR
(Lambert 1865)

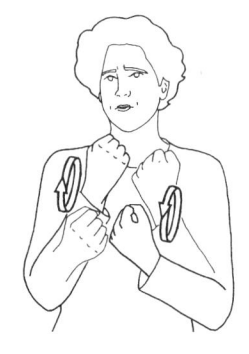

ASL SUFFER 2

turned away from the body, were a consequence of the difficulty in turning both fists simultaneously "in front of the stomach." After a century in the U.S., SUFFER also expanded in meaning to the more generic gloss DIFFICULT (Long 1910).

SUMMER

SUMMER comes from the old Parisian sign ÉTÉ (summer). Although both signs are commonly interpreted as representing the act of wiping sweat from the forehead, the original etymology is entirely different. Pélissier (1856) notes in his entry AOÛT (August) that the sign is produced by the hooked index finger tracing the forehead to represent a crown of laurels. The month of August, according to French custom, was the time when awards of new books and crowns of laurels were presented to the best students in school. What was once the sign AOÛT during Pélissier's time later took on the broader meaning of "summer." Another LSF sign for *août* used in Paris until the 1970s maintained the hooked index finger representing the crown of laurels. The proximity between the form and the gesture of wiping one's brow allowed for the reinterpreted etymology in both ASL and LSF.

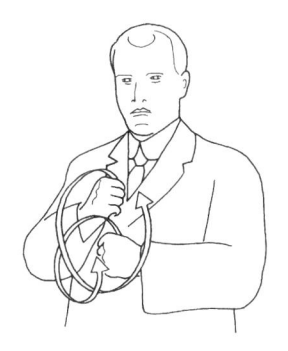

ASL DIFFICULT
(YD from Long 1910)

ASL SUMMER

Distribution of prizes
(from *La Semaine de Suzette* 1935)

LSF AOÛT
(YD from the ALSF archives)

SUMMON

The original sign for SUMMON, first documented by Long (1910), consisted of two parts—tapping the back of the left hand and then making a beckoning motion. Higgins (1942) has an almost identical description: "tapping the hand for attention and motion to come." At present, this sign is produced with two principal segments: the fingertips of the right flat hand tap the back of the left and then pull back while contracting into a fist with a raised thumb.

ASL SUMMON

SUN

❶ Starting in the nineteenth century, this variant form was a compound consisting of the index finger tracing a circle in the air followed by the sign BRIGHT directed at the signer's face (Clark 1885; Long 1910). The circle is no longer evident in the contemporary sign; however, the rotation of the wrist with the bundled handshape constitutes a trace of this part of the sign's etymon.

ASL SUN 1

❷ This older variation is dropping out of use. It more closely resembles Long's (1910) entry for the sign MOON, which he describes as "hold the right 'C' hand over the side of the right eye and looking up at the sky lift the hand, still in position of 'C' upward toward an imaginary moon."

ASL SUN 2

SUNDAY

All of the signs for the days of the week in ASL, other than SUNDAY, are represented by their first (or first and second) letter. Clark (1885) notes that Deaf Americans "denote a day of rest, or a holy day" for SUNDAY. Higgins (1923) interpreted the form to represent "the large opened doors of the church building." The description in Michaels (1923) leaves no doubt as to its etymology: "Hold [up] both hands . . . ; close your eyes; move the lips as if in prayer." The contemporary sign, similar in form to WONDERFUL as well as the old LSF ADORER (worship), symbolizes the gesture of praise to God seen in certain Christian congregations.

ASL SUNDAY

SUPERIOR

This sign incorporates the LSF sign UN (one), where the upward movement of the thumb signals superiority or "firstness" (Lambert 1865; see "UN (One): The Hidden Number," p. 239). In Saint-Laurent-en-Royans, raising the thumb upward is the sign CHEF (chief, leader). Among Trappist monks, the thumb also designates the Superior—one of the brothers who has been elected to direct the monastery. In this and other ASL signs, the meaning behind the extended thumb and notions of uniqueness or superiority has been obscured by the use of the extended index finger to indicate the number 1.

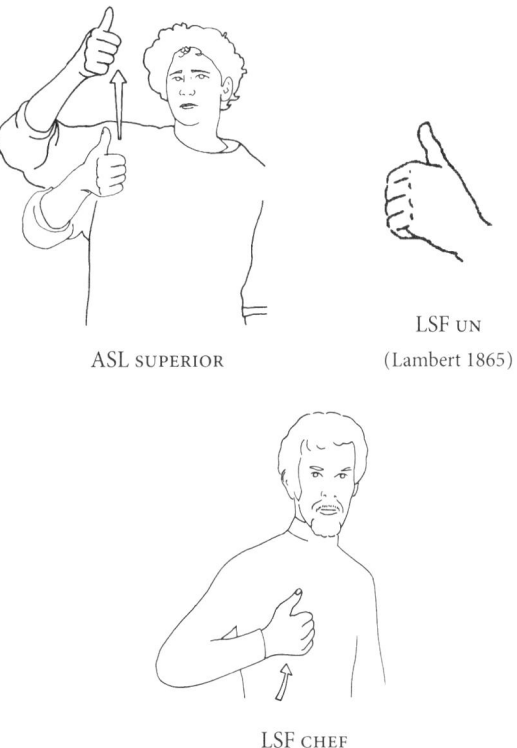

ASL SUPERIOR

LSF UN
(Lambert 1865)

LSF CHEF
(YD from St-Laurent 1979)

SUPPOSE

In an older form of SUPPOSE (E. Shaw, field observation), the little finger moves up and away from the forehead, the metaphoric location for intellectual faculties. The meaning of SUPPOSE corresponds to the idea of "issuing a hypothesis"; the movement away from the face also contributes to the symbolism that hypotheses portend something about the future (see "Axis of Time," p. 286). This doubly motivated sign is likely an initialized variant inherited from the LSF sign AU CAS OU (in case of), with the location lowered from the forehead to the cheek—a common evolution in both ASL and LSF.

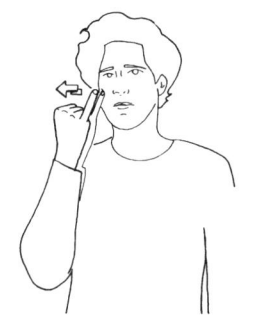

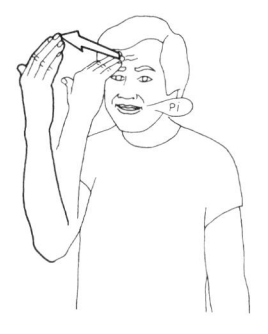

ASL SUPPOSE

LSF AU CAS OU
(IVT 1986)

SWEET

Once produced with the paintbrush handshape (Long 1910; Higgins 1923), which gave rise to the sign CUTE (see entry), the contemporary form of SWEET uses the flat or mitten handshape. Michaels (1923) describes the sign as "move the fingers of one hand downward over your lips two or three times; lick your lips a little with the tongue." SWEET likely derives from the old French sign BIEN (well) that also uses the paintbrush handshape. Ferrand (circa 1785) describes BIEN as "bring the index and the middle fingers of the right hand to the mouth while making the natural sign of a good thing with the lips." The ASL sign's meaning has expanded over time to include such things as personal characteristics, an animal's sweet disposition, and the medical condition diabetes.

ASL SWEET

SWEETHEART

❶ This old variant of the sign (e.g., Alabama; E. Shaw, field observation), where both little fingers make brushing contact as the wrists rotate, comes from the French sign PETIT AMI (sweetheart). In the Mediterranean basin, rubbing the index fingers together is a symbol of intimacy and can also mean "friend." In SWEETHEART 1, the little fingers replaced the index fingers, which added to the notion of smallness expressed in the French phrase *petit ami* (literally, *little friend*).

❷ As this sign evolved, the little fingers no longer brushed each other but linked together while the thumbs bent and straightened. This variant form remains in limited use today, especially among older Deaf people (e.g., Indiana; E. Shaw, field observation).

❸ In the final step of SWEETHEART's evolution, the little fingers lost all prominence. Now, the two fists, side by side, are placed close to the heart while the thumbs bend and straighten. Long (1910), Higgins (1923), and Michaels (1923) all document this sign. Both Long and Higgins glossed it MAKE LOVE. Michaels suggests that the movement of the thumbs mimics how "sweethearts do their heads when conversing or courting," a reinterpreted etymology that probably precipitated the alteration in form from SWEETHEART 2. Higgins (1923) also notes that "the hands close together would indicate imprudent courtship." For this reason, Edward Miner Gallaudet may have produced the sign with the two fists far apart from each other in his signed, filmed monologue about Lorna Doone (1910).

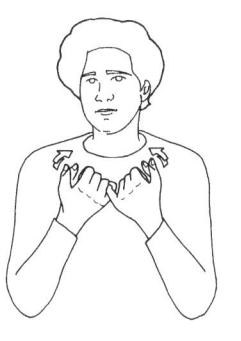

ASL SWEETHEART 2
(YD)

ASL SWEETHEART 3

SYMBOL

Often mistaken as an initialized sign, SYMBOL's etymon is the complex religious LSF sign SYMBOLE (symbol) documented by Ferrand (circa 1785) and Lambert (1865), whose entry reads "SYMBOLE: faithful apostles: résumé of the articles." The Apostles' Creed consists of twelve articles (or statements) of belief representing the central doctrine of the Christian faith. In LSF, the extended fingers of the left hand represent these articles that are gathered by the right hand, which then closes into a fist and then touches the left palm, symbolically uniting the articles and inscribing them into the Bible. The circular movement of the right hand was not maintained in ASL; instead, there is a short repeated movement away from the body, similar to SHOW (see entry). This endows the sign with its contemporary meaning, that of showing or presenting a symbol. Its likeness to an initialized version of SHOW obscures the sign's link with its religious etymon.

ASL SYMBOL

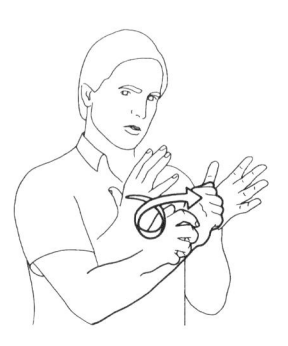

LSF SYMBOLE
(IVT 1986)

T

TAKE ADVANTAGE OF

The etymology of this sign remains unknown. One possibility is that the middle finger symbolically takes something from the left palm, much like in the LSF sign GAGNER (win; see WIN) and the ASL GRAB A CHANCE (see entry). The sign aligns semantically with the idea of advantage as a gain. It generally has negative connotations in ASL and is related to the English concepts of being ripped off or being taken advantage of. It is not surprising, then, that the sign can also mean "molest." In ASL, the bent middle finger also denotes physical or emotional sensations (see EXCITED, PITY, and TEND TO).

ASL TAKE ADVANTAGE OF

TALK

❶ The two upright index fingers alternately moving back and forth from the mouth represent an exchange of discourse between two interlocutors. Higgins (1923) interprets the form as "the nodding of the heads." TALK 1 shares the same form and meaning as the French sign DISCUTER, CAUSER (discuss, speak), and was documented by Long (1910) as meaning "conversation." Several semantically related signs have been derived from TALK 1 by initialization, including COMMUNICATE, INTERVIEW, and NEGOTIATE.

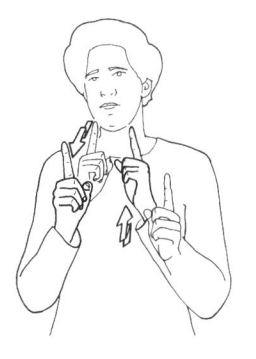

ASL TALK 1

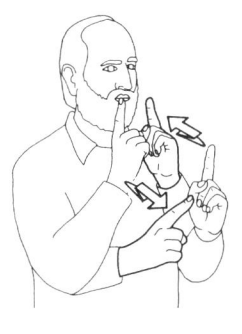

LSF DISCUTER, CAUSER (IVT 1986)

❷ In the second sign, the extended fingers of the right hand symbolize the flow of words from the mouth. In LSF, the same sign means "lecture." The symbolism of the fingers as flowing words was already present in Ferrand's entry DÉCLARER (declare), which he describes as "agitate the fingers of the open right hand in front of the eyes" (circa 1785). Likewise, the Brothers of St. Gabriel (1853–1854) gloss this sign as BAVARD (chat), and explain that "the fingers oscillate several times to indicate loquaciousness." In ASL, the hand can stay fixed at the mouth while the fingers oscillate or it can tap the mouth several times like the LSF variant CONFÉRENCE (lecture).

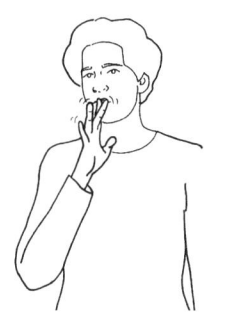

ASL TALK 2

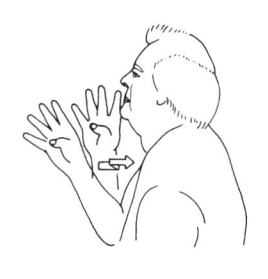

LSF CONFÉRENCE
(YD, fieldwork)

TASTE

TASTE is inherited from the LSF sign GOÛTER (taste), described by the Brothers of St. Gabriel (1853–1854) as "bring the index of the right hand over the extremity of the tongue and take on the air of tasting something." In the early twentieth century, the index (Long 1910) or bent middle finger (Higgins 1923) touched the tip of the tongue, as if placing something on it. In later years, the sign moved from the tongue to the chin, a change that also occurred in the signs DRY and LIE (see entries). Also, the bent middle finger became metaphorically associated with both emotional and tactile senses (see FEEL and TOUCHED).

ASL TASTE

A cook tasting the soup
(Blanchet 1864)

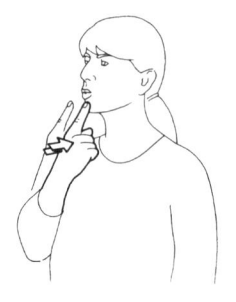

LSF GOÛTER
(IVT 1986)

276   TASTE

TEACH

This sign comes directly from the French sign ENSEIGNER (teach). Blanchet (1850) describes the form as "the fingers of the hand open and close into a bundle; bringing them toward the front: simulates the action of taking something from the head and throwing it into the head of another in closing and opening the fingers." Lambert (1865) uses a more lyrical description, explaining that one must "take the fists of intelligence from one's forehead and toss them to the forehead of another who is in front of you." In an LSF variant, the hands do not open until the end of the movement. These same two forms coexisted in ASL in the early twentieth century; in one, the hands opened (Long 1910; Roth 1941), and in the other, now more common form, the hands remain closed (Higgins 1923).

ASL TEACH

LSF ENSEIGNER
(Pélissier 1856)

TEASE

Clark (1885) includes the gloss TEASE under his entry ACCOST in which he explains that one must "strike the horizontal left forearm near wrist, with palmar surface of finger of right hand; point right index at person, and then crook same, drawing hand slightly to rear." In ASL, hooked index fingers convey the notion of harshness or aggression (see WITCH and MEAN 2) but also invoke the image of poking someone with a stick (see URGE). The same sign is glossed in LSF as TAQUINER with the meaning "tease" or "torture," depending on the co-occurring facial expression. The meaning of the ASL

ASL TEASE

LSF TAQUINER
(IVT 1986)

sign has not changed, but when the left hand repeats the same movement over the right hand, it is glossed TORTURE.

TECHNICAL

The outer edge of the left hand has represented a sharp edge since at least the early twentieth century (Long 1910; Higgins 1923). The English expression *cutting-edge technology* employs the same metaphor. The bent middle finger, known to symbolize the sense of touch, taps the outer edge of the left fist. In the ASL signs SKILL 1 and SKILL 2 (see entries), literal sharpness transformed into the notion of intellectual sharpness; here, the meaning extended to technological sharpness.

ASL TECHNICAL

TELL

The contemporary ASL sign TELL is the old French sign DIRE (tell, say), which was produced by "plac[ing] the index finger on the mouth and direct[ing] it towards the person to whom one says something" (Lambert 1865). Pélissier (1856) illustrated the sign with a repeated movement. Documented in the U.S. since the early twentieth century (Long 1910; Michaels 1923) the sign remains unchanged to this day.

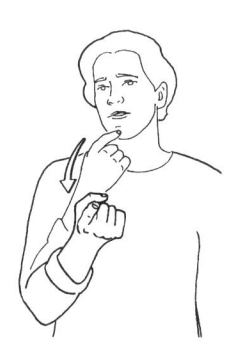

ASL TELL

LSF DIRE
(Pélissier 1856)

TEMPT

Documented since the late nineteenth century in the U.S. in the Lord's Prayer (A. Clark 1899), TEMPT is the old French sign TENTER (tempt) where "the end of the index taps the elbow of the left arm several times" (de Gérando 1827). The point of contact under the elbow refers to concealment and underhandedness, as is also the case in the signs STEAL 1 and CHEAT 4 (see entries). Also, the hooked index finger in ASL and LSF metaphorically associates the sign with negative or harsh things.

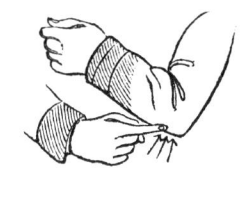

ASL TEMPT

LSF TENTER
(Pélissier 1856)

TEN

TEN originates from the old LSF compound DIX (ten), which was composed of UN (one), the extended thumb (see "UN (One): The Hidden Number," p. 239), and ZÉRO (zero). Today, the ASL sign has been reduced to the handshape of UN with the twisting of the wrist as the only trace of ZÉRO.

ASL TEN

TEND TO

Long (1910) documents this sign under his entry INCLINED, DISPOSED TO, which he describes as "touch the heart with the bent finger of the right '5' hand (as in 'feel'), then extend the left open hand toward the left and bring the right open hand just back of it also pointing toward the left; carry both hands toward the left, thus indicating the inclination of one's feelings." The

ASL TEND TO

form, then, is a gestural demonstration of projecting one's feelings outward. Today, the sign can be produced with either one or two hands, and is usually accompanied by the mouthed *pih* configuration. It is also common to see the possessive pronoun following this sign, especially when describing the tendencies of a certain person or group of people. This particular instantiation of the possessive pronoun (e.g., the one used in the expression DEAF WAY) also exists in LSF with the same mouthed configuration, suggesting that there may have once been a historical link (see HIS, HERS, ITS).

THAN

THAN comes from the French sign QUE (than), which is one of the methodological signs invented by de l'Épée (1784) that was strictly relegated for use in Signed French. The movement of the right hand from high to low conveys the inequality between two things that are compared. De l'Épée used the two bent hands to indicate the difference in size between two people: "I explain *que* by placing the left hand lower and indicating myself while my right hand is higher to show that Pierre [is bigger than me]." In ASL, the change in movement—to the right hand slapping down the left fingertips—ultimately obscures the origin of this invented sign. Higgins (1942) interpreted the movement in the ASL sign as resembling "pushing something down." THAN has come to be used in ASL to mean "instead of" or "rather than." The fact that the

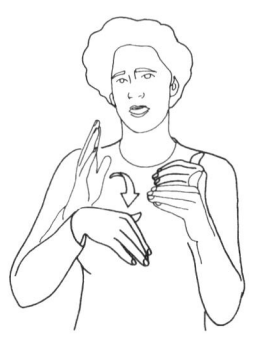

ASL THAN

sign predates the invention of Signed English may explain why it has become fully integrated in ASL discourse.

THANK YOU

❶ This sign hails directly from LSF, and is still used today in both languages. Jamet (circa 1830) describes its production as "the right hand touches the mouth by the tips of the fingers, and is graciously drawn toward the front." Long (1910) cites the same sign and notes that signers greet, thank, or bid farewell by "throwing a kiss."

ASL THANK YOU 1

❷ Higgins (1923) describes a compound where the right hand moves away from the mouth while the left hand moves away from the heart. He translates this sign as "good from the lips and heart" (1942). In contemporary ASL, signers typically reserve the two-handed variant for use in formal settings. Since the left hand has raised closer to the right hand, the sign's connection with projecting thanks from the heart has ruptured.

ASL THANK YOU 2
(YD from Higgins 1923)

ASL THANK YOU 2

THING

❶ The right flat hand moves laterally, tracing successive points "as if placing several things" (Higgins 1923) in front of the signer. We recognize a similar motivation in the old LSF sign CHOSES (things), in which the signer "pass[es] around the hand showing

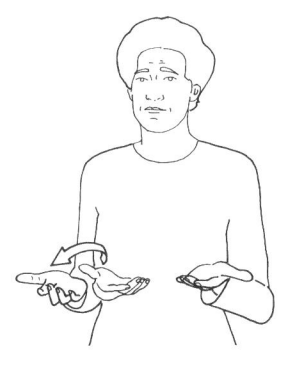

ASL THING 1

THING   281

things" (Ferrand circa 1785). Clark (1885) documents the sign as having a "sinuous motion" from right to left, whereas today the hand moves in one short jump from left to right. Both George Dougherty (*Discovery of Chloroform*, 1913) and Edward Allen Fay (*Dom Pedro's Visit to Gallaudet College*, 1913) signed the contemporary form in their stories for the NAD film series, showing that the sign had evolved by the early twentieth century.

❷ At one time in history, a variant form existed where the hand was configured in a bundled handshape to symbolize an ensemble of things (see "The Bundled Handshape," p. 217). This variant, documented by both Long (1910) and Higgins (1923), has since disappeared from mainstream ASL.

ASL THING 2
(YD from Long 1910)

(ONE) THOUSAND

(ONE) THOUSAND hails directly from the French sign MILLE (thousand), which is "expressed like the Roman number by an M" (de l'Épée 1784). Similar to (ONE) HUNDRED (see entry), (ONE) THOUSAND must be preceded by a number or another qualifier, like SEVERAL, unless it is repeated to express "thousands and thousands." The eventual extension of the thumb ultimately obscured the sign's link with the initialized *M* in both ASL and in LSF.

ASL (ONE) THOUSAND

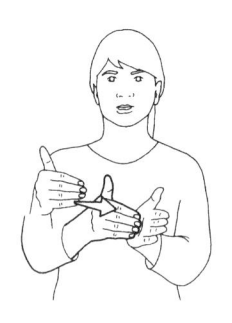

LSF MILLE
(IVT 1986)

TICKET

Higgins (1923) documents TICKET as being produced with the left palm up rather than upright, and cites "the bent index and middle used... to punch the left hand as if it were a ticket." This is a visual representation of how train conductors validate tickets.

ASL TICKET

TIME

❶ In the earliest form, the bent index finger taps the back of the left hand (Clark 1885; Long 1910; Higgins 1923). Though universally believed to be the gesture of pointing to one's watch, TIME hails from the old French sign HEURE (time). Ferrand (circa 1785) described the sign as "show the hammer which hits the bell," and Lambert confirmed this eighty years later (1865), noting "with the right index tap the time on the back of the hand as does a bell." Clark (1885) first documented TIME in the U.S., saying that signers "tap back of left hand near knuckles with tip of slightly-curved index of right hand." This description of the form is consistent with the era since wristwatches had not yet been invented.

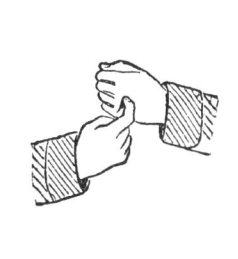

ASL TIME 1, LSF HEURE
(Pélissier 1856)

Old clock with a hammer
(Jean-Javal 1925)

❷ Once wristwatches became widely available in the U.S. in the 1920s, the point of contact for the index finger shifted from the back of the hand to the wrist, thus subtly obscuring the etymon of this seemingly transparent sign.

ASL TIME 2

TIME 283

TIME PERIOD

First documented in the U.S. by Long (1910) and Michaels (1923), this sign is etymologically linked to the LSF sign DATE (date), which is produced with the key handshape today. The symbolism behind the LSF etymon is revealed in the Belgian variant, where the key or ring handshape of the right hand touches the left palm, as if marking a date on a calendar or notepad. In ASL, due to the influence of the English word *time*, the sign was later initialized with the T handshape. Consequently, the left hand is generally interpreted as representing the face of a clock (e.g., Stokoe et al. 1965, p. 219), rather than a piece of paper. This may be a reason for the change in the sign's orientation over time.

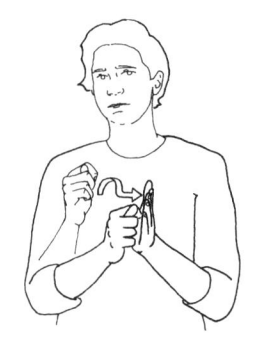

ASL TIME PERIOD

LSF DATE (Belgium)
(CFLSB 1989)

TODAY, NOW

TODAY, NOW originated from the French compound sign AUJOURD'HUI (today), which once consisted of JOUR (day; see DAY) followed by MAINTENANT (now; Lambert 1865). Over time, the sign reduced, probably for ease of production, so that only the second component, MAINTENANT, is still used. In formal registers, however, some signers still return to the original compound. The semantic distinction between *today* and *now* is made through movement; reduplicated movement means "today," and a single drop of the hands means "now." In LSF, the homonymy between MAINTENANT and AUJOURD'HUI has been established for some time. The change from the flat

ASL TODAY, NOW

LSF MAINTENANT
(Lambert 1865)

hands in the etymon to the modified horn handshape in ASL (which is the letter *Y*) perhaps was motivated by the last letter in the English word *today*.

TOMATO

TOMATO was once a compound comprised of the sign RED followed by the sign SLICE. The second part of the compound was produced with either the thumb (Long 1910) or the flat hand (Sternberg 1994). Over time, the extended index finger from the sign RED compounded with the left handshape. Frishberg (1976) cites TOMATO as a classic example of the compounding process in ASL, where select elements of two distinct signs—in this case, the handshapes of RED and SLICE—merge into one.

ASL TOMATO

TOMORROW

Identical to the French sign DEMAIN (tomorrow), TOMORROW means "one day in the future" where the extended thumb represents the LSF number UN (one; see "UN (One): The Hidden Number," p. 239) projected forward along the axis of time (see "Axis of Time," p. 286). This sign was first documented by Clark (1885), who notes that the right hand moves "to front from right shoulder." This movement is consistent with the French etymon, which also never touched the cheek. In contemporary ASL, the sign's initial location has raised from the shoulder to the cheek.

ASL TOMORROW

LSF DEMAIN
(Pélissier 1856)

Axis of Time

Linguists typically describe signs according to their main components (or *parameters*): handshape, orientation, location, movement, and nonmanual markers (namely, facial expressions). Handshape tends to receive the most attention in discussions of the metaphorical or symbolic meanings that link signs to sign families (e.g., Frishberg 1976). However, movement and location are the central features linking a family of signs that depict the passing of time.

In the earliest documentations of LSF, de l'Épée (1784) noted that the signer's body represented the present, while the past and future were denoted by displacing the hand behind or in front of the body, respectively (78). Thus, an invisible, contiguous timeline was conceived of as running horizontally along the side of the signer.

Four French signs have influenced a set of vocabulary in ASL relating to the passing of time along this axis: RESTER (stay), DURÉE (last), CONTINUER (continue), and JUSQUE (until). In RESTER, "the image is one of an object that is fixed on another" (Lambert 1865, 244) and the right thumb presses down on the left to hold it in place. The hands drop straight down, indicating no movement along the axis of time. DURÉE, first described by de Gérando (1827), is identical to RESTER in all parameters save for movement: "press the right thumb in a cross over the left and advance them as far as the arms can reach" (585). The forward movement, then, expressed the concept of something that endures or *stays* over time. JUSQUE was described by several authors as one or both hands configured in the letter *J* moving forward along the axis of time. A derivation of this sign, also through initialization with the letter *P,* is PENDANT (while).

The movement (or lack of movement) distinguishes each sign in this ensemble; it is also the primary feature that has remained consistent throughout history. Handshape, on the other hand, does not provide as uniform a trace to link these signs together. The range of configurations has, in fact, helped to obscure the etymologies of each sign. Consider first the sign STAY, once described by Higgins (1942) as "one thumb holds the other down so it stays." Both Long (1910) and Higgins (1923) describe the hands as configured in the letter *A,* identical to its French etymon. The contemporary form, however, contains both an extended thumb and extended little finger. In contrast, Higgins (1942) described the sign CONTINUE as "right thumb holding down left thumb nail for 'Stay' and both hands move forward. . . . The forward movement brings in the idea of continuity" (20). Here, the original handshape that we see in LSF and early ASL is maintained. The movement of these signs remained consistent over time, but the shift in handshape in STAY contributed to its distinction from CONTINUE. The evolution of the handshape in this family of signs is proved incomplete in Edward Miner Gallaudet's story about Lorna Doone (1910), where he signs CONTINUE with the little fingers extended, thus combining elements of the sign STAY with CONTINUE.

Stokoe et al. (1965) were the first to semantically link the signs STILL, CONTINUE, and STAY with the sign SAME AS, lending some understanding as to how the group of signs is linked etymologically. All of these "express the concept of continuity, or duration, or lack of change" (11). SAME AS incorporates the modified horn handshape thrust downward much like STAY. Signers can inflect this sign with movements to convey concepts such as "monotonous," which is SAME AS with a vertical, circular movement; "all the same," SAME AS tracing a wide horizontal circle in front of the signer; "nothing has changed," SAME AS produced with short, downward taps in front of the signer (this is similar to the LSF sign TOUJOURS PAREIL [always the same]). Today, SAME AS is used as a comparative—moving the sign back and forth between two entities indicates similarity.

In the last sign under this family, STILL, we see both hands configured in the handshape of STAY and SAME AS moving in parallel away from the signer's body to indicate the passing of time (much like the sign DURING and the LSF PENDANT [during]). The notion of continuity is imbued in both the handshape and the movement along the axis of time.

The ubiquity of these signs in ASL likely contributed to the variety of forms and the evolution of meanings that we see after transmission to the U.S. by Clerc. By analyzing them as a lexical family, we are able to see more clearly the linguistic resources, such as movement and location in addition to handshape, that allow signers the ability to express highly specific concepts in subtle ways. Both ASL and LSF contain an array of signs that employ the location and movement along this invisible line to convey some aspect of the passage of time.

TOUCHED

The ASL sign TOUCHED is similar in form and meaning to the French sign TOUCHÉ (touched) drawn by Lambert (1865) with the caption "touched heart" and the accompanying translations "be touched," "have pity," and "moved." Traditionally, the heart is the site of emotions. In this sign, the heart is touched by the bent middle finger, which is the handshape in ASL and LSF that indicates physical and emotional sensations (see CONCERN and PITY and "Handshape Change," p. 148).

ASL TOUCHED

LSF TOUCHÉ
(Lambert 1865)

TOUGH

The sign TOUGH combines two metaphorical associations with hardness: the fist handshape (see METAL 1) and the sternum. The downward thrusting movement denotes a tearing of or attack on the heart, as Blanchet (1850) described in his entry ATROCITÉ (atrocity). There are no historical documents linking the ASL sign with the LSF sign ABÎMÉ, ASSASSIN (ruined, murderer); however, the proximity in form and meaning indicates a likely connection. Today, the meaning of the LSF sign has expanded to include "criminal," "murderer," and "ruined," while the ASL sign has retained the original meaning "tough," in addition to "gang."

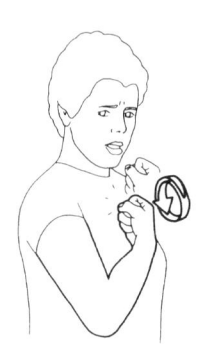

ASL TOUGH, LSF ABÎMÉ, ASSASSIN
(IVT 1986)

TRAIN

This sign originates from the old French sign TRAIN (train), which is still used in Saint-Laurent-en-Royans. The left hand represents the tracks while the right hand represents the passage of a train. Clark (1885) was the first American author to record this sign under his entry RAILWAY CAR, stating that it "indicate[s] the iron rails and movement over same." That sign was originally produced with forked handshapes instead of the paintbrush configuration we see today, and the right hand was held parallel to the left to depict the movement of the train over the tracks. Higgins (1923, 1942) notes that at one point the right hand was configured with two hooks "show[ing] the wheels moving along the rails" (1942). The short, repeated movement in contemporary ASL evolved from the single long movement, and, as a result, it no longer reveals much of the original iconicity.

ASL TRAIN

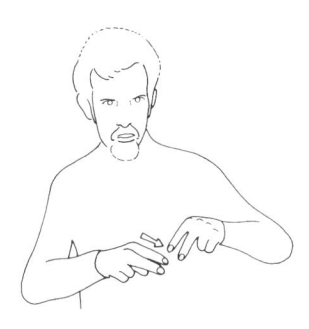

LSF TRAIN
(YD from St-Laurent 1979)

TRASH, GARBAGE

A sign of uncertain origin, TRASH, GARBAGE is possibly a homonym of the sign LETTUCE, CABBAGE (see entry) where the resemblance between the mouthing of the English words "cabbage" and "garbage" led to the link between the semantically distinct signs. Coincidentally, the same correlation between *cabbage* and *garbage* occurred in English in the seventeenth century, when *cabbage* had two alternate spellings: *garbage* and *carbage* (Hoad 1996).

ASL TRASH, GARBAGE

TRIP

❶ The source of TRIP 1 is uncovered in the LSF sign ALLER (go), which is produced by "roll[ing] the index fingers around each other" (Sicard 1808). This same form was first recorded in the U.S. in Veditz's film *Preservation of the Sign Language* (1913), and it has remained unchanged since. The location of TRIP 1 tends to be a bit higher than neutral signing space, in contrast to the more banal sign GO 1 (see entry), suggesting visits to faraway places.

❷ A second variant has since emerged in ASL where the bent middle fingers articulate the same circular movement. Both TRIP 1 and TRIP 2 can also mean "tornado."

ASL TRIP 1

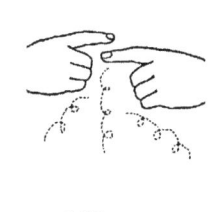

LSF ALLER
(Lambert 1865)

ASL TRIP 2

TRIVIAL, UNIMPORTANT

Undocumented by older authors, the ASL sign likely derived from the French sign IL N'Y A PAS (there's nothing). Instead of the circular movement in the LSF sign, TRIVIAL, UNIMPORTANT exhibits a straight back and forth movement of the hands toward the center of the signing space. The meaning has become quite specific in ASL and is used only to characterize something as inconsequential, whereas the LSF sign is taken literally to mean "nothing."

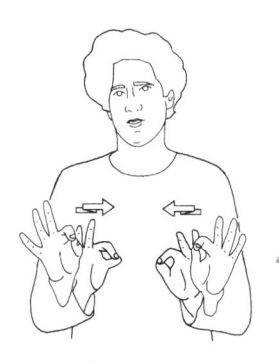

ASL TRIVIAL,
UNIMPORTANT

LSF IL N'Y A PAS
(IVT 1986)

TROUBLE

❶ TROUBLE 1 comes directly from the French sign TROUBLÉ (troubled). Sicard (1808) explains "this sign is produced with both hands that serve to imitate the confusion, the darkness that obfuscates the eyes, and that halfway covers the view of objects in the environment." First documented in the U.S. by Clark (1885), the sign is produced in this earlier form by Robert McGregor in the film *A Lay Sermon—The Universal Brotherhood of Man and Fatherhood of God* (1913). The ASL sign WORRY is derived by initialization with the W handshape.

ASL TROUBLE 1

LSF TROUBLÉ
(IVT 1986)

❷ A derivative of TROUBLE 1, TROUBLE 2 begins with the hands on either side of the head and the right hand above the left. Then both wrists bend down in a single movement. Higgins (1942) characterizes it as "so many things are happening to me that I am almost swamped."

ASL TROUBLE 2

TRUE

TRUE is inherited from the LSF sign VÉRITABLE (true), which Ferrand (circa 1785) described as "move the index directly outwards from the mouth." The direct path of movement represents evenness, while moving the sign away from the mouth symbolizes sincerity. The sign has long been a substitute for the copula verb *to be* (Clark 1899; Higgins 1923), linking the notion of existence with that of truth—a connection that was also inherited from the LSF ÊTRE (be): "sign LIFE, sign TRUE"

ASL TRUE

(Blanchet 1850). Today, the ASL sign TRUE has expanded in meaning to include "real," "really," and "sure."

TRY

❶ In the earliest records of TRY (Long 1910; Veditz 1913) we see the old French sign COURAGE (bravery, fortitude) which signers produced by "bending the arms and closing their fists" to demonstrate the "sign of force" (Sicard 1808). The symbolism behind the closed fists projected away from the body is consistent with the French meaning "courage" and the American meaning "try." In both cases, the sign represents "an effort made" (Higgins 1942). The movement away from the body reinforces this symbolism, as if the signer were encountering and then overcoming an obstacle.

ASL TRY 1
(YD from Long 1910)

LSF COURAGE
(Lambert 1865)

❷ In TRY 2, the sign's arced movement doubly reinforces the idea of making an intense effort at overcoming an obstacle. The initialization of the sign with the T handshape also appeared in Higgins (1923), and this has obscured the sign's original etymology. Likewise, the noninitialized variation of TRY, now produced with the extended thumb handshape, further ruptures the link with the original symbolic meaning associated with the fists.

ASL TRY 2

TURN

TURN is not documented in historical texts; however, a similar sign exists in contemporary LSF as TOUR (turn), where the small crescent handshape rotates out toward the individual who is granted a turn. It is possible that the crescent handshape in the LSF sign is a modified form of the LSF number DEUX (two). If these forms are indeed related, the extended thumb and index finger in the ASL sign are also traces of DEUX, while the movement symbolizes taking turns, as in "first me, then you."

ASL TURN

LSF TOUR
(IVT 1986)

TWENTY, TWENTY-ONE

Inherited from LSF, the signs TWENTY and TWENTY-ONE both maintain traces of the French number DEUX (two), where the index finger and thumb are raised. The bending of the thumb (rather than the index finger) in TWENTY-ONE exhibits an integration of the French and American counting systems, where the raised index finger (not the thumb) is the number sign ONE.

ASL TWENTY

ASL TWENTY-ONE

U

UGLY

❶ UGLY 1 is used when a signer is emphatic, and it most closely resembles the etymon documented by the older authors (Clark 1885; Long 1910; Higgins 1923). Long characterized UGLY as "the hands going up and down alternately as if distorting the face." In contemporary ASL, this sign is glossed as FACIAL EXPRESSION and is embellished with an unattractive expression. Long (1910) documented the first step in the evolution of this sign in a second variant, which he described as "bring [the forefingers] up in front of the face so that the fingers are . . . barely crossed . . . draw the hands apart toward the sides."

ASL UGLY 1

❷ Over time, signers dropped the nondominant hand and the right index finger maintained the movement of UGLY 1. The iconicity of an ugly facial expression inherent in UGLY 1 has since dissipated in the contemporary form, having been replaced by two metaphorical abstractions associated with negative aspects in ASL—the hooked index finger and the nose.

ASL UGLY 2

UNDERSTAND

This sign derives from the old French sign COMPRENDRE (understand), described as "press the index on the forehead then draw it out suddenly" (Lambert 1865). To Lambert, this form symbolized the sprouting of the spirit from the head. In early descriptions of UNDERSTAND (Clark 1885; Long 1910; Higgins 1923), the curved index finger pointed to the forehead then moved out as it straightened. Today, the sign's initial handshape is a fist from which the index finger subsequently flicks up. The hand does not contact the head except in emphatic instances.

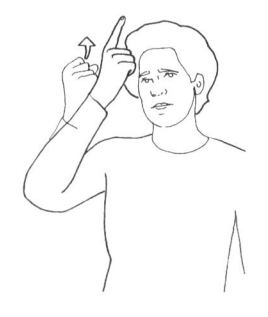

ASL UNDERSTAND

LSF COMPRENDRE
(Lambert 1865)

UNSKILLED

The etymology of this sign comes from Long (1910), who cites it in his entry DULL, STUPID. He explains that the signer must "place the right C hand so the thumb is directly under knuckle of the forefinger of the left [mitten handshape] and the C measures the imaginary thickness of the skull; move the hand along to the end of the forefinger." This earlier form of the sign, then, depicted someone with a thick skull, which in Western culture represents a lack of aptitude or intelligence. Later, the left hand closed around the right thumb, and the horizontal movement of the right hand along the length of the forefinger was replaced by a rotation of the wrist, likely to ease production. In addition, the right hand opened, further obscuring the metaphor of a thick skull.

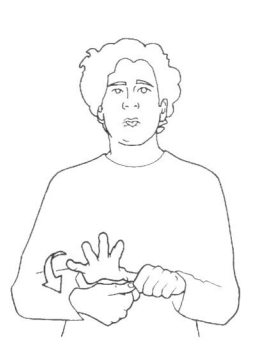

ASL UNSKILLED

UNTIL, TO

This sign hails from an invented French sign for the preposition *to*. Sicard (1808) first cites it under the entry JUSQUE (until), describing it as "1) Determine a point on the left. 2) Trace a horizontal line from the right ending at that point." This sign continues to be used today in ASL with a slight reduction in movement. However, in formal registers or emphatic contexts, a much larger signing space can be utilized, as was the case in the etymon.

ASL UNTIL, TO

URGE

URGE comes from the French sign FORCER (stimulate), similar in meaning to the French word *aiguillonner* (spur on), which figuratively means "incite." The key handshapes depict hands holding a stick to prod cattle.

ASL URGE

LSF FORCER
(IVT 1997)

Farmer prodding oxen
(from *La Semaine de Suzette* 1919)

USE, WEAR

USE, WEAR derives from the old French sign HABITUDE (habit), where the index finger spiraled upward to symbolize repetition (Lambert 1865). The borrowing of the French sign HABITUDE to mean "use" is due to the semantic proximity of the French words *habitude* (habit), *usage* (use), *utile* (useful), and *utiliser* (use). In Lambert's (1865) entry UTILE, he refers the reader to the entry USAGE, where he then refers the reader to the entry HABITUDE. Similarly, Blanchet (1850) refers the reader to USAGE in his entry for HABITUDE. Additionally, the old LSF sign became initialized with the letter *H,* which is close in form to the letter *U*. Once transmitted to ASL, the sign assumed a circular movement in lieu of a spiral and lowered in the signing space. In older ASL variants, the sign is produced near the stomach (e.g., in Veditz's film *Preservation of the Sign Language,* 1913). The addition of the left flat hand as a base on which the signing hand is centered, has further obscured the sign's etymological relationship with HABITUDE. The alternate meaning of "wear" likely stems from the false association of the English word *habit* with the French word *habit* (clothes).

ASL USE, WEAR

LSF HABITUDE
(Lambert 1865)

V

VACATION

Several signs, both old and contemporary, have slightly different forms, but they share the common meaning "off from work." Higgins (1923) glossed the sign as IDLE, NO WORK or HOLIDAY and described it as the thumbs resting on the chest "under imaginary suspenders" with the "other fingers hanging down loosely." Long (1910) described a similar sign glossed as IDLE, but with the fingers wiggling. Higgins (1923) had another sign glossed as HOLIDAY in which the thumbs alternately contacted the chest. All of these variations are essentially gestural translations of a social stereotype describing the posture of a person who is unemployed, standing with their thumbs under their overalls. The immobile fingers reinforce the symbolism behind the sign—idle or nonworking hands.

ASL VACATION

VAIN

Long (1910) was the first American author to document this sign. The two forked hands represent either the regard of others that vain people desire or looking at oneself in the mirror. Higgins (1923) wrote that "the finger tips are one's eyes gazing at one's features." The same sign exists in LSF, where it can be translated by the French expression *m'as-tu-vu?* (did you look at me?).

ASL VAIN

VEHICLE (PARKED)

This sign depicts vehicles that move on the ground (cars, buses, and trains) and through water (boats). The latter type of vehicle is responsible for the trident hand configuration. At one time, the three fingers raised vertically represented the three masts of a ship. This etymology is explicit in Long (1910), Higgins (1923), and Michaels (1923). Higgins describes the etymon as "upright fingers and thumb are the masts of the ship as it rides the waves." From the founding of ASD in 1817 until the early twentieth century, ships and trains were the most widely used vehicles for transportation. Once automobiles became more popular, American Deaf people applied the form of the sign SHIP to the newfound mode of transportation. Today, the unusual, and presumably arbitrary, handshape that depicts a variety of vehicles is, in fact, rooted in a definitively iconic form. One sign, SHIP, retains the hand configuration and iconicity of the etymon.

ASL VEHICLE (PARKED)

ASL SHIP
(Michaels 1923)

ASL SHIP

VIRGIN

❶ This sign, initialized with the V handshape, originally represented the Virgin Mary's halo (Long 1910; Higgins 1923).

❷ Due to the pressure of gestural economy, the movement of the contemporary sign has been reduced to the V gliding down the cheek. As the sign's production simplified over time, its meaning broadened from referring exclusively to the Virgin Mary to referring to any virgin, male or female.

ASL VIRGIN 1
(YD from Higgins 1923)

Mary and her halo
(Alain 1924)

ASL VIRGIN 2

VOLUNTEER, APPLY FOR

The sign as it exists today was first mentioned in Long (1910) as "catch the lapel of the coat (or imaginary lapel) with thumb and forefinger . . . and lift up as if selecting and offering oneself for service." Although the contemporary ASL form still means "volunteer," its use has expanded to include applying for a job as well as the actual application itself.

ASL VOLUNTEER, APPLY FOR

W

WAIT

The fingers of both open hands wiggle in the sign WAIT, which is documented by Long (1910), Higgins (1923), and Michaels (1923). It comes from the old French sign ATTENDRE (wait), in which the fingers repeatedly bend "as if pulling something towards the self" (Blanchet 1850). The signs WAIT and HOPE (see entry) are closely linked in form and meaning, and they are founded on the same metaphor—one pulls toward the self that which one waits for or hopes to receive. WAIT has evolved in ASL such that the fingers alternately wiggle instead of bend.

ASL WAIT

LSF ATTENDRE
(Pélissier 1856)

WALK

❶ Higgins (1923) clearly depicts the sign still in use today as "prone hands pointing outward, moved up and down alternately as if walking with them." The sign, therefore, is an iconic representation of feet walking.

❷ In another variant, the trident handshape is used. This form comes from the LSF sign PAYSAN (peasant), which depicts the stereotypically awkward gait of a country peasant. The existence of WALK 2 in ASL reinforces the etymology of the sign AWKWARD (see entry), which derives from the same LSF etymon.

ASL WALK 1

ASL WALK 2

WANT

The sign WANT is based on the gestural metaphor of drawing toward the self that which is desired. This sign is similar in form and meaning to the old French sign VOULOIR (want), produced as follows: "clench the fingers of the two hands . . . draw them together towards yourself" (Blanchet 1850). Both Long (1910) and Higgins (1923) document the ASL sign with a similar description. The only change in the contemporary form is that the inward movement has shifted to a downward movement. This evolution also occurred in LSF. The original form of WANT continues to be used in ASL.

ASL WANT

LSF VOULOIR
(Pélissier 1856)

WAR

The contemporary ASL sign WAR derives from the old French sign GUERRE (war), which has been maintained without modification in Saint-Laurent-en-Royans, France. Ferrand's (circa 1785) characterization of the form furnishes its etymology: "armies lined up for battle on two sides," where the movement of the hands symbolizes the attack and retreat of troops in battle.

ASL WAR

LSF GUERRE
(YD from St-Laurent 1979)

WARM

❶ The etymon of this variant is the old French sign CHAUD (hot), described by Blanchet (1850) as "the open hand, palm placed in front of the mouth, simulates the action of warming the hand with one's breath." Clark's (1885) description of the first part of HOT consists of the "nearly-closed right hand"—the bundled handshape found in WARM 1. The opening of the hand in the second part of WARM 1 represents the movement of the breath, a common gesture from the nineteenth century.

❷ In the first part of this regional variation (Alabama; E. Shaw, field observation), we see traces of the first part of the LSF sign CHAUD. There is no documented evidence accounting for the closed hand at the end of the sign, though it is possible that the movement depicts grasping the warmth of the breath in the hand.

ASL WARM 1

LSF CHAUD
(Pélissier 1856)

ASL WARM 2

WARN

This sign originated in the old French sign AVERTIR (warn), which depicted the act of "push[ing] the arm of someone with the intent to say 'pay attention, be careful'" (Ferrand circa 1785). Higgins (1923) documented the sign in his entry ADVISE. As a result of the widely documented evolutionary tendency to reduce complexity, the long, single movement of the original sign transformed into a short and repeated one in both LSF and ASL.

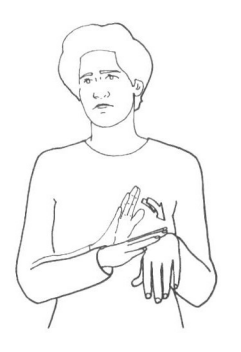

ASL WARN

LSF AVERTIR
(Pélissier 1856)

WEEK

In the ASL sign WEEK, the left hand is widely believed to represent the four weeks in a calendar month, while the extended index finger of the right hand depicts the passing of one of those weeks. The origin of this sign, however, does not correspond to the image of a calendar. In LSF, SEMAINE (week) was simply the French number SEPT (seven) shaken in space (Pélissier 1856). Conforming to the French gestural system for numbering, SEPT was produced by presenting the five fingers of one hand and the extended thumb and index finger of the other hand (the French DEUX [two]). A regional sign used in Saint-Laurent-en-Royans is an intermediary form between the earlier LSF and the ASL signs—the left hand, representing the number 5, rested under the right hand, representing the number 2, and together they symbolized the seven days in a week. The original shaking movement noted by Pélissier reduced to a slight back-and-forth movement. Roth (1941) confirms this etymology in his entry WEEK, in which he states that signers "hold the left hand with the fingers spread before you. (This is to represent the five days.) Lay the thumb and index finger of the right hand in the left palm. (This is two more, to make the seven days of the week.) Push the hands out, letting the right hand slip off the left palm a little farther out." The fact that the French number DEUX was not used in ASL (see "UN (One): The Hidden Number," p. 239) easily allowed for the thumb to contract, resulting in the extended index finger of the right hand. This simple evolution in form ultimately triggered (or was triggered by) the reinterpreted etymology.

ASL WEEK

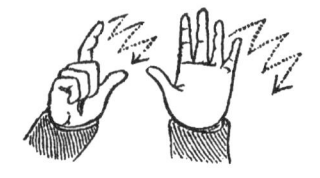

LSF SEMAINE
(Pélissier 1856)

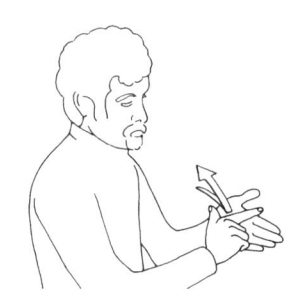

LSF SEMAINE
(YD from St-Laurent 1979)

WHAT

❶ Long (1910) and Michaels (1923) note that WHAT 1 was a compound composed of striking "the index finger of the left hand with the right index finger" (the sign TO) and then moving "the right hand with the palm turned up out in front of you" (Michaels). The second part of the compound is the "natural sign" (Ferrand circa 1785) the older French authors described that one uses "each time one questions" (Brouland 1855). This gesture is also used by Trappist monks (Y. Delaporte, field observation). At the beginning of the twentieth century, the second part of the compound was used for the meanings "where," "what," and "which." For example, Long cites this form under his entry WHERE, and Higgins (1923) notes "which" as a translation under his entry WHAT. Eventually, the first part of the compound disappeared in ASL.

ASL WHAT 1 (second part of compound)
LSF QU'EST CE QUE C'EST?
(Pélissier 1856)

❷ Over time, distinct ASL signs developed to convey each interrogative (e.g., *where, which*, etc.). WHAT 2 is likely the result of assimilation of the original components of WHAT 1, such that the right index finger of the first part now traces over the fingers of the open left hand. WHAT 1 and WHAT 2 co-existed in the early twentieth century (Long 1910; Higgins 1923); however, WHAT 1 was already falling out of use. Long notes that WHAT 2 "is preferable" to the compound. Today, the fingers of the left hand are no longer spread and there is no obvious indication that the form was once a compound.

ASL WHAT 2

WHATEVER

Higgins (1923) documents this sign under his entry INDIFFERENT, which he describes as "left hand supine fingers bent upward, palm of fingers leftward, right hand fingers downward, brush back and forth against the left fingers, left fingers yielding to the brushing." Watson (1964) shows this same sign with the right hand slightly elevated over the left as meaning "it makes no difference" or "never mind." WHATEVER derives from the gesture attributed to Pontius Pilate consisting of rubbing the hands to wash away guilt or responsibility. It conveys the meaning "I wash my hands of this" in both English and French. Proof of this etymology can be seen in the contemporary LSF sign BONHEUR (happiness), which is very similar to WHATEVER, and comes from a gesture homonym consisting of rubbing the hands as a sign of satisfaction. In both ASL and LSF the action of rotating the hands over each other changed into brushing against each other.

ASL WHATEVER

Etymon of WHATEVER
(Illustration by Pat Mallet)

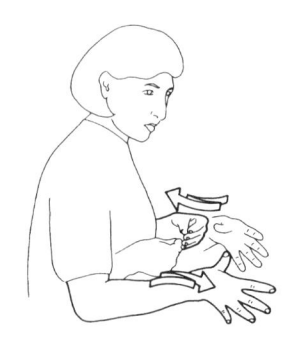

LSF BONHEUR
(IVT 1986)

WHEN

Colloquially interpreted as outlining the face of a clock (Higgins 1942), WHEN is described in one of the earliest accounts of ASL as "intended to represent an interrogation-mark" (Clark 1885). Higgins (1923) illustrates Clark's form, showing the right hand held horizontally and moving in a circle toward the left upright index finger. The imagery of a clock and a question mark are equally suited to

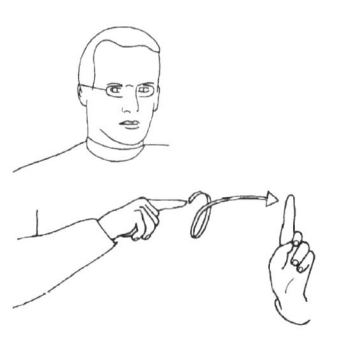

ASL WHEN
(YD from Higgins 1923)

this interrogative sign that can request the time. Today, the right index finger traces a half circle above the left index finger before making contact with the fingertip. The changes from the sign described in Clark and Higgins to the contemporary form have obscured the etymological origin.

ASL WHEN

WHERE, WHAT

Though historically used for all sorts of interrogatives (Long 1910; Higgins 1923; Michaels 1923), this form is now commonly used to mean "where." However, in some areas (e.g., Ohio and Alabama; E. Shaw, field observation) it means "what." The polysemy of this sign stems from the fact that *what*, *where*, and *which* were all conveyed with the same form at the beginning of the twentieth century (see WHAT 1). The extended index finger was originally the second part of a compound that Michaels (1923) documents in his entry WHAT. He explains that it is produced by signing TO, followed by moving the index finger "in a roundabout way in front of you," essentially inquiring "to which of these things do you refer?" Today, the first part of the compound has been dropped.

ASL WHERE, WHAT
(YD)

WHICH

The etymon of this sign is the old LSF sign OU (or), where the extended thumbs symbolize the French number UN (one) (see "UN (One): The Hidden Number," p. 239). The alternating movement of the hands visually conveys the question, *Which one?*

ASL WHICH

LSF OU
(Pélissier 1856)

WHITE

The early French authors report that the location of the sign BLANC (white) on the chest was an indication of the articles of clothing with this color, such as *blouse* (Blanchet 1850), *tie* (Pélissier 1856), *shirt* (Jamet circa 1830), *linen of a blouse* (Lambert 1865), and *the shirt of deaf students' uniforms* (Pellet 1938). An older variant of BLANC corresponds exactly to the contemporary ASL sign WHITE and is described by Blanchet as "simulate the action of seizing a shirt high on the chest with the fist and the fingers of one hand."

ASL WHITE

LSF BLANC
(Pélissier 1856)

WHO

❶ WHO 1 is a very old sign first documented in the nineteenth century by Abel Clark (1899). He describes the form as "the index finger is moved in a circle around the face." Signers continued to use this form into the early twentieth century. In the film *Preservation of the Sign Language* (1913), George Veditz introduces

ASL WHO 1
(YD from Michaels 1923)

himself by producing this form and then pointing to his chest.

❷ WHO 2 emerged at the same time as WHO 1. The large circular movement that traced the outline of the face in WHO 1 is reduced to a small circle outlining the mouth. Higgins (1923) interprets this form as "the pursing of the lips to say 'who.'"

ASL WHO 2

ASL WHO 3

❸ Today, in the most evolved form of WHO, the thumb rests on the chin and the once circular movement of the index finger has reduced to only a small up and down movement in front of the mouth.

❹ This is a rare variant used in Maryland (E. Shaw, field observation), in which the index and middle fingers open and close. The use of two fingers, as opposed to only the index finger, suggests that the open hand may have once been used to circumscribe the face.

ASL WHO 4

WHY

❶ The old LSF sign POURQUOI (why) was once composed of two parts, POUR (for) and QUOI (what) (Pélissier 1856). Ferrand (circa 1785) documented it as "sign POUR sign QUOI accompanied by an advancement of the body and the hands." In Long (1910), WHY is a product of that original compound where the two separate movements— the outward movement of the index finger from the forehead in FOR and the horizontal shaking of the hand in

ASL WHY 1
(YD, from Long 1910)

LSF POURQUOI (POUR + QUOI)
(Pélissier 1856)

WHY 309

WHAT—merged into a single arched movement away from the forehead.

❷ The contemporary ASL sign is produced with the bent middle finger handshape, and the same sign is still used in Saint-Laurent-en-Royans. Higgins (1942) lists *because* as an alternate translation of the sign, which is interesting since WHY and BECAUSE (see entry) are both rooted in French compounds that began with POUR (for)—POUR + QUOI (why) and POUR + ÇA (for that).

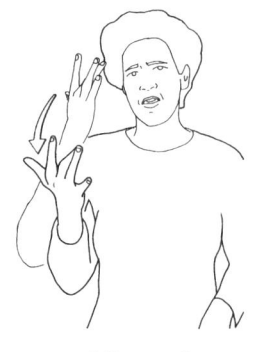

ASL WHY 2

LSF POURQUOI
(YD from St-Laurent 1979)

WILLING

Related to the semantically similar sign ADMIT (see entry), WILLING is a gesture for unburdening the heart toward another by offering one's goodwill (Higgins 1923). The meaning has become somewhat restricted today, so instead of offering goodwill, signers typically use the form to convey they are reluctantly prepared to do something.

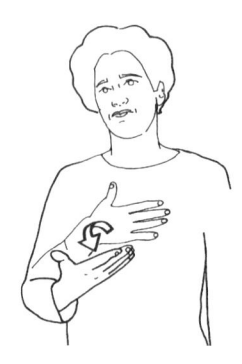

ASL WILLING

WIN

WIN is inherited from the old French sign GAGNER (win), which is similar in form to the gesture of seizing something with the hands, "as if catching a fly in flight" (Lambert 1865; see GET). This sign is also a possible reference to the game of dice, as in "throw the dice, take them" (Jamet circa 1830). Today, due to assimilation, both hands open and close through the course of the sign's production.

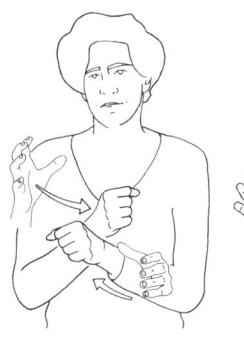

ASL WIN

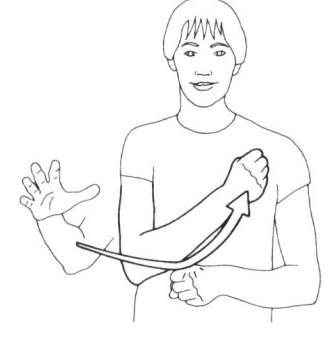

LSF GAGNER
(IVT 1986)

WINE

This form derives from the old French sign VIN (wine), which is produced by "roll[ing] the manual letter V on the cheek" (Lambert 1865). In both ASL and LSF, the placement of the sign on the cheek "indicates the color of wine" (Pélissier 1856). The movement of the ASL sign has remained unchanged; however, the W handshape replaced the V handshape for the English *wine*. It is likely that Clerc and Gallaudet made this change when they introduced the sign in America.

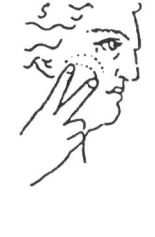

ASL WINE

LSF VIN
(Lambert 1865)

WISE

This is a very old sign that has been documented in the U.S. since the nineteenth century. Clark (1885) recorded WISE as "place the back of curved index against the center of forehead, other fingers and thumb closed; move the index up and down few times." While the location at the head is clearly symbolic of the place where intellectual faculties reside (see KNOW), the handshape and movement are less transparent. Early twentieth-century documents show that WISE was originally a compound. Long (1910) glossed the sign DEEP WISDOM under the same entry as SCIENCE (see SCIENCE 1) and described it as "bring the end of the right forefinger from the head and pierce it through or between the fingers of the [left] hand, indicating that the wisdom goes down deep." In the contemporary sign, the left hand has been dropped completely and the long movement of the right hand has become a short, redoubled one in front of (but not on) the forehead.

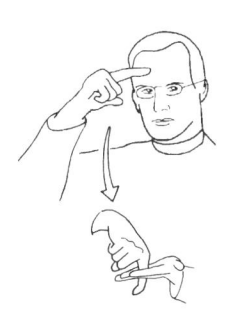

ASL DEEP WISDOM
(YD from Higgins 1923)

ASL WISE

WISH

WISH is metaphorically derived from the sign HUNGER, which originates from LSF. Both signs indicate a yearning for something and are differentiated only by the number of times the sign is produced.

ASL WISH

WITCH

The first part of the sign represents the crooked nose of a witch. There are two possible explanations for the second part of the sign. The hooked index fingers could have derived from the LSF sign MÉCHANT (mean). It is also possible that the end of the sign is a variant of the signs PICK ON or REVENGE (see entries). In either case, the hooked index fingers are used to evoke harshness (see METAL 2 and TEASE).

ASL WITCH

LSF MÉCHANT
(IVT 1986)

WOMAN

❶ WOMAN 1 derives from the compound of GIRL followed by FINE (see entries), which is similar to the old French compound sign MADAME (woman) followed by JABOT (ruffles). Higgins (1923) translates this form with the English word *lady*, denoting a woman of some prestige.

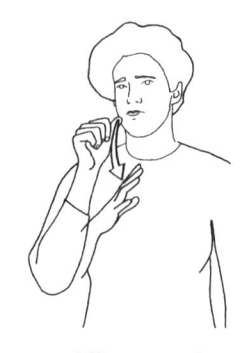

ASL WOMAN 1

LSF MADAME + JABOT
(Lambert 1865)

❷ The handshape of the first part of the compound in WOMAN 1 later modified in anticipation of the open handshape of FINE. The evolution of this form allowed for the emergence of the semantically related sign MOTHER (see entry).

ASL WOMAN 2

WONDER

This sign is inherited from the French sign RÉFLÉCHIR, MÉDITER (reflect, meditate), where the signer would bring the index finger to the forehead and trace small circles on this area (Blanchet 1850). Documented as THINK by Clark (1885), Long (1910), and Higgins (1923), WONDER has changed only slightly in the contemporary form so that the index finger no longer touches the forehead.

ASL WONDER

WON'T, REFUSE

In older forms (Higgins 1923), the closed fist is thrown behind the shoulders, indicating the gesture of a petulant child. Today, the sign is produced with the thumb handshape, rather than the fist. The symbolism behind the movement is literally "throw something away," a gesture widely used by hearing people in Western European cultures. The semantically related signs PROTEST and RESIST (see entries) have retained the original fist handshape.

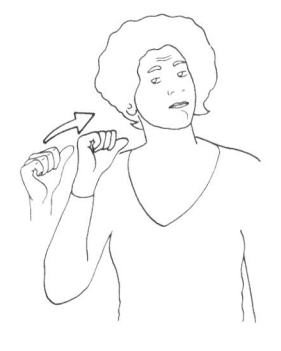

ASL WON'T, REFUSE

"That boy is angry and bad."
(Jacobs 1869)

WORD

This form is identical to the second part of the old LSF compound sign MOT (word), which was composed of the sign NOM (name) followed by a move to "specify the length on the left index finger with the thumb and index of the right hand" (Lambert 1865). Long (1910) observed that, in referring to a word, the placement of the right hand against the left index finger was acting "as if to measure its length." The sign remains unchanged to this day.

ASL WORD

WORK

❶ WORK 1 is widely used in sign languages throughout Europe (France, Germany, Spain, and Greece, to name a few). It has also been used for centuries by Cistercian monks and, more recently, in International Sign. The outer edge of the right fist strikes the inner edge of the left fist much like a manual laborer would employ a tool. The etymon is the LSF sign TRAVAILLER (work), which is also the etymon of the semantically related sign MAKE (see entry). Today, the form remains unchanged in some ASL dialects (for instance in Hawaii; Shroyer and Shroyer 1984) and in some communities of African Americans (E. Shaw, field observation).

ASL WORK 1, LSF TRAVAILLER
(IVT 1986)

❷ In this more frequently used form, which is documented by Long (1910) and Higgins (1923), both wrists have rotated so that the palms are now face down. All of the American authors interpret this sign as representing manual activity. For example, Higgins

ASL WORK 2

314   WORD

(1923) wrote that "one wrist hammered on the other to show effort." This form has become a highly productive base from which many signs have developed via initialization, including BUSINESS, BUSY, DUTY, EMPLOY, ENTERPRISE, FUNCTION, and INDUSTRY, INTERN.

WORK OUT

In this sign, we see a visual motivation similar to that in the sign MACHINE (see entry), where cogs fit into a wheel, thereby allowing a machine to run. By metaphorically abstracting that image, WORK OUT reflects the process by which events transpire smoothly over time.

ASL WORK OUT

WORLD

This sign represents the contours of the globe. The right hand has been initialized since the early twentieth century (Long 1910; Higgins 1923). At the time, the left hand assumed the fist handshape, but later it took on the same handshape as the right, so that both are initialized with the letter *W* today. Several other initialized signs have evolved from WORLD, including INTERNATIONAL, KIND (meaning "type"), ORBIT, and UNIVERSE.

ASL WORLD

WORSE

WORSE is identical to the old French sign MAUVAIS (bad), which was also used as the first part of the old French compound sign PIRE (worse): MAUVAIS followed by PREMIER (first; Lambert 1865). In French culture, the forked handshape often represents the Devil, as is seen in Lambert's 1865 illustration of the sign DIABLE (devil). In an American variant noted by Sternberg (1994), WORSE was followed by an extended thumb, thus retaining the second part of PIRE. (see "UN (One): The Hidden Number," p. 239). The ASL sign MULTIPLY is an unrelated homonym of WORSE.

ASL WORSE

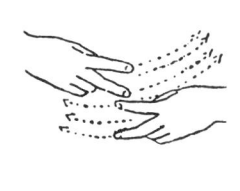

LSF DIABLE
(Lambert 1865)

LSF PIRE: MAUVAIS   +   PREMIER
(Pélissier 1856)   (Lambert 1865)

WORTH, PRICE

Given the sign's composition (its handshape, location, movement, and so on), WORTH, PRICE most likely derived from its antonym WORTHLESS (see entry), which came from the LSF sign SANS, RIEN (without, nothing). Following this reasoning, the ASL sign WORTHLESS was treated as a compound, where Deaf Americans interpreted the initial position of the LSF sign to mean "worth" and the opening of the hands at the end to mean "less" (an analogous relationship exists in the complementary signs WITH and WITHOUT). Indeed, Stokoe et al. (1965) translate WORTHLESS as a compound meaning "worth nothing." Deriving the sign WORTH, then, was a result of back formation where signers simply dropped the second part of the sign WORTHLESS. The semantically and

ASL WORTH, PRICE

etymologically related sign IMPORTANT 2 (see entry) split from the etymon via a shift in movement.

WORTHLESS

WORTHLESS is identical in form to the French sign SANS, RIEN (without, nothing), except that it has lowered from the mouth to the center of the signing space. The two ring handshapes have the value of two zeros, which is reinforced by the opening of the hands to show that they are empty. We also see traces of SANS, RIEN in the ASL sign NOTHING 2 (see entry), where the fists open as they move out from the chin. The ASL sign WORTH, PRICE (see entry) likely derives from WORTHLESS.

ASL WORTHLESS

LSF SANS, RIEN
(IVT 1997)

WRONG

This very old sign was inherited from the LSF TROMPER (deceive), which itself comes from the evil eye gesture widely used throughout the Mediterranean basin by hearing people to mock someone (see "The Veiled Devil," p. 176). In the nineteenth century, the meaning of the French sign would change depending on its orientation: when directed toward the self, it meant "I am wrong;" when directed at someone else, it meant "you are wrong." The shift in meaning from "deceive" to "wrong" was driven by the quasi-homonym in French of *tromper* (deceive) and *se tromper* (wrong). After the loss of

ASL WRONG

its directionality, the sign took on the absolute meaning, in both LSF and ASL, of *se tromper* or "wrong." While the gesture used by European hearing people is made with the horn handshape—the index and little fingers raised—this configuration is rarely seen in LSF and was replaced early on by the raised thumb and little finger. Clerc imported this variant to the U.S. Slight modifications have since emerged that result in distinct meanings in ASL: with a twisting of the wrist, the sign means "accidentally"; with repetitive movements, it means "make repeated mistakes"; and with each hand alternately touching the chin, it means "make many mistakes."

A. LSF se tromper
B. LSF tromper
(Lambert 1865)

Y

YEAR

This sign derives from the French sign ANNÉE (year) recorded by Sicard (1808) and illustrated by Pélissier (1856). Sicard writes that "with the left hand, make the globe of the sun that must be shown as fixed in the center of the movements of our earth and other planets; with the right hand, make the globe of the earth, traversing a big circle around the sun." Its form has remained relatively unchanged in ASL; however, the sign also can be produced with an abbreviated movement where the right fist rotates above the left fist before it is brought to rest on the left hand.

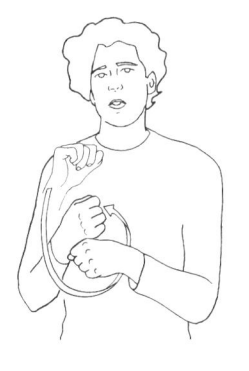

ASL YEAR

LSF ANNÉE
(Pélissier 1856)

YELLOW

The etymon of YELLOW is the old LSF JAUNE (yellow), which Blanchet (1850) described as made with the letter *J*, the first letter of the French word *jaune*. Fortuitously, that handshape is the same as the ASL letter Y, the first letter of the English word *yellow*. This sign has remained unchanged since its inception.

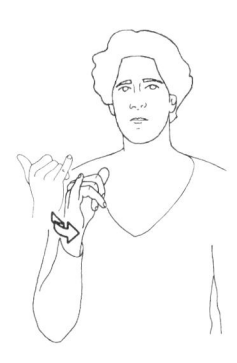

ASL YELLOW

YES

This sign has existed in LSF since the nineteenth century. Lambert (1965) illustrated it initialized with the letter O, the first letter of *oui* (yes). The fist handshape used in the ASL sign likely represents a head nodding in affirmation.

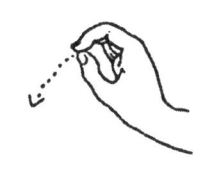

ASL YES

LSF OUI
(Lambert 1865)

YESTERDAY

YESTERDAY comes from the French sign HIER (yesterday) that symbolically represents "one day in the past." The thumb handshape is the LSF number UN (one), and the hand projected behind the body indicates moving along the axis of time (see "UN (One): The Hidden Number," p. 239; and "Axis of Time," p. 286).

❶ In this variant used in Maryland (E. Shaw, field observation), the thumb drops from the base of the cheek to the upper chest. This form retains a trace of the French etymon HIER (yesterday), where the thumb made no contact with the body but moved from near the front of the face to the shoulder.

❷ YESTERDAY 2 is the most commonly used variant in ASL. Long (1910) described it as "place . . . the thumb at the corner of the mouth; throw the hand back and bring the thumb against the cheek again near the ear." This movement is an abbreviation of HIER.

LSF HIER
(Pélissier 1856)

ASL YESTERDAY 1

ASL YESTERDAY 2

YOUNG

This sign derives from the French sign JEUNE (young), which Ferrand (circa 1785) characterizes as "raising the hands on either side by gradation, manual letter J, sign of gaiety, life, and strength." As in the sign LIVE (see entry), YOUNG is motivated by the metaphor that youthfulness is characterized by vigor and the healthy flow of blood through the body. Unlike the LSF sign, the ASL sign is not initialized, and the movement is reduplicated.

ASL YOUNG

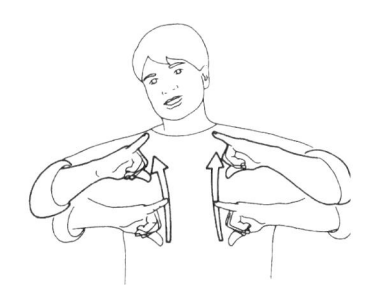

LSF JEUNE
(IVT 1986)

ILLUSTRATION CREDITS

ASL Alphabet	Webster, Noah, and Loomis J. Campbell. 1877. *A Handy Dictionary of the English Language*. New York: Ivison, Blakeman, Taylor.
BOSS	Clamaron, Jérôme. 1875. *Alphabet dactylologique orné de dessins variés*. Paris: Institution nationale des sourds-muets.
BOY	Piroux, Joseph. 1830. *Vocabulaire des sourds-muets*. Nancy, France: L'établissement des sourds-muets.
BREAD	Nineteenth-century engraving from the collection of the Musée du Blé et du Pain, Verdun-sur-le-Doubs.
DOCTOR	Goust, François. 1954. *Médecine pour tous*. Paris: Larousse.
DUMB	Calbris, Geneviève, and Jacques Montredon. 1986. *Des gestes et des mots pour le dire*. Illustrations by Zaü. Paris: Clé International.
FINE	Piroux, Joseph. 1830. *Vocabulaire des sourds-muets*. Nancy, France: L'établissement des sourds-muets.
GIRL	Chazottes, Louis. 1864. *Méthode de Toulouse pour l'instruction des sourds-muets*. Poitiers: Henri Oudin.
HEIGHT	Pastouriaux, Louis, and Victor Régnier. 1954. *Leçons de Sciences*. Paris: Delagrave.
HONOR, RESPECT	Bardy, France de. 1937. *Chansons enfantines du bon vieux temps*. Liège, Belgium: Gordinne.
JUSTICE	Pinloehe, Auguste. 1922. *Vocabulaire par l'image*. Paris: Larousse.
MACHINE	Basquin, René. 1947. *Mécanique*. Paris, Delagrave.
MAN	Agron, Suzanne. 1970. *Précis d'histoire du costume*. Paris: Jacques Lanore.
MANAGE	Hallynck, Pierre, and Maurice Brunet. 1948. *Histoire*. Paris: Masson.
MOON	Blanchet, Alexandre L. P. 1864. *Enseignement des sourds-muets*. Paris: Hachette.
NOISE	*Le Journal de Bébé*, March 1938. Paris: Albin Michel.
OLD	Renard, Marc, and Yves Lapalu. 2000. *Sourd, cent blagues*. Vol. 2. Les Essarts-le-Roi: Éditions du Fox.

PAPER	Blanchet, Alexandre L. P. 1864. *Enseignement des sourds-muets*. Paris: Hachette.
	Clamaron, Jérôme. 1875. *Alphabet dactylologique orné de dessins variés*. Paris: Institution nationale des sourds-muets.
PRESIDENT	Clamaron, Jérôme. 1875. *Alphabet dactylologique orné de dessins variés*. Paris: Institution nationale des sourds-muets.
SAVE	"How the Slaves of Morphine Can Break Their Chains." 1914. *Nos Loisirs*, May.
SILLY	*Le Réveil des Sourds-Muets,* July 1901.
SKINNY	Virolle-Souibès, Marie. 1985. "Gestes emblématiques masculins et mixtes à Alger et en Kabylie." *Geste et image*, 4: 69–107.
SUMMER	Anonymous illustration. 1935. *La Semaine de Suzette*, January.
TASTE	Blanchet, Alexandre L. P. 1864. *Enseignement des sourds-muets*. Paris: Hachette.
TIME	Jean-Javal, Lily. 1925. *Bricolin ou les sept métiers*. Paris: Éditions Gedalge.
URGE	*La Semaine de Suzette*, July 1919.
VIRGIN	Alain, Louis. 1924. *Bible scolaire illustrée*. Paris: Bloud and Gay.
WON'T, REFUSE	Jacobs, John. A. 1867. *Learning to Spell, to Read, to Write, and to Compose,—All at the Same Time. Part I*. New York: D. Appleton.

REFERENCES

Agron, Suzanne. 1970. *Précis d'histoire du costume.* Paris: Jacques Lanore.

Alain, Louis. 1924. *Bible scolaire illustrée.* Paris: Bloud and Gay.

Annual Report of the Directors and Officers of the American Asylum at Hartford, for the Education and Instruction of the Deaf and Dumb. 1887. Hartford, CT: Press of Case, Lockwood and Co.

Bahan, Ben, and Joan C. P. Nash. 1996. "The Formation of Signing Communities," in *Deaf Studies IV: Visions of the Past—Visions of the Future,* 1–26. Washington, DC: Gallaudet University College of Continuing Education and Outreach.

Baker-Shenk, Charlotte, and Dennis Cokely. (1980) 1991. *American Sign Language: A Teacher's Resource Text on Grammar and Culture.* Washington, DC: Gallaudet University Press.

Bakhtin, Mikhail M. 2008. *L'œuvre de François Rabelais et la culture populaire au Moyen Âge et sous la Renaissance.* Translated by Andrée Robel. Paris: Gallimard.

Barakat, Robert. 1975. *Cistercian Sign Language: A Study in Non-verbal Communication.* Kalamazoo, MI: Cistercian Publications.

Bardy, France de. 1937. *Chansons enfantines du bon vieux temps.* Liège, Belgium: Gordinne.

Battison, Robbin M. 1978. *Lexical Borrowing in American Sign Language.* Silver Spring, MD: Linstok Press.

Benoît de Nursie. 1992. *Règle de saint Benoît.* Collection Témoins du Christ. Dourgne: SODEC-AIM.

Berthier, Ferdinand. 1868. *Le Code Napoléon, code civil de l'Empire français, mis à la portée des sourds-muets, de leurs familles et des parlants en rapport journalier avec eux.* Paris: Petit Journal.

Blanchet, Alexandre L. P. (1850) 2007. *Petit dictionnaire usuel de mimique et de dactylologie.* Archives de la langue des signes française. Limoges: Lambert-Lucas.

———. 1864. *Enseignement des sourds-muets.* Paris: Hachette.

Bosworth, Rain G., and Karen Emmorey. 2010. "Effects of Iconicity and Semantic Relatedness on Lexical Access in American Sign Language." *Journal of Experimental Psychology: Learning, Memory, and Cognition* 36(6): 1573–81.

Brdys, Marie-Agnès, et le Groupe de recherche sur le langage gestuel. 1982. *Les mains qui parlent. Éléments de vocabulaire de la langue des signes.* Poitiers: Association des sourds de la Vienne.

Brien, David, ed. 1992. *Dictionary of British Sign Language/English.* London, Boston: Faber & Faber.

Brothers of St. Gabriel. (1853–1854) 2006. *Iconographie des signes.* Archives de la langue des signes française. Limoges: Lambert-Lucas.

Brouland, Joséphine. 1855. *Spécimen d'un dictionnaire des signes.* Poster of 132 illustrations. Paris: Institution impériale des sourds-muets.

Brown, J. S. 1856. *A Vocabulary of Mute Signs.* Baton Rouge: Morning Comet Office.

Cagle, Keith. 2010. "Exploring the Ancestral Roots of American Sign Language: Lexical

Borrowing from Cistercian Sign Language and French Sign Language." PhD diss., University of New Mexico. ProQuest (UMI number 3409321).

Calbris, Geneviève, and Jacques Montredon. 1986. *Des gestes et des mots pour le dire*. Illustrations by Zaü. Paris: Clé International.

Calbris, Geneviève, and Louis Porcher. 2002. *Geste et communication*. Paris: Didier.

Carénini, André. 1991. "La symbolique manuelle." In *Histoire des mœurs II, vol. 1*, edited by Jean Poirier, 75–162. Paris: Gallimard.

Centre Francophone de la Langue des Signes de Belgique. 2002. *Lexique de signes*. Bruxelles: Centre Francophone de la Langue des Signes de Belgique.

Chazottes, Louis. 1864. *Méthode de Toulouse pour l'instruction des sourds-muets*. Poitiers: Henri Oudin.

Clamaron, Jérôme. 1875. *Alphabet dactylologique orné de dessins variés*. Paris: Institution nationale des sourds-muets.

Clark, Abel S. 1899. *The Lord's Prayer in the Sign Language*. Hartford, CT: Connecticut Magazine Co.

Clark, William P. 1885. *The Indian Sign Language: With Brief Explanatory Notes of the Gestures Taught Deaf-Mutes in Our Institutions*. Philadelphia: L. R. Hamersly and Co.

Costadau, Alphonse. 1720. *Traité historique et critique des principaux signes qui servent à manifester les pensées*. Lyon: Frères Bruyset.

Costello, Elaine. 1994. *American Sign Language Dictionary*. New York: Random House.

———. 1995. *Signing: How to Speak With Your Hands*. New York: Bantam Books.

———. 1999. *Concise American Sign Language Dictionary*. New York: Random House.

Davis, Anne. 1966. *The Language of Signs*. New York: Domestic and Foreign Missionary Society of the Protestant Episcopal Church in the United States of America.

Davis, Jeffrey E. 2010. *Hand Talk: Sign Language among American Indian Nations*. Cambridge: Cambridge University Press.

De Jorio, Andrea. (1832) 2000. *Gesture in Naples and Gesture in Classical Antiquity*. Translated by Adam Kendon. Bloomington, IN: Indiana University Press.

Delaporte, Yves. 2007. *Dictionnaire étymologique et historique de la langue des signes française. Origine et évolution de 1200 signes*. Les Essarts-le-Roi: Éditions du Fox.

———. 2008. "Quand le pouce se fixe sur le corps. Continuité et discontinuité dans l'histoire des signes." *Patrimoine Sourd* 23: 18–24.

Delaporte, Yves, and Yvette Pelletier. 2012. *Signes de Pont-de-Beauvoisin. Le dialecte du quartier des filles de l'Institution nationale des sourds-muets et sourdes-muettes de Chambéry 1910–1960*. Limoges: Lambert-Lucas.

de l'Épée, Charles M. (1784) 1984. *La véritable manière d'instruire les sourds et muets, confirmée par une longue expérience*. Collection Corpus des œuvres de philosophie en langue française. Paris: Fayard.

Dougherty, George T. 1913. *Discovery of Chloroform*. Washington, DC: National Association of the Deaf.

Dudis, Paul G. 2004. "Body Partitioning and Real-Space Blends." *Cognitive Linguistics* 15(2): 223–38.

Fay, Edward Allen. 1913. *Dom Pedro's Visit to Gallaudet College*. Washington, DC: National Association of the Deaf.

Ferrand, Jean. (ca 1785) 2008. *Dictionnaire à l'usage des sourds et muets*. Archives de la langue des signes française. Limoges: Lambert-Lucas.

Frishberg, Nancy. 1975. "Arbitrariness and Iconicity: Historical Change in American Sign Language." *Language* 51: 696–719.

———. 1976. "Some Aspects of the Historical Development of Signs in American Sign Language." PhD diss., University of California, San Diego.

Gallaudet, Edward Miner. 1910. *The Lorna Doone Country of Devonshire, England*. Washington, DC: National Association of the Deaf.

Gannon, Jack. (1981) 2012. *Deaf Heritage: A Narrative History of Deaf America*. Washington, DC: Gallaudet University Press.

Gérando, Joseph M. de. 1827. *De l'éducation des sourds-muets de naissance*. Paris: Méquignon.

Gordon, Joseph C. 1892. *Education of the Deaf: Notes and Observations, with Revised Index*. Washington, DC: Volta Bureau.

Groce, Nora E. 1985. *Everyone Here Spoke Sign Language: Hereditary Deafness on Martha's Vineyard*. Cambridge, MA: Harvard University Press.

Guy, Jean-Claude. 1993. *Les apophtegmes des Pères*. Paris: Cerf.

Hadley, Lewis F. 1893. *Indian Sign Talk*. Chicago: Baker and Co.

Hallynck, Pierre, and Maurice Brunet. 1948. *Histoire*. Paris: Masson.

Higgins, Daniel D. (1923) 1942. *How to Talk to the Deaf*. Chicago: Paluch.

Hoad, Terry F., ed. 1996. *The Concise Oxford Dictionary of English Etymology*. Oxford: Oxford University Press.

Hotchkiss, John B. 1913. *Memories of Old Hartford*. Washington, DC: National Association of the Deaf.

International Visual Theater. 1986–1997. *La langue des signes. Dictionnaire bilingue LSF/français*. 3 vols. Vincennes: Centre socio-culturel des sourds.

Jacobs, J. A. 1869. *Learning to Spell, to Read, to Write, and to Compose,—All at the Same Time. Part I*. New York: D. Appleton and Company.

Jamet, P. ca 1830. *Dictionnaire des signes*. Two unpublished manuscripts. Caen, France: Communauté du Bon Sauveur; Albi, France: Institution des sourds-parlants.

Jean-Javal, Lily. 1925. *Bricolin ou les sept métiers*. Paris: Éditions Gedalge.

Kendon, Adam. 2004. *Gesture: Visible Action as Utterance*. Cambridge: Cambridge University Press.

Klima, Edward S., and Ursula Bellugi. 1979. *The Signs of Language*. Cambridge, MA: Harvard University Press.

Labov, William. 1972. "Some Principles of Linguistic Methodology." *Language and Society* 1: 97–120.

Lambert, Louis-Marie. (1865) 2005. *Dictionnaire de la langue des signes française d'autrefois*, edited by Yves Delaporte. Paris: Éditions du CTHS.

Lane, Harlan. 1984. *When the Mind Hears: A History of the Deaf*. New York: Random House.

———. 1999. *The Mask of Benevolence*. San Diego: Dawn Sign Press.

La Providence. 1979. *Langage gestuel*. Saint-Laurent-en-Royans: La Providence, Institut médico-pédagogique pour déficients auditifs.

Laveau, François. (1868) 2006. *Petit dictionnaire de signes illustré*. Archives de la langue des signes française. Limoges: Lambert-Lucas.

Liddell, Scott. 2003. *Grammar, Gesture, and Meaning in American Sign Language*. Cambridge: Cambridge University Press.

Liddell, Scott K., and Robert E. Johnson. 1986. "American Sign Language Compound Formation Processes, Lexicalization, and Phonological Remnants." *Natural Language and Linguistic Theory* 4(4): 445–513.

Littré, Émile. 1863–1872. *Dictionnaire de la langue française*. Paris: Hachette.

Long, J. Schuyler. 1910. *The Sign Language. A Manual of Signs*. Iowa City: Athens Press.

Lubar, Steven. 1992. "'Do Not Fold, Spindle or Mutilate': A Cultural History of the Punch Card." *Journal of American Culture* 15(4): 43–55.

Lucas, Ceil. 1995. "Sociolinguistic Variation in ASL: The Case of DEAF." In *Sociolinguistics in Deaf Communities*, edited by Ceil Lucas, 3–25. Washington, DC: Gallaudet University Press.

Lucas, Ceil, Robert Bayley, Ruth Reed, and Alyssa Wulf. 2001. "Lexical Variation in African American and White Signing." *American Speech* 76(4): 339–60.

McCaskill, Carolyn, Ceil Lucas, Robert Bayley, and Joseph C. Hill. 2011. *The Hidden Treasure of Black ASL: Its History and Structure*. Washington, DC: Gallaudet University Press.

McGregor, Robert P. 1913. *A Lay Sermon—The Universal Brotherhood of Man and Fatherhood of God*. Washington, DC: National Association of the Deaf.

Meir, Irit. 2010. "Iconicity and Metaphor: Constraints on Metaphorical Extension of Iconic Forms." *Language* 86(4): 865–96.

Michaels, John W. 1923. *A Handbook of the Sign Language of the Deaf*. Atlanta: Home Mission Board, Southern Baptist Convention.

Mitchell, Ross E., and Michael A. Karchmer. 2004. "Chasing the Mythical Ten Percent: Parental Hearing Status of Deaf and Hard of Hearing Students in the United States." *Sign Language Studies* 4(2): 138–63.

Mitchell, Ross E., Travas A. Young, Bellamie Bachleda, and Michael A. Karchmer. 2006. "How Many People Use ASL in the United States? Why Estimates Need Updating." *Sign Language Studies* 6(3): 306–35.

Mitton A. 1949. "Le langage par gestes." *Nouvelle Revue des traditions populaires* 2 (Mars-Avril): 138–51.

Nomeland, Melvia M., and Ronald E. Nomeland. 2012. *The Deaf Community in America: History in the Making*. Jefferson, NC: McFarland.

Oléron, Pierre. 1974. *Éléments de répertoire du langage gestuel des sourds-muets*. Paris: Éditions du Centre national de la recherche scientifique.

Parmentier, Richard J. 1987. "Peirce Divested for Non-intimates." *Recherches Sémiotiques/Semiotic Inquiry* 7(1): 19–39.

Pastouriaux, Louis, and Victor Régnier. 1954. *Leçons de Sciences*. Paris: Delagrave.

Paulmier, Louis-Pierre. 1844. *Considérations sur l'instruction des sourds-muets*. Paris: Chez l'Auteur.

Peirce, Charles S. (1893) 1955. "Logic as Semiotic: The Theory of Signs." In *Philosophical Writings of Peirce*, edited by Justus Buchler, 98–119. New York: Dover Publications.

Pélissier, Pierre. 1856. *Iconographie des signes faisant partie de l'enseignement des sourds-muets*. Paris: Paul Dupont.

Pellet, René. 1938. *Des premières perceptions du concret à la conception de l'abstrait. Essai d'analyse de la pensée et de son expression chez l'enfant sourd-muet*. Lyon: Bosc and Riou.

Pinloche, Auguste. 1922. *Vocabulaire par l'image*. Paris: Larousse.

Piroux, Joseph. 1830. *Vocabulaire des sourds-muets*. Nancy, France: L'établissement des sourds-muets.

———. 1855. *Méthode de dactylologie à l'usage, de lecture et d'écriture, des sourds-muets. Livre de l'élève*. Paris: Hachette.

The Preservation of American Sign Language. 2003. Burtonsville, MD: Sign Media, DVD.

Presley, Delma E. 1976. "The Crackers of Georgia." *Georgia Historical Quarterly* 60(2): 102–16.

Puybonnieux, Jean-Baptiste. 1846. *Mutisme et surdité*. Paris: Baillière.

Radutzky, Elena. 2001. *Dizionario bilingue elementare della lingua italiana dei segni*. Rome: Edizioni Kappa.

Renard, Marc, and Yves Lapalu. 2000. *Sourd, cent blagues*. Vol. 2. Les Essarts-le-Roi: Éditions du Fox.

Richardin, Claude J. 1834. *Réflexions et citations sur l'état moral des sourds-muets*. Paris: Hachette.

Riekehof, Lottie L. 1987. *The Joy of Signing*. Springfield, MO: Gospel Publishing House.

Roth, Stanley D. 1948. *A Book of Basic Signs Used by the Deaf*. Rev. ed. Fulton, MO: Missouri School for the Deaf Press.

Saussure, Ferdinand de. 1959. *Course in General Linguistics*. New York: Philosophical Library.

Schmitt, Jean-Claude. 1995. *La Raison des gestes dans l'Occident médiéval*. Paris: Gallimard.

Shaw, Emily. 2013. "Gesture in Multiparty Interaction: A Study of Embodied Discourse in Spoken English and American Sign Language." PhD diss., Georgetown University, Washington, DC.

Shroyer, Edgar H., and Susan P. Shroyer. 1984. *Signs across America*. Washington, DC: Gallaudet University Press.

Sicard, Roch Ambroise. 1808. *Théorie des signes ou introduction à l'étude des langues, où le sens des mots, au lieu d'être défini, est mis en action*. Vol. 2. Paris: Institution des sourds-muets.

Srage, Mohamed Nader. 1991. "La communication gestuelle illustrant la variété de strates sociales au Liban." *Geste et Image* 8/9: 161–85.

Sternberg, Martin L. 1994. *American Sign Language Dictionary*. New York: HarperCollins.

Stokoe, William C. 1960. *Sign Language Structure: An Outline of the Visual Communication Systems of the American Deaf*. Studies in Linguistics: Occasional Papers No. 8. Buffalo, NY: Dept. of Anthropology and Linguistics, University of Buffalo.

Stokoe, William C., Dorothy C. Casterline, and Carl G. Croneberg. (1965) 1978. *A Dictionary of American Sign Language on Linguistic Principles*. Silver Spring, MD: Linstok Press.

Supalla, Ted. 2008. "Sign Language Archeology: Integrating Historical Linguistics with Fieldwork on Young Sign Languages." In *Sign Languages: Spinning and Unraveling the Past, Present and Future. Papers from the 9th Theoretical Issues in Sign Language Research Conference*, edited by R. M. de Quadros, 575–83. Petrópolis/RJ, Brazil: Editora Arara Azul.

Taub, Sarah F. 2001. *Language from the Body: Iconicity and Metaphor in American Sign Language*. Cambridge: Cambridge University Press.

Thompson, Robin L. 2011. "Iconicity in Language Processing and Acquisition: What Signed Languages Reveal." *Language and Linguistics Compass* 5(9): 603–16.

Thompson, Robin L., David P. Vinson, and Gabriella Vigliocco. 2009. "The Link between Form and Meaning in American Sign Language: Lexical Processing Effects." *Journal of Experimental Psychology: Learning, Memory, and Cognition* 35(2): 550–57.

———. 2010. "The Link between Form and Meaning in British Sign Language: Effects of Iconicity for Phonological Decisions." *Journal of Experimental Psychology: Learning, Memory, and Cognition* 36(4): 1017–27.

Us des Cisterciens réformés de la Congrégation de la Grande Trappe. 1890. Toulouse: Privat.

Veditz, George. 1913. *Preservation of the Sign Language*. Washington, DC: National Association of the Deaf.

Virolle-Souibès, Marie. 1985. "Gestes emblématiques masculins et mixtes à Alger et en Kabylie." *Geste et Image* 4: 69–107.

Watson, David O. 1964. *Talk with Your Hands*. Menasha, WI: George Banta.

Wilcox, Phyllis P. 2000. *Metaphor in American Sign Language*. Washington, DC: Gallaudet University Press.

Wilcox, Sherman. 2009. "Symbol and Symptom: Routes from Gesture to Signed Language." *Annual Review of Cognitive Linguistics* 7: 89–110.

Woodward, James C. 1976. "Signs of Change: Historical Variation in American Sign Language." *Sign Language Studies* 10: 81–94.

Wylie, Laurence. 1977. *Beaux gestes*. Cambridge, MA: Undergraduate Press.